What people are saying about Cheap Tricks:

"It's the most useful pennypinching guide I've seen. Right on the money..."
—*The Whole Earth Review*

"Covering everything in the world about saving money, this book should be on everyone's bookshelf. You can't afford not to own it."
—Chuck Carter, People's Radio Network

"A fascinating book that pays for itself over and over again."
—Money in the Morning, KCEO Radio, San Diego

"...this well-written guide will save you time while it saves you money."
—Jack Hart, Writing Coach, *The Oregonian*

"The cheapest American alive? I think Andy Dappen can make a genuine claim."
—Erik Lacitis, *The Seattle Times*

"...the perfect book for the No-Go '90s: If you can't make big bucks, at least make your little ones last."
—Rob Lovitt, Contributing Editor, *Skiing Magazine*

"...this book pays for itself on every page."
—Bob Hise, satisfied reader

"I love your book... Please send one to my daughter who is living in her own apartment and needs this desperately."
—Meggie Dirnberger, reader from St. Louis

"... the most complete guide I've seen on cutting costs in your daily life. It covers everything from appliances to wills and, spiked with wry humor, is just fun to read."
—*The Thrifty Companion Newsletter*

"...this book is written with self-deprecating humor and, best of all (given the cost of books today), it's CHEAP!"
—*Booklist*

"It's like owning a huge coupon book, except you don't have to tear out the pages."
—KIRO-TV, Seattle

Cheap Trick$

100s of Ways You Can Save 1000s of Dollars!

by

Andy Dappen

Brier Books, Brier, Washington

Cheap Tricks
100s of Ways You Can Save 1000s of Dollars!

By Andy Dappen

Illustrated by Art Dappen

Published by:

Brier Books
Post Office Box 180
Mountlake Terrace, WA 98043
U.S.A.

Cover designed by Bob Hise
Edited by Florence Hansen

Publisher's Cataloging in Publication Data
Dappen, Andrew R.
Cheap Tricks: 100s of Ways You Can Save 1000s of Dollars/ by Andy Dappen -- 1st edition.
Includes Index.
1. Consumer education. 2. Thrift and saving. 3. Finance, personal.
1992 640.73—dc20   CIP 92-90592
ISBN 0-9632577-0-6 (pbk.): $13.95

Contents

To my parents,
who made me the cheapskate I am,
and my wife,
who tolerates me that way.

Acknowledgements

My thanks to the many people who made this book possible by sharing their secrets of saving money.

Because this book was produced with a sharp eye toward cutting costs (how could you trust me if I did not practice what I preach?), my special thanks go to my brother, Art, who provided the cartoons. His work is good, his price is unbeatable. Thanks also to my wife and Florence Hansen for all those aggravating hours of editing: Without their contributions, *Cheap Tricks* would have cost you a few bucks more.

About The Author

Andy Dappen is a journalist who has written hundreds of magazine articles about adventure, sports, travel, and health, but he is first and foremost a cheapskate.

He can't help himself. His grandmother crocheted door mats out of old plastic bags and made her holiday decorations from discards in the trash. His father still walks the stairs bowlegged to spread out the wear spots on the carpet. His mother does most of her Christmas shopping the week after Christmas to capitalize on sales, his brother supports a family of 10 on a missionary's pay, his sister sends him photocopied birthday cards.

This combination of genetics and environment have molded Andy into a third generation penny-pincher who continues to perfect the art. He has to. Supporting a family on a writer's income—an income that would appear enviable only in a third-world country—he must practice what he preaches.

From the offbeat anecdotes that enliven this book, to the hundreds of practical tricks from which everyone can benefit, Andy shares the secrets of his art on the pages that follow.

Warning — Disclaimer

This book is meant to help you live frugally and it can save you thousands of dollars.

Great effort has been taken to ensure that the following information is accurate. However, there may be mistakes—both typographical and in content—so it is up to you, the reader, to treat this book **only** as a source of ideas and **not** as the unquestionable truth.

Equally important, the writer and the publisher cannot anticipate every circumstance and condition under which information from this book will be used and cannot predict all possible outcomes of applying this information. Under some circumstances specific tips could be invalid or false. It is, therefore, the reader's responsibility to evaluate whether the advice given is appropriate for the circumstances. It is the reader's responsibility to weigh the associated risk surrounding a course of action and to accept that risk if he or she proceeds. It is also the reader's complete responsibility to test and verify the book's advice before applying that advice in ways that could result in physical harm and/or financial loss.

The author and Brier Books shall have neither liability nor responsibility to any person, group, or entity with respect to any loss or damage caused, or alleged to be caused, directly or indirectly by information contained in this book.

If you are unwilling to be bound by all of the above, please return this book to the publisher for a full refund.

Introduction

A leaky bucket holds no water. You fill it, but it won't store the water needed to quench your thirst, douse the garden, or wash the car.

When it comes to saving money, you too may be a leaky vessel incapable of storing funds for the things you want: a house, a vacation, your children's education, your retirement.

Many books address this problem by advising you to boost your earning power, by telling you to pour more water into the bucket. But this usually leads to more of the very thing you wish to avoid—work. More work means less time for the joys of life—family, friends, travel, sports, or killing slugs in the garden.

This book takes a different approach. It is a cork (or rather a hundred corks) to plug the holes draining your savings account of thousands of dollars each year. Each dollar saved equals a dollar of wealth you needn't earn. In fact, after adding federal and state income taxes to the equation, a dollar saved equals over a dollar-and-a-half earned. Use the "corks" in this book and you'll quickly appreciate the wisdom of Cicero who said in 46 B.C., "Men do not realize how great an income thrift is."

Much later, Thoreau exaggerated, "Almost any man knows how to earn money, but one in a million knows how to spend it." Look around and you'll see the evidence—Americans who earn $60,000 a year but have no savings; neighbors with swanky cars *and* credit cards leveraged to the hilt; couples who "own" big houses but whose children live at child-care centers. Follow even a third of the suggestions in this book and you'll join the minority who know how to spend wisely.

A Spanish proverb says, "The wise and their money go to market twice." Most of the suggestions in this book make you wiser—they help you buy more for less. And most suggestions do this without compromising your lifestyle.

Some of my suggestions, however, do involve lifestyle adjustments. People of modest means can purchase what they need *and* save for the future if they put their materialism on a diet. Somewhere between the Trump attitude of the 1980s (He with the most toys wins.) and Thoreau's disdain of materialism (The man doesn't own the house, the house owns the man.) there is a middle ground. Most of us can live happily here with far less money than we would believe.

At times, therefore, I make suggestions which represent a downshift from Trumpism toward Thoreauism. Implement those suggestions that make sense to you—that don't ask too great a sacrifice. And chuckle at those suggestions that go too far. After all, there is comic relief in fanatics like me who are so possessed (or deranged?) that they actually walk up the stairs bowlegged to wear the carpet more evenly, or who photocopy birthday cards for their wives.

Throughout the book a few themes of wise spending repeat themselves. Themes like patience. For every purchase, turn, turn, turn, there is a season. Need something today and it usually costs you dearly. Bide your time and you'll stumble across a sale, used product, friend with a connection, wholesale outlet... where the price is right.

Ignoring advertising is another repeating theme. We are all influenced, if not brainwashed, by advertising. We get so bombarded that we eventually believe Nike shoes will transform us into Michael Jordans, that *Head and Shoulders* shampoo will have the babes (or dudes) swarming us. We believe that brand-name corn is superior to a store brand, even though one cannery may have slapped different labels onto identical cans. We believe Vuarnet sunglasses give superior eye protection over those costing a quarter as much; in fact, they don't. The list is long and I may attack some of your sacred products. But read with an open mind and, if you're lucky, you'll grow cynical and suspicious of advertising.

Other themes you'll see repeated throughout the book? Research large expenditures. Get several price quotes before you pay. Don't overbuy: Why buy a 16-cycle washer when three cycles is all you use? If it's a bargain but isn't what you want, it's not a bargain. Preventing a problem is much cheaper than repairing one. When the price is right, stock up. Double up: Use things twice or thrice before trashing them.

All these themes, which in concert comprise a body of wise spending habits, are summed up in a word in my family. They are part of the great policy we call "Dappenomics." My grandmother fostered the first tenets of Dappenomics, my father enlarged and refined them, and now I'm documenting them. I hope my documentation will someday help my daughter take up the cause and plug the leaks in her bucket. I hope it does the same for you now.

Industry is Fortune's right hand, and frugality her left.

Thomas Fuller, M.D.

Using This Book

Readers new to *Cheap Tricks* should browse the book quickly to become familiar with its scope and to recognize where these pages can lead in the quest of becoming a frugal guru. You'll notice the chapters are presented alphabetically as an organizational tool; this will help you find topics of interest and relocate valuable hints later.

After your preview, tackle the book in any order you wish. Each chapter is self-sufficient, so skip around and pluck the topics that offer you the best prospects for profit. Remember the book's vast scope, however, whenever you're faced with a major outlay. If your vehicle dies abruptly, read the appropriate car chapters before repairing or replacing the car. If you need a homeowner's policy on a new house, check out the insurance chapter. If a family member is about to undergo elective surgery, look over the medical chapter. If you're about to sprout a bud, read the chapter on babies and children. And if it's tax time—well, find a bridge to jump off.

While this book shares the tenets and practices of becoming a master Cheapnik, there is also great benefit in just dabbling. After all, frugality is nothing like a game of golf where a haphazard level of commitment earns you a poor score. In this arena, even aimless dabbling will leave you much richer.

But be careful. The rewards can inspire you to dive deeper into the game; in turn, those new rewards can lure you deeper still. Soon the foundations of previous economic principles warp as you wrestle with the paradox that a millionaire who spends foolishly is a pauper while a pauper who spends wisely is already wealthy. Later, you may find yourself enjoying not only the financial rewards but the actual game of getting more for less. And when you become inextricably hooked, frugality becomes an art form and walking the stairs bowlegged or weaving door mats from old plastic bags is an expression of that art. That's when others classify you as part of the lunatic fringe—a euphemism for "nuts."

So if you find yourself getting excited as you read these tips or you look at them and see gold, stop to monitor yourself. Is your heart racing, your breath short and shallow? These are the first symptoms of an addiction that can lead to the fringe. I've warned you now: It is up to you to decide whether it's safe to read on.

He who has money has the whole world.
                                        Yiddish proverb

Fortune knocks at the door but the fool does not invite her in.
                                        Danish proverb

Appliances

Guess how many electrical appliances you have in the house. I got to thinking about it recently when, among the coffee maker, crock pot, microwave, blender, popcorn maker, and electric skillet, I couldn't find counter space to lay down a cutting board. Which reminded me of my office where I must unplug one appliance to use another, despite the fact that each outlet has an adapter to accept six plugs.

So I wandered the house counting the video and stereo components, kitchen appliances, office equipment, cleaning machines, and bathroom paraphernalia. Not counting lamps, I was up to 54 and I hadn't reached the garage with its bevy of electric tools.

The cost of buying, maintaining, and running these machines can tear apart your wallet like a school of piranhas. Following are tips for slowing the feeding frenzy.

AIR CONDITIONERS (window-mounted)

♦ The EnergyGuide tags put on all new air conditioners tell the machine's Energy Efficiency Rating (EER), or the amount of cooling obtained from the electricity used. A rating of eight is good and a machine with such a rating might run 700 hours for $55, but a machine with an even better rating of 10 will provide the same cooling for only $44. Consequently, a cheap air conditioner to buy may be an expensive one to own.

♦ Install air conditioners on north- or east-facing windows. South- and west-facing windows receive more sun and will make the unit work harder.

AIR PURIFIER

♦ Will a good purifier make you less allergic to home? Controlled studies show that air purifiers have little effect on reducing allergies. The *University of California at Berkeley Wellness Letter*, rated by many newspapers and magazines as the country's best health newsletter, says, "Unfortunately, even the best air purifiers are no better than air conditioners at ridding indoor air of allergens and pollutants." And air conditioners have never rated as a miracle cure for allergies.

Why? Because pollutants and allergens are not airborne for long. They settle onto the walls, furniture, and carpet where even $600 purifiers can't touch them.

Save yourself a big chunk of change and use other approaches to reducing allergens in the house. Mop, dust with a damp cloth, and vacuum often. When fumes or gases irritate you, open windows and turn on exhaust fans. Ban pets from the bedroom. Replace the furnace filter monthly. Wash all bedding often. On warm days, cool the house with an air conditioner—it recycles the inside air and keeps new allergens out.

CLEANLINESS AND CHEAPNESS

♦ Dust, whether it is inside or outside the appliance, contributes to overheating, and heat is one of the main enemies of electrical appliances. Vacuum the vents and dust the casings of all your appliances regularly so they can shed heat. Cover valuable equipment (computers, stereos) when they are not in use.

♦ Computers, tape recorders, compact-disc players, and VCRs all have moving parts needing occasional cleanings. Use a cotton swab dipped in photographic-lens cleaner (or *Windex*) to clean the lens of a CD player. A *Q-tip* dipped in isopropyl alcohol cleans the heads of tape recorders.

CLOTHES DRYERS

♦ Gas dryers are so much cheaper to operate than electric ones that you'll recoup their higher cost (about $50) in about a year. Electric dryers perform slightly better than gas, but the lower cost of gas more than compensates for these minor differences. As a group, gas dryers break down more often than their electric brethren, but by studying the frequency-of-repair records published in *Consumer Reports*, you'll find a few gas machines that are more reliable than most electric models.

If you get a gas dryer, buy one with an electronic ignition. A dryer with a pilot light uses 30% more gas and ups your fuel bill $25 a year.

♦ Moisture sensors that turn off your machine when the clothes have dried save you money. Why? Because without them most people ensure that the clothes get dry by adding an extra 10 or 15 minutes to the timer.

♦ Drying clothes with the air-fluff setting does not require heated air and saves energy. It also keeps clothes from shrinking.

♦ Take advantage of preheated air and dry clothes in consecutive loads.

♦ Dryers devour both energy and life from your clothing. Clotheslines solve both problems. Hang the clothes outside in fair weather, in the basement during foul weather. I have no basement so I placed a long dowel above my washer and dryer. Clothes come out of the washer, onto a hanger, and onto the dowel. Once dry, I move the garments, hangers and all, into my closet.

Note: Smoothing clothes as you hang them saves lots of ironing. Pants hung by the cuff also minimize ironing.

♦ Dryers run best when the lint screen is clean.

COMPACT DISC (CD) PLAYERS

♦ To quote a *Consumer Reports* product evaluation, "There's no need to spend a lot of money on a CD player. All of them sound splendid, and all come with more features than most people will ever use."

♦ Component CD players won't have any better sound quality than inexpensive portable CD players. Why? Because

CDs don't store music per se, but the digital code of the music.

Drew Kaplan, owner of DAK Industries, writes in his mail-order catalog, "Every computer (which is what a CD player really is) reproduces the bits (which represent the sound) exactly the same. I've tested dozens of CD players. And, to be honest, I can't tell the difference between a $1000 component and a $150 portable."

Pay more for a component if you like the features, but not for the false hope of purchasing better sound quality.

DISHWASHERS

♦ Many people are so antiseptic they don't let a dishwasher do its job—clean dirty dishes. They waste prolific quantities of hot water and time, rinsing the dishes before trusting them to the machine. If your dishwasher is worth its keep, it will clean your dishes without this falderal, so do yourself (and your utility bill) a favor: stop prewashing.

The saniphobic may find this hard, but I challenge you to this test: Simply scrape off the food scraps and excess sauces before stacking the dishes in the washer, even if it will be days before you run the machine. Same goes for silverware, just get the excess food off. Wait until the dishwasher is full, then run it. First you'll be amazed by the results, then depressed about the countless hours of life you've wasted to prewashing.

♦ If your dishwasher fails this test, it is probably old and has lost its muscle. This is still no reason to waste copious quantities of hot water, prewashing dishes. Here is the cheap (and fast) solution for geriatric machines: Keep dirty dishes piled in the sink with cold water covering the eating surfaces. When you've got a machine-load of dishes, pour off the water (no added scrubbing) and load them.

♦ After testing your machine as described above, try the same test using the "Short Wash" cycle, an option using 25% less hot water. Many machines will still pass.

♦ The "Energy Saver" setting of your dishwasher will save you $10 to $15 a year. This feature lets dishes air dry and, in a few dishwashers, employs cold water for one of the rinse cycles. Yes, air drying is perfectly sanitary—in today's lawsuit-happy climate, no manufacturer would give you this option if the odds of health problems were worse than 1 in 5 billion. To improve drying, crack open the washer's door after the last rinse cycle.

♦ Hand-washing dishes is said to be cheaper than machine washing because you use less water. If you really pack your dishwasher before running it, however, you can clean just as many dishes with the nine to 12 gallons of hot water used.

♦ To run a dishwasher every day with 140°F water costs a family with average electric rates about $90 a year ($45 dollars for families owning gas water heaters). Obviously, if you run the machine less frequently, you'll spend less. In my family, we cut dirty dishes by using some of them more than once. We each have a spot on the kitchen counter for dishes we plan to reuse. After breakfast I rinse my cereal bowl, spoon, and glass with a cup of cold water and put the lot in my spot. I can use them all again at lunch. After lunch, the bowl may be greasy from soup so it goes in the dishwasher. But my glass can be rinsed for another use. Meanwhile, if we only boiled or steamed vegetables in a pot, we rinse it and leave it on the stove for another job. All told, the process cuts our dishwashing in half. Equally nice, it saves time.

If the suggestion sounds unsanitary, let me point out that most people use the same drinking glass in the bathroom for weeks at a time. They also use the same toothbrush day after day without ill effect.

♦ You can cut your dishwashing costs a few dollars a year by resetting the main water heater from 140° to 120°F. Not all dishwashers clean well at this temperature, but it is worth an experiment.

If you are buying a new dishwasher, the extra $30 spent on a booster heater that raises the temperature of incoming water to 140° is well spent. The booster heater lets you turn the main water heater down to 120°, a trick that saves you $20 to $30 a year and pays for the booster heater in under two years.

EXTENDED WARRANTIES

♦ Should you get extended warranties on your stereo, computer, television, or other appliances? In a word: no. Why not? Insurance, which is what an extended warranty is, is a losing gamble because the insuring company takes in more money than it pays out. Taking a loss to protect yourself from a disaster makes sense. Taking a loss to insure yourself against minor mishaps you can afford to fix does not. So play the odds. The odds say you'll come out ahead ignoring these policies.

For electronic retailers, extended warranties are usually the most profitable "product" they sell. In fact, many businesses would not survive save for the profitable warranties they sell to 40% of their customers. The cost of these warranties is substantial, yet only 15% to 20% of warranty owners ever use them. As a result, for every dollar taken in on these policies, the retailers pay back only 10¢ to 15¢. Even if you are bad at math, you'll realize that's no deal.

Furthermore, you don't know whether your retailer will still be in business or whether you will still live in the area should you need to make a claim.

Forget the extended warranties. Research your purchases and buy gear with a record for reliability. Ignore the arm twisting from salespersons professing the value of these warranties. Altruism does not motivate their persistence, it's the commission (up to 20%) they want.

FREEZERS

♦ Chest freezers use 10% to 15% less energy than uprights: Partly because they are better insulated, partly because the heavy, cold air does not flow out when the door is opened.

♦ Auto-defrost freezers use about 40% more energy than manual-defrost models. Manual models should be defrosted when they accumulate 1/4 inch of ice.

♦ Freezers packed with lots of food are more efficient than nearly empty ones.

INFORMATION

♦ For additional free information about purchasing and maintaining computers, printers, telephone products, VCRs, camcorders, televisions, and audio equipment, contact the Consumer Electronics Group of the Electronic Industries Association (2001 Pennsylvania Avenue, NW, Washington, DC 20006, 202-457-4919) and request their *Consumer Publications List*. The list contains over 20 different educational booklets you can order.

MICROWAVES

♦ Most Americans now own a microwave oven but many of them are unhappy that they purchased small, underpowered machines. Medium-sized microwaves get much better marks for customer satisfaction—they hold much more food and are powerful enough to cook it quickly.

Buy at least a 600-watt oven if you want your unit's cooking times to correspond to most cookbooks. Keep in mind that most people use their microwaves for simple tasks (heating leftovers, cooking vegetables, defrosting, fixing prepared meals, heating drinks) so the bells and whistles of high-end microwaves go unused. Adequate size and power, an accurate timer, and five to 10 cooking levels are all that most people require of a microwave.

♦ Knowing your microwave's power compared to the power of those used in cookbooks can reduce mistakes that ruin food. Don't know your unit's power? Use this simple test. Pour exactly eight ounces of water into a glass measuring cup and place the cup (uncovered) in your unit. Microwave on "high," timing how long it takes for the water to boil. If it boils in under three minutes, your microwave is a 600- to 700-watt unit; in three to four minutes, its power is 500 to 600 watts; in more than four minutes, its power is less than 500 watts.

♦ A conventional oven uses two to three times more energy than a microwave. Stove top burners are even more inefficient. Use your microwave whenever possible.

♦ Wondering if your glass and ceramics are safe for the microwave or whether you need new cookware? The FDA recommends this test: Microwave the empty container for one minute. If it is warm or hot, don't use it in the microwave; if it is lukewarm, it is okay for reheating foods; if it is still cool, use it for microwave cooking.

♦ Covering food with a loose lid speeds up microwave cooking. Paper plates make cheap lids: Reuse them until they are dirty.

OVENS

♦ If your baking times never jibe with the cookbooks, the temperature-control knob of your oven needs adjusting. You don't need a pro for this, just an oven thermometer. Place the thermometer in the oven, turn the oven to 350°F, and wait 20 minutes. A reading that is more than 10° off should be corrected.

Pull the temperature-control knob off the stove panel by pulling straight out. You'll find either a diagram describing how to adjust the temperature or a disk under the control knob. To adjust the disk, loosen the screws on the back of the knob and then rotate the disk. Rotating the notches clockwise lowers the temperature 10° per notch. A counterclockwise rotation raises the temperature 10° per notch. Now tighten the disk screws and slide the knob back on its stem.

♦ Stop peeking. Every time you open the oven door, you lose a quarter of the entrapped heat.

♦ A nail through a baking potato reduces its cooking time by 15 minutes. Slicing potatoes in half and laying them, cut surfaces down, on a greased cookie sheet, cuts baking time by a third.

♦ Turn off the oven about 30 minutes before your dish is done. The trapped heat will finish the job.

♦ Get organized and bake several dishes at once while the oven is hot.

♦ Based on the average cost of energy (8¢ per kilowatt-hour), running the cleaning cycle of a self-cleaning oven costs between 50¢ and 75¢. Chemical oven cleaners for standard ovens cost about $1 per cleaning. Over time, a self-cleaning oven will help pay for itself, especially if your electric rates are below average.

♦ When you run the cleaning cycle of a self-cleaning oven, do it after baking or broiling. The oven is already fired up.

♦ Gas ovens with a pilot light make excellent food dehydrators. Chop up the food you wish to dry, put it on a foiled tray, and leave it in the oven for a day or two.

If dehydrating food isn't a passion and you are in the market for a gas range, buy one with electronic ignition. Eliminating the pilot light will cut your fuel consumption by nearly 40% and save you $25 to $30 a year.

PURCHASING TIPS

♦ As a rule, you get the best bang for your buck buying mid-priced appliances. Low-end products are often not as well made and may lack truly useful features. High-end products flaunt expensive features few people really need—features that are also prone to breaking.

Mid-priced dishwashers, for example, cost around $350. Some machines cost twice this amount because they offer a plethora of special cycles. In product reviews, however, the expensive machines were no better for everyday dishwashing than their $350 brethren. Mid-priced dishwashers usually have a light, normal, and heavy cycle, and that is all most people need.

♦ The true cost of an appliance is the sum of the sticker cost, lifetime maintenance costs, and lifetime operating costs. A refrigerator costing $150 less than a competitor is actually much more expensive if it has a poor maintenance history and uses 40% more energy.

You can guesstimate maintenance costs of competing appliances by comparing their frequency-of-repair records in magazines like *Consumer Reports.*

Calculating the lifetime operating costs is even more important. With appliances like refrigerators, this cost may be as low as 1.5 times the retail cost (for an efficient unit) and as high as three times the retail cost (for an inefficient unit). Compare the EnergyGuide tags attached to refrigerators, freezers, dishwashers, air conditioners, furnaces, water heaters, and washing machines to obtain the yearly cost of running different machines, and multiply this figure by the number of years the appliance should last.

Note: The EnergyGuide will have a chart calculating the yearly cost of running the machine at different electric rates. Use your local electric rates (ask a salesperson if you don't know them) to determine the yearly operating costs.

♦ If you're considering a new appliance, especially one that consumes lots of energy (refrigerator, water heater, freezer, air conditioner, washer, dryer), look at the *Consumer Guide to Home Energy Savings* by Alex Wilson (reserve it from the library or order it from the American Council for an Energy-Efficient Economy, 1001 Connecticut Ave. NW, Suite 535, Washington, DC 20036). This guide lists and rates high-efficiency appliances and helps you pick the most economical.

♦ When buying a dishwasher, refrigerator, freezer, washing machine, or gas range, used appliances may not be your cheapest option. Over the last decade, the efficiency of all these appliances has increased by more than 30%, making the long-term costs of running old appliances quite high. If you can't afford to buy new, look at used appliances that are only a few years old.

REFRIGERATORS

♦ Refrigerators are real power pigs, scarfing up 8% of your electric bill (16% in gas-heated homes). With this kind of appetite, you want to avoid running two machines. It is much cheaper to operate one big refrigerator/freezer than two small units.

♦ Prolong the life of the gasket sealing the refrigerator by wiping it regularly with warm water. Once the gasket starts deteriorating, you're in for a big waste of energy and money. Test the seal by closing the door on a sheet of paper. The sheet should be firmly anchored. Repeat the test along the length of the gasket. Adjust the door hinges or replace the gasket if the seal is bad.

♦ A dusty condenser coil (on the bottom or back of the refrigerator) reduces a refrigerator's efficiency and shortens its life. Clean it several times a year with a coil brush (from a hardware store) or a soft-bristle attachment on a canister-style vacuum cleaner. Unplug the refrigerator first.

♦ The convenience of a frost-free refrigerator is great, but it costs you—its energy consumption can be twice that of a manual-defrost model ($100 versus $45 a year to operate).

♦ Top-freezer refrigerators are cheaper to buy *and* run than side-by-side refrigerator/freezers. The average side-by-side unit uses 35% more energy and will cost an extra $30 a year to run. Historically, top-freezer units also have fewer repair problems. Either type of refrigerator will give you fewer repair problems if you avoid frills like ice makers. Dispensers for both water and ice are particularly prone to meltdown and can increase refrigerator repairs by 50%.

♦ Each degree drop in the temperature of your refrigerator or freezer increases power consumption by 2.5%, meaning you don't want the temperature lower than necessary. However, keeping temperatures too high greatly reduces the shelf life of your food. Use a thermometer to keep the freezer at 0°F and the refrigerator at 37°F.

♦ Installing refrigerators away from heat sources like stoves, dishwashers, and direct sunlight reduces their operating costs. If it is impractical to move the refrigerator away from heat sources, place an aluminum foil heat reflector between the two.

REPAIR

♦ When my General Electric dishwasher broke down last year, I learned the GE Answer Center (800-626-2000) would give customers repair instruction over the phone. A technician analyzed my problem and gave me a test to conduct. When I called back with the results of my test, he told me which part was most suspect and where to get it locally. Unfortunately, the local outlet did not have the part in stock so I ordered it through the Answer Center using my credit card.

The part arrived two days later and, with the instructions the technician had given me, I soon had the dishwasher fixed. That saved me at least $60 in service fees.

GE gives repair instruction on all of its major appliances except microwaves and gas ranges. They also offer repair instruction on their consumer electronics, though a high percentage of these products will need to be serviced professionally.

♦ The following manufacturers also offer repair instruction over the phone.
- Hotpoint, and RCA major appliances. These are actually manufactured by General Electric. Call (800-626-2000).
- Whirlpool, Roper, KitchenAid. Call the Whirlpool Consumer Assistance Center (800-253-1301). The center gives repair instruction on all its major appliances except microwaves.
- RCA. Receive technical support and troubleshooting for RCA's consumer electronics (800-336-1900).
- Maytag. Contact Maytag Customer Relations for over-the-phone repair instruction (800-688-9900).
- Amana. Gives instruction on minor repair problems but not for problems that may involve parts replacement (800-843-0304).

STOVES

♦ Cooking on top of a range is an inefficient use of electricity so, if you own them, use appliances like microwaves, rice makers, electric skillets, crock pots, and popcorn cookers. These appliances use less power.

♦ Match your pans to the burner size. A small pot on a big burner lets heat disappear into thin air.

♦ A watched pot never boils—probably because the lid is off. A lid decreases boiling times (and electricity use) some 20%. To make the lids even more efficient at trapping heat, lay hot pads over the lid as makeshift cozies.

♦ Once water boils, turn the heat to low: A slow boil is as hot as a rolling boil.

♦ Pressure cookers reduce stove-top cooking time by two-thirds, saving you time and money. Use them.

TELEVISIONS

♦ Spraying glass cleaner on the surface of a TV screen can cause damage. Apply the spray to a soft, lint-free rag, then wipe the screen.

♦ Televisions often have ventilation slots on the bottom, so keep your tube off soft surfaces like carpet.

♦ Pet hair and dander inside a TV contributes to break downs. Don't let cats lie on the television (or VCR).

VCRs and CAMCORDERS

♦ To clean or not to clean—that is the controversy. Many repairmen condemn all cleaning cartridges for VCRs and camcorders, saying that the abrasiveness and improper tension of these cleaning devices often damage the heads and guide rollers. An added danger, according to one repairman, is the public's perception that, "If using a cleaning tape once is good, using it often must be gooder." Wrong—unless sanding the face off the heads is the intent.
Other repairmen generally agree with the above but concede that the *Scotch Cleaning Tape* (about $10) is safe for VHS systems: Tests conducted by *Electronic Servicing and Technology*, a trade magazine for professional technicians, found that the damage inflicted by this tape is negligible and that it does clean your heads. According to my repairman at Guy's Electronic Service in Seattle, all

video tapes have cleaning agents bound to the oxides in the tape. The *Scotch Cleaning Tape* cleans the heads because it has a higher ratio of these cleaning agents and a lower ratio of oxides. But because it is a normal magnetic tape, it is not abrasive.

For 8mm camcorders, the *Sony Cleaning Cassette* works along similar principles and preserves your heads.

Use these cleaning tapes for 15 or 20 seconds when you notice a degradation (snowy image, lines in the screen) of your picture quality. Take the machines in for servicing if tape fails to improve the image.

♦ Repairmen will tell you to bring your VCR and camcorders in for cleaning a minimum of once a year (semiannually for heavy users). Are these cleanings (costing between $20 and $40) necessary?

Yes and no. More important than the months or years between cleanings is the hours of use. Most manufacturers recommend that the heads, guide rollers, pinch roller, pressure rollers, impedance rollers, capstan, idlers, pulleys, etc. be cleaned every 500 hours. For people using their VCR once or twice a week, it may take two or three years to amass 500 hours.

And if you wait more than 500 hours between professional cleanings, are you destroying your machine? Some parts, like the pinch roller, may need replacement sooner than normal but the money saved by not cleaning as often may offset replacement costs.

Not everyone agrees with me, but here are my thoughts on professional cleanings. If you own a low-end machine, schedule professional cleanings less often (every 600 to 700 hours) because the benefits may not justify the cost. With a high-end machine costing $500 to $600, the relative cost of the cleanings is a much smaller percentage of the machine's value, so a stricter maintenance schedule makes more sense.

♦ Wear the neck strap while filming with a camcorder. This sounds like trivial advice, but gravity is among the main causes of damaged camcorders. Because these machines are only a little more durable than egg shells, a short fall can shatter them.

♦ Hair can clog up this machinery, but that's nothing compared to a peanut butter and jelly sandwich down the hatch. Train cats and kids to steer clear of these toys.

WARRANTIES

♦ If you forgot to send in your registration card, will the manufacturer repair an appliance that would still be under warranty? Yes, but you need a receipt or cancelled check as proof of purchase. Save those precious paper slips.

♦ You must use an authorized service center for warranty work on an appliance. Call the manufacturer or the dealer who sold you the appliance for the address of a local center. Most major manufacturers will also have toll-free numbers you can get from directory assistance (800-555-1212).

WASHING MACHINES

♦ Because 90% of the electricity for washing clothes is used to heat water, washing is much cheaper if you chill out. Warm-water washes and cold rinses clean all but the filthiest clothes as well as hot washes and warm rinses. If your water is soft, cold-water washes also clean all but the dirtiest, greasiest clothes. Despite the temperature used for washing, always use cold-water rinses.

♦ Inefficient washing machines use three times more energy than efficient ones. It pays to study the Energy-Guide labels when making a new purchase.

♦ Wash only when you have a full load. You'll save on electricity, water, and detergent.

WATER HEATER

♦ Is the water in your area hard? If so, drain several quarts of water and sediment from the faucet-like valve near the bottom of the tank twice a year. Eliminating the sediment prolongs the heater's life and allows it to heat water more efficiently.
Even if your water is soft, perform this chore annually. Read the manufacturer's instructions before beginning.

♦ If you're in the market for a new water heater, study the EnergyGuide and purchase an energy-efficient model. It may cost more up front but will pay off later. Also, get the size that matches the size of your family. The larger the heater, the more it costs to run.

♦ **Finally**, consider simplicity. Sure, many appliances make life easier, but a quarter of my home appliances are expensive dust collectors. A little vision before purchasing would have left me wealthier and my house less cluttered. Like Sir Rabindranath Tagore said, "...people of this modern age are more eager to amass than to realize."
What do you mean, who is Rabindranath Tagore?

Babies and Children

I choked recently over a statistic stating that the average couple now spends $225,000 on *each* of their children before shoving them from the nest. Made me wonder if I was foolish in refusing the camels I was once offered in trade for my daughter. It also shed new light on my oldest brother's motivation. He claims his calling is to establish Christian schools in Mexico, but I suspect Mexico is the only place in North America where he can afford to raise eight children. I mean eight kids times $225,000—he'd have to be a multi-millionaire to raise them in the United States.

That is if he raised them like "average" Americans. Fortunately, anyone with a penny's worth of sense can raise average children without spending anything near an average amount of money. I'm not saying raising kids is cheap, but it needn't make you regret having them. Children themselves will bring you to that conclusion when they become teen-agers, but that's another story. Right now we're talking about saving money.

GIVING BIRTH

Besides dying, giving birth is the average woman's costliest medical expense. Most women pay $3000 to $5000 to bear children but expenses can easily hit the $7000 mark if minor complications require a cesarean section. Women with comprehensive maternity coverage as part of their health insurance may not worry about the cost. But what if you have no coverage, or your health insurance has a cap (e.g., $2000) on maternity coverage and doesn't cover minor complications like cesarean sections? Then the big bills can hurt as much as the birthing process itself. Following are a few ways to cut costs.

♦ Use a hospital that encourages early discharge (i.e., barring any complications you leave after 24 hours).

♦ Keep the baby in the hospital room with you, rather than in the nursery. You'll save money and your child will be less likely to contract a respiratory infection in the nursery.

♦ Consider the possibility of using a certified nurse-midwife at a birthing center (check Birth Centers and Midwives in the *Yellow Pages*). This option is particularly valid for low-risk women (women who don't have high blood pressure, have had successful vaginal births, whose babies are not breech, and whose babies are neither too large nor too small). Complete costs (prenatal, labor and delivery, newborn and postpartum exams) average around $1800.

The main concerns revolve around what happens if the delivery doesn't progress normally. You need confidence that the staff of your center is competent *and* comfortable in turning you over to a hospital or doctor if the delivery progresses abnormally. You want to know the staff will rely on their backup before a problem becomes a crisis.

And just what or who is that backup? Which hospitals are used and can the birthing-center staff transport you there in five minutes? Exactly what happens if you are transferred to the hospital and who will attend to you there? If doctors are the backup, who are they, are they always available, how quickly can they intervene, and what facilities do they have at their disposal?

♦ Women who are self-insured should take stock of their maternity coverage *before* they become pregnant. If your traditional policy places a cap on your maternity coverage, the total coverage offered by an HMO could be easily worth slightly higher premiums—at least until after your child is born.

Recently when my wife and I got serious about having another child, we debated switching to the local HMO—it s maternity coverage was far superior and the premiums were only a few hundred dollars more than our Blue Shield plan which has a maternity cap. To my dismay, we stayed with Blue Shield—my wife was comfortable with her obstetrician and didn't want to switch doctors. Loyalty is wonderful, but I didn't find it worth the extra $2000 it cost us.

♦ Cesarean sections can add greatly to the "average" cost of giving birth. The Health Insurance Association of America says the process increases doctors' fees about $500 and hospital fees more than $2000. About a quarter of American babies are delivered by cesarean sections and experts deem many of them unnecessary. Scheduling problems caused by a protracted labor, the profit incentive for doctors, and the fear of getting sued (the CYA-effect) combine to make many doctors quick to cut.

That's not to say there aren't legitimate reasons for cesarean sections, simply that many women receive them unnecessarily. For example, 85% of women who previously delivered by cesarean have repeat surgery despite the results of major studies in which 75% of the women who had previously had a low horizontal incision (the common cesarean incision now) were able to deliver vaginally.

In the hospital environment, prolonged labor also may result in cesareans because hospitals don't always differentiate between "the average" time of delivery and what is "normal." Women whose labor progresses beyond average become cause for concern, even though many protracted deliveries were combined with many short deliveries to derive that average.

Certified nurse midwives staffing birth centers are more likely to view the prolongation of labor as normal and several studies have shown that low-risk women delivering at these centers undergo far fewer cesareans without an increased incidence of bad outcomes. In one of these studies, less than 5% of the 12,000 low-risk women using birth centers had cesareans.

To lower your risk of an unnecessary procedure, ask your doctor what percent of his or her babies are delivered by cesarean. Call the hospital you intend to use and ask the same question—you'll get shuffled around in the bureaucracy but with persistence you may find the statistic. Many authorities believe that cesareans are unnecessary more than 12% to 14% of the time, so you have cause for alarm if your doctor's or hospital's rates are over 20%.

Ask the doctor when, in his or her opinion, a cesarean becomes necessary and whether he or she seeks a second opinion in the decision. Make sure the doctor understands your preferences and your budget constraints. You want a doctor who will be flexible, who will work with and around your needs. If you sense this cooperation, your partnership is likely to be a good one. If you don't sense it, consider another doctor.

For more information about cesarean sections consult: *Consumer Reports* (February 1991); *Unnecessary Cesareans: Ways to Avoid Them* by Dr. Charles Mahan and Diony Young; C/SEC Inc. (22 Forest Road, Framingham, MA, 01701, 508-877-8266); Cesarean Prevention Movement (P.O Box 152, Syracuse, NY 13210, 315-424-1942).

♦ Name-brand prenatal vitamins can cost as much as $16 per 100 while store brands cost about $6.50 per 100. Compare the labels and you are unlikely to find significant difference in the products.

♦ Get my wife talking about maternity hose and she rants that the designers must have cut them to fit baboons. Me? I rant that manufacturers overcharge for anything with the word "maternity" in front of it.

During her latest pregnancy, Jan, who normally wears medium-sized L'eggs, solved the hose dilemma by simply ordering large sizes of standard hose. She found these fit much better than maternity hose. Me? I found they fit our budget better.

INFANTS AND TODDLERS

♦ Many baby products are luxuries at best, wastes of money at worst. Following are some you may wish to avoid:

- **Bassinets**. If you're given one, use it. But don't go out and buy one. Clothes baskets or a large drawer covered with a quilt will do the job. Or just place your child in a crib from day one.

- **Formula**. Pediatricians usually prefer that babies be breast fed. This minimizes food allergies, infections, and perhaps the likelihood of childhood obesity. It's also free.

- **Jarred baby foods** are convenient for occasional use but expensive for everyday use. It's easy and much more economical to mash or puree foods you've prepared for the rest of the family (use a fork, blender, or food processor). It's also easy to puree larger quantities of food and freeze the excess in ice-cube trays. Once frozen, pop the cubes into a freezer bag. Later, you can place a cube in a dish, defrost it, and serve.

- **Baby food grinders** are sometimes useful for pureeing your fare into food an infant can stomach, but most foods can be mashed quite easily by hand.

- **Baby juices** cost two to three times more than the juices marketed to adults. And if you follow the pediatrician's advice of diluting adult juices half and half with water, adult juices are cheaper still. Admittedly, some infant juices are fortified with additional vitamins, but if you're feeding your child properly, the added vitamins are overkill anyway.

- **Baby applesauce** is considerably more expensive than normal applesauce. Buy the adult version.

- **Traveling crib**. An inflatable plastic wading pool (available at most department stores) makes an inexpensive replacement for a portable travel crib. Inflate it, cover it with a sheet, tuck the edges of the sheet under the bottom of the pool, and put your infant (or young toddler) in it.

- **Bibs**. Avoid terrycloth bibs or you'll be forever washing them. Get a few inexpensive plastic ones and sponge them clean after use.

- **Baby bathtubs**. The kitchen sink works fine for infants if you line it with a towel. Infants are about as mobile as a plant and don't collect dirt all that quickly, so don't bother with the mutual torture of bathing too often. Toddlers can be washed in a tub, but placing them in a plastic clothes basket (inside the tub), keeps them from sliding around.

- **Baby soaps** are costly and unneeded. Use a plain-Jane soap that is low in scents, additives, and antibacterial agents.

- **Baby shampoo** does have fewer additives and while it may sting less when it gets in the eyes, the "No Tears" claim is more hype than fact. Adult shampoos won't melt baby's hair or eyes, so use them. Babies don't have much hair, so go lean on the amount of shampoo used.

- **Talcum powder** on an infant's bottom will neither prevent nor cure diaper rash. In fact, an infant's skin is sometimes irritated by powder. Talcum powder is also potentially dangerous—airborne particles can damage an infant's lungs and have caused pneumonia and death.

- **Commercial diaper wipes** are another unnecessary purchase. The economical alternative: Use warm wash clothes, or make your own wipes from paper towels (see *Formula* chapter). If you do opt for commercial wipes, avoid those with alcohol in the ingredients.

- **Full-sized cribs** are more expensive and less versatile than portable cribs. Portable cribs can be rolled between rooms in the house and pack into a small bundle for travel. Not all portable cribs are safe, however, so research before you purchase.

- **Infant swings.** Generations of parents managed to pacify children during the first months of life without this Yuppie rage. Consequently, infant swings are on my thumbs-down list. Nonetheless, some parents swear by them and if their opinions override my good advice, at least have the good sense to buy a windup model—they are cheaper to buy and operate (no batteries needed). Buy the windup model with the longest running time.

- **Walkers** have the highest accident rate of any group of baby products (nearly 25,000 injuries per year). While using them, children routinely crash down stairs, tumble into pools, and tip over onto concrete floors. Save your money (and your child).

- **Changing tables** rate high on the unneeded list. Any elevated surface will do—the top of a dresser, washer, or dryer. Worried about kids falling off an unofficial changing table? Then build a rail around the top of the dresser. The best solution, however, is to not leave a child unattended. Gather everything you need for a diaper change before you set the child down.

- **Diaper wraps.** You'll hear radically different opinions about the fancy (and expensive) diaper wraps used with cloth diapers: everything from 'Made in Heaven' to 'Cursed by Hell.' I side with the latter group. As far as I'm concerned, the reason these wraps 'breathe' (a quality the manufacturers tout), is because they leak. After trying several brands, my wife and I reverted to the old-standby—cheap, plastic overpants. Coated-nylon overpants are also excellent and, though more expensive, last longer. Neither of these simple and inexpensive overpants 'breathe' but I've yet to hear a doctor or nurse object to their use.

♦ For diaper rash, get a 10-ounce tin of *Bag Balm*, a product made to protect cows' utters, but sold at many pharmacies. It works extremely well, despite instructions stating, "For veterinary use only." Ounce for ounce, it's four times cheaper than *A&D Ointment* or *Desitin*.

Besides using it for diaper rash, parents who are constantly washing their hands after diaper changes should use *Bag Balm* as a hand cream. It prevents and cures chapped hands.

♦ You can make a nice, inexpensive changing table for infants from a trolley cart. Lay a piece of foam on the top shelf for the baby (cover the foam with fabric if you want) and put changing supplies on the bottom shelves.

If you're concerned about your baby squirming off the top shelf, insert two lengths of 1/2-inch doweling between the trolley's handles to create a rail around the perimeter of that shelf.

One of the beauties of this "changing table" is that the trolley cart can be put to another use after your child is out of diapers. Ours is now in the office supporting our new "baby"—a computer printer.

♦ A good bib (a large plastic one with pockets to catch food slithering floorward) greatly reduces the number of clothes you'll wash and the outfits your child will ruin.

♦ Use a car seat for children weighing under 40 pounds—for safety and to avoid the hefty fines you can receive in any of the 50 states for an infraction.

Save money by buying one convertible car seat instead of an infant car seat plus a larger seat for toddlers. This is not a compromising. Convertible car seats are well-rated for all children up to 40 pounds in weight.

♦ Few parents relish feeding toddlers without use of a high chair, but that doesn't mean you need to invest in a throne. An inexpensive alternative to a true high chair is a portable high chair that grips the edges of tables and counters. Portable high chairs work well and are about half the price of high chairs. They also travel with you when you visit friends and keep the dining room uncluttered.

♦ If you have a daughter, you're likely to receive more little dresses as presents than you can possibly use. Keep several, exchange the rest for items you still need.

You are also likely to receive duplicate outfits or widgets you can't use. Don't know where to return them? My wife sometimes uses this trick when she knows a gift should go back: While thanking the gift-giver, she'll effuse, "What a cute widget/outfit. Where did you ever find it?"

Unable to learn where to return an item? Save it, unused, and give it as a baby gift to someone else.

♦ Young children grow so fast you're smart to buy clothes that are one or two sizes too large and to let your child grow into them.

♦ Babies and young children don't care if what they wear is Gucci or gauche, new or old. Take advantage of the innocent years (up to age six or seven) to dress children in used clothing from friends, thrift shops, garage sales, rummage sales, and bazaars. Do it now and save for the expensive years ahead when children go to school and get "educated."

When buying used clothing at rummage sales, garage sales, thrift shops and the like, you won't always find what you want when you want it. Think ahead. If you find something that is a few sizes too large that will be useful later, buy it and store it.

♦ If you purchase a number of unisex outfits and colors for your first child, you'll have the basis of a wardrobe for your next child, whatever its sex.

♦ Dirt and stains stick to babies and young children as naturally as big bills stick to dry-cleaned goods. If you buy children's clothing labeled "dry-clean only," don't say you weren't warned.

♦ Children have their diapers changed about 5300 times during the first two-and-a-half years of life. Disposable diapers, at an average cost of 26¢ each, are the most convenient but most expensive diapering option and will cost you about $1378.

Services that clean your cloth diapers each week are a little less convenient and, on average, a little less expensive. The average cost for 2 1/2 years of service is about $1260. Find out more about these services by looking them up in the *Yellow Pages* (under Diaper Service) or by contacting the National Association of Diaper Services (2017 Walnut St., Philadephia, PA 19103, 215-569-3650)

The cheapest option is to wash diapers yourself. Assuming costs of $240 for diapers and overwraps, three washes per week, average electric rates for the appliances involved, and detergent fees of 40¢ per load, home laundering costs about $570 for a first child. That's a cost of 10.7¢ per diaper. For a second child, the cost drops to about 6¢ per diaper because you already own the diapers.

♦ With our first child, my wife and I initially opted for the diaper service because the daily changing of 10 to 12 diapers gave us enough exposure to diapers. After about a year, however, we found the monthly bill harder to stomach than the stench of washing diapers—especially since our daughter's diaper use had dropped to six or seven diapers per day.

If you make such a switch, do it as your child is growing into a new diaper size. You'll be steamed if you invest in the needed diapers only to discover they are soon too small.

♦ Washing diapers, while not high on the list of fun jobs, is not as repugnant a chore as legend has it: As parents are fond of saying, it's not so bad when it's your kid. Talk to a few mothers and glean their tricks for making the job short and sweet.

Besides the money saved from washing diapers, I've noted that parents who wash diapers get their children potty-trained sooner than parents using disposables or a diaper service. Coincidence? Probably, but it holds true among our friends.

♦ Purchase used diapers cheaply through diaper services. These diapers will be slightly tattered, but they have plenty of life left.

♦ Sterility-minded Americans usually use a hot/warm cycle to wash diapers. Warm rinses, however, don't get your diapers any cleaner. Save money and rinse with cold water.

A friend uses cold water to wash *and* rinse her children's diapers. She uses the prescribed amount of detergent, adds 1/3 to 1/2 cup of bleach, washes, and then throws the diapers in the dryer. "Never had a problem getting the diapers perfectly clean," she reports.

Don't believe it? Try a test load. If you're satisfied with the results, you'll save money from here on in. If you're dissatisfied, you've lost little—but don't let that stop you from comparing my ancestry to a foul, festering diaper.

♦ Brittle plastic pants and bibs can be softened by rubbing the plastic with baby (or mineral) oil.

♦ Baby oil is just mineral oil with a little added fragrance. Buy whichever one is cheapest.

CHILDREN

♦ The knees go first in children's pants. Double the life of these pants by reinforcing the knees with iron-on patches. Iron the patches to the inside of the knee and you won't alter the pants' appearance.

♦ Lengthen the arms of a child's winter coat by adding knitted cuffs to the sleeves. Get these cuffs at the notion counters of department stores and make the coat last another season.

♦ Shorten the legs of old tables and chairs and, *voilà*, you're left with children's furniture.

♦ Old, adult T-shirts make nightgowns for grade-school girls.

♦ Make necklaces for little girls by staining elbow macaroni in food coloring for several minutes. Let the macaroni dry and then string them on fishing line.

♦ A children's modeling compound can be made from 2 cups of clean sand mixed with 1 cup of water and 1 cup of cornstarch. The figures and forts built with this compound will harden into permanent structures. Cost is about 35¢ versus upwards of $10 for commercial product.

♦ Inexpensive chalkboards can be made by painting a piece of masonite (like a 4-foot by 8-foot sheet) with blackboard paint (available from paint and hardware stores). Paint the board thoroughly, then apply a second coat just after the first coat dries. Glue or nail a piece of trim to the bottom of the board to hold chalk. Clean the chalkboard periodically with white vinegar.

♦ Don't take your kids to toy stores with you. Even if you think you can resist their pleading, why risk it?

♦ Take advantage of the early years (age 0 to about 6) to give your children inexpensive, used merchandise as gifts (birthdays and Christmas). At this age kids aren't aware of whether something is used or new. Nor are they aware of brand names. Once you get into the school years, gift giving may not be so simple or cheap.

♦ Garage sales are the place to find used toys, high chairs, strollers, bicycles, books, sports equipment, and clothing for your children. By the time another family is ready to usher a possession out the door, the price is likely to be dirt cheap. Finding items you want is a hit-and-miss proposition so buy anything of possible interest when you find it and store it. Because the prices at garage sales are about a tenth of what you'll pay for new goods, you can afford the luxury of storing items.

To work the garage sales like a professional, check Friday's paper (under "Garage Sales" in the classified ads) and locate a neighborhood where you can shop many sales with a minimum of driving. Arrive first thing Saturday morning and quickly make the rounds of each sale you intend to visit.

♦ Wearing used clothing is something many children may not be proud of, so you may opt to buy new garments for school clothing. But don't forfeit the entire game. Get rough-and-tumble clothing for home use or for sports from rummage sales, thrift shops, and second-hand stores. Make sure to pull out old name tags before presenting this clothing to your children.

♦ Older kids will accept used clothing with more enthusiasm if the item has a trendy label. Get your hands on labels that impress by: extracting them from your own clothing, pirating them from the clothes of older siblings, requesting them from friends who are donating clothes to charity... Sew these labels into the used clothes you've bought and children are suddenly much happier. Okay, it's underhanded—but so is lying about Santa Claus and the Easter Bunny.

It's an option—you decide whether the end justifies the means.

♦ Through a little positive reinforcement, you can foster fond feelings in your children about rummage sales and thrift shops. Give the kids a dollar or two of their own to spend. Don't complain about their taste—better they blow a buck than a ten spot at Toys R Us on more expensive junk. Make shopping at these places rewarding and they won't mind returning.

♦ Masking tape around crayons becomes a cast that keeps them from breaking so easily.

♦ Emergency rooms around the country see several hundred cycling-related head injuries each day. We're talking about more than dollars and cents here, but the money saved from preventing head injuries is added incentive to make your kids wear helmets whenever they saddle up. Buy helmets that are ANSI or SNELL approved.

Naturally, older kids are likely to object—they believe they are immortal. But imagine what happens to an egg-like head moving at 20 miles per hour when it stops instantly against the tarmac and you'll understand the transitory nature of immortality.

♦ Teaching kids to be money wise and advertising savvy will save *you* thousands of dollars. After all, some of the 20,000 TV advertisements targeted at kids will hit their mark, meaning your children will be begging for money.

Unfortunately, as your children grow, they may become less inclined to listen to you (a teen-age belief is that no one is stupider than parents), so it may be hard to teach them the facts of smart spending.

A possible solution? Buy your children a subscription to *Zillions—Consumer Reports for Kids* (Box 51777, Boulder, CO 80321-1177). The magazine appeals most to children ages 10 to 14 and reports on things they care about: clothes, skateboards, videos, shoes, fast food... Products are tested by kids and advice comes across as kid-to-kid gospel.

The magazine will not only help children spend money wisely, it will teach them about earning and investing money. Try it awhile. If your kids read it, the magazine will save you much more than you pay for it.

♦ Allowances are very educational and, when properly used, will save you more than they cost. Through allowances you can teach your children one of the facts of life: no money, no spending. Let them use their own dollars to buy snacks, gifts, toys, superfluous clothing, and entertainment. And when a child pleads, "I want a new bike, new Levis, or new...," take the pressure off yourself. Tell them, "Sure, if you can afford it."

When they spend their allowance, give them your advice, but don't bail them out of the troubles they create. Along with those troubles come some valuable lessons.

♦ While children should have chores that are expected of them, it's not unreasonable to hire children for chores that are beyond the call of duty—e.g., painting the house. Giving children the opportunity to build their savings accounts in this way also gives you more of an excuse to refuse their frequent pleas for money.

Note: With younger children, don't be overly critical of imperfect work or short attention spans. Reward their desire to help and gently work on the job's execution.

♦ Teach children that turning lights and appliances off, using hot water conscientiously, and turning down the heat are all big energy savers.

Reinforce the idea that energy saved equals money saved: Set up a chart that measures each child's contribution to saving energy. Then, when you pay utility bills, share the savings with your children or do something special for them (e.g., pizza dinner). When there's a payback, kids will get far more excited about helping.

♦ Many experts believe it is unwise to attach cash incentives or penalties to routine chores and schoolwork. I believe there are exceptions to the rule. The rewards of flossing and brushing teeth, for example, are not terribly tangible. Rewards (monetary or otherwise) are a pat on the back that will keep a child's motivation up and their dental bills down.

♦ Consider including teen-agers in family financial planning meetings. Make them aware of the family's financial restrictions, of where the money goes each month, of which expenses are discretionary and which are not, of opportunities that are simply not possible for the family at this time. Your children don't need to know all the details, but an understanding of the generalities is likely to make them less demanding and more willing to help.

♦ Give your children incentive to drive responsibly with some reality therapy—have them sign an agreement stating that they will pay the insurance deductible if they cause an auto accident.

♦ State universities can educate your children for about $31,000 less than private colleges can. In 1990, tuition, room, and board cost $14,403 at the average private college versus $6,523 for in-state residents at public universities ($9832 for out-of-staters).

What's more, a growing body of experts assert that top-quality public schools will educate your children as well as the big-name private schools and that reputation is not synomous with quality. Learn about the quality and cost of over a thousand American colleges and universities by consulting *Money Guide: Best College Buys* (order from: P.O. Box 30626, Tampa, FLA 33630, $4.50).

♦ For more child-related money savers see the *Formula* and *Reuse* chapters.

♦ Finally, treat your children well—not just because you love them, but because later in life they may become your independent retirement account (IRA). Maybe the $225,000 you put into each child will pay off. Then again...

Interest works night and day, in fair weather and in foul. It gnaws at a man's substance with invisible teeth.

Henry Ward Beecher

Banking Matters

Borrowing and investing money are opposite sides of the same coin. The money you borrow is money someone else has invested—with a middleman (a financial institution) to coordinate transactions and glean profits.

No one denies that financial institutions have the right to make a buck for their role, but neither do you want to be victimized by these institutions at every flip of the coin. And that can happen. Whether you're investing or borrowing, it's easy to stumble into pits designed to pay you less (when you're investing) or wring you for more (when you're borrowing). Following is a listing of pits to avoid and practices to consider when attending your money matters.

AUTO LOANS

♦ Avoid adjustable-rate auto loans— many of these auto loans don't have annual caps and in a volatile market you could be looking at rocketing rates. Another reason to avoid adjustable rates: In most cities you can find fixed-rate auto loans offering rates that are just as low.

♦ In most cities you'll get a lower interest rate (often as much as 1%) on auto loans through a credit union. As with any loan, make sure you compare the annual percentage rate (APR) of different loans.

♦ Each month the "Money Scorecard" column in *Money* magazine lists which banks in the 24 largest metropolitan areas offer the best rate on auto loans. Note: This list does not monitor credit unions.

BILL-PAYING

♦ A bank offering you pay-by-phone service can save you hours of time and many dollars each year. My wife and I pay eight different utility and credit-card bills by phone each month. One quick call authorizes the bank to cut checks to those eight different firms. This saves us hours of time, eight 29-cent stamps, and the cost of envelopes and checks.

♦ Let the bank automatically pay as many bills as possible (e.g., mortgage payments, medical insurance). Saves you time, postage, envelopes, and the cost of checks.

CERTIFICATES OF DEPOSIT (CDs)

♦ Certificates of deposit (CDs) are an investment scheme for money you want to keep relatively liquid. The return from a CD is much simpler to estimate than that from money markets and savings accounts. Fees are rarely charged, so when you compare different CDs, concentrate on the interest rates and the penalties (if any) for early withdrawal.
Shop around for the best rate at different banks before tying up your money. The fastest and easiest way to shop for high-yield CDs on a national level is to consult the Money Scorecard in *Money* magazine. Here you'll find a listing of banks (phone numbers included) offering the best rates on CDs. If regional rates are low, go national: Use the phone to open an account with a distant bank, then mail in your check for a CD. It's fast and cheap.

♦ Not many of us need to worry about it, but don't put more than $100,000 in one bank's CDs. That's the limit of your insurance should the bank go belly up—something happening quite regularly these days.

CHECKS

♦ If you buy replacement checks from your bank, you are paying twice what you should. Bypass the bank and get your checks from *Current* in Colorado Springs (800-426-0822) or *Checks in the Mail* in Los Angeles (800-733-4443).

These companies guarantee your checks will work with your financial institution. I can give testimony that I've had no trouble with my mail-order checks—now if I can get these guys to pay my bills!

♦ If you run out of checks, use the deposit slip in the back of your checkbook. These slips have all the vital information found on a normal check—the bank's identification number, the account number, your name and address—and are valid tender if the vendor accepts them.
Whenever you write a check to the bank, use these deposit slips to save your normal checks.

CHECKING ACCOUNTS

♦ In most cities credit unions offer the best deals on checking accounts. You've gotta learn the right lingo, though—credit unions call the accounts "share-draft accounts."
Even if you don't have a credit union at work, you are probably eligible to join the union of a relative or in-law. A few credit unions let anyone in the geographic area join.
You can't assume, however, that because it's a credit union it offers the best deal. Input the variables like interest rates, fees, penalties, convenience, required balances; then let your wetware (brain) sort out the best deal.

♦ Sometimes you need to float a check for an extra day (e.g., maybe you're not sure you have sufficient funds). Accomplish this by writing the check for a charge in red ink. Bank computers processing checks are unable to read red ink and will set your check aside for manual processing. Typically, this buys you an extra day or two before your account gets charged.

♦ You've been looking for your checkbook the last week and finally conclude it's lost or stolen. What do you do? Close your account and tell the bank not to pay the outstanding checks? That gets expensive—the bank may charge you over $10 for each stop payment ordered.
The inexpensive solution is to notify the bank of the loss, then refuse to pay the bank for any checks it approves with counterfeited signatures. It is the bank's responsibility

to inspect the John Hancock on your checks against your real signature (a copy of your signature is kept on file at the bank). If the bank refuses to pay a counterfeited check, then the business that accepted the check is held responsible—their penalty for not verifying the credentials of the crook who forged your signature.

♦ There are occasions when it is worth ordering a stop payment on a check. If a business fails to provide the service it promised or a product falls short of the advertised claims, stop payment if the vendor is callous toward your grievance. Businesses are more responsive to problems when they learn payment has been withheld. You can only play this option for a few days before your account is charged, so quickly inspect the goods and services you purchase.

DEBIT CARDS

♦ These 'cash' cards don't draw from a line of credit but take money out of your checking account. They are equivalent to writing a check to your account for cash (when drawing money from a machine) or writing a check to a vendor (when paying for goods or services).

The fee involved for using your cash card in an automated teller machine (ATM) depends on your account. A few banks gouge you for using these cards, but the average transaction fee of 25¢ to 50¢ is low compared to using credit cards for cash advances.

♦ Given the option between paying a vendor with a credit card or with cash drawn from a debit card, opt for the credit card (assuming you're not carrying an outstanding balance). With the credit card, you won't actually pay the bill for another month; during that time your money can be earning interest.

♦ Unlike credit cards that have a maximum liability of $50 on lost cards, in some states you can lose much more if someone gets hold of your debit card. Typically, your liability for unauthorized withdrawals doesn't start until you receive your statement. If you don't respond to problems within several days, however, you risk up to $500 in unauthorized charges. The moral? Review your statement promptly upon its arrival.

HOME EQUITY LOANS

♦ If you own a home and have considerable equity in it, you probably qualify for a home equity loan. Use such loans to build an addition to the house, finance cars, take vacations, pay for a child's education, or even to make another investment. The banks consider these low-risk loans (they've got your house as collateral) so the interest rates are several percentage points better than unsecured loans. Furthermore, the interest on a loan under $100,000 is tax deductible.

Check the current rates in *Money* magazine's "Money Scorecard." It lists the banks offering the best rates in the 24 largest metropolitan areas.

♦ Need a cheap way to escape the financial strain from the monthly balances on your credit cards? Take out a home equity loan. Use the loan to pay off all your credit cards. The advantage? At the time of this writing, you'll pay the bank 9.5% on your loan versus the 18% or 19% you may be paying the credit card company.

Warning: Don't employ this trick if you'll run up the outstanding balance on the cards again. Otherwise, you'll just be piling new debt on top of old.

MONEY MARKET FUNDS AND SAVINGS ACCOUNTS

♦ Put money that must remain liquid in a non-bank money market fund rather than a bank savings account. You can get your cash out fast, write large checks against it, and will earn 1.5% to 2% more on your funds.

One word of caution: Money placed in these funds is not insured by the FDIC so invest with a top-rated fund. Back issues of *Money* magazine (visit the library) will help you zero in on several funds worthy of your money.

♦ Although you can net more money using a non-bank money market fund as a savings account, most people let a bank manage their savings accounts. Some people do this to have their money insured, others value the simplicity of having their savings and checking accounts under the same roof (one-stop banking).

Deciding whether to use a bank's standard savings account or its money market savings account (which often boasts a higher interest rate) is no easy task. Fees associated with many money market funds or the larger minimum balances required (to have fees waived or to qualify for the higher interest rates) can play Pacman with your profits.

There is no easy way to generalize here. To get the best deal you must carefully study each savings program: its return, fees, minimum balances... If it all seems too complicated, use the bank's traditional account (either a statement or passbook account). The actual return on traditional accounts is most always competitive with, and often much better than, the actual return on the bank's money market savings accounts.

HOME LOANS

♦ "It's like pouring money down a rat hole," home owners are fond of saying of renting a house. But home owners have a rat hole of their own—interest. By the time a home owner pays off a 30-year, $100,000 loan, he will have paid a total of $264,000 at 8%, $316,000 at 10%, and $370,000 at 12%. That's a huge rat hole.

If your financial institution allows it (and most do) put whatever extra money you can each month toward a principal payment on your house. We're talking about big savings here. For example, if you have a 30-year, $100,000 loan at a rate of 10%, your monthly payment is $877.50. If, however, you paid $900 each month (only $22.50 more), you'd pay off the loan in 26 years (instead of 30) and, therefore, pay *$33,328 less* in interest. That's no misprint: you'd save 33 grand.

The same mathematic principles explain why you save so much with a 15-year loan versus a 30-year loan. Paying off a 15-year, $100,000 loan at 10%, you'd pay $1075 per month (versus $877.50 per month for 30 years). Over 15 years you'd pay a total of $193,000 (versus a total of $316,000 for a 30-year loan). Your saving: $123,000.

Instead of signing a 15-year note, however, my wife, who worked in the mortgage banking industry for years, recommends getting a 30-year loan. Shop extensively for the lowest interest rate and be sure the loan allows you to make extra principal payments whenever you choose. Then, treat your loan exactly like a 15-year loan, making those larger payments that save you a ton of money. Why bother getting a 30-year loan if you intend to pay it off in 15 years? Because if times get tight, you are not trapped into higher payments—you can drop back to the required smaller payments until the family's cash flow increases.

♦ Shop the market extensively before settling into a particular loan. In the same city, the cheapest home loan is likely to be 1% lower than the highest. Doesn't seem like much, but for a $100,000, 30-year loan, the lower rate saves you at least $25,000 over the life of the loan.

Shop the credit unions, too—in many cities they offer the best rates.

SAVINGS INVESTMENT PLANS (SIPs)

♦ People have the amazing capacity to spend whatever they earn. Protect yourself from yourself by using an employer deduction plan that automatically places some of your paycheck in a savings investment plan. Such plans— often referred to as a 401(k)—have additional benefits: They can reduce your annual tithing to Uncle Sam by hundreds of dollars because they defer taxes until the time the plan matures (or is cashed in). Furthermore, many employers contribute to your plan at a percentage of what you invest.

Many people avoid these plans, believing them to be complicated. They really aren't, as a knowledgeable friend or a supervisor in the human resources or benefits departments will prove to you if you ask questions. You should ask questions—the money these accounts both earn and save justifies the research.

♦ Many companies let you take a hardship withdrawal against your SIP (or your profit-sharing account) amounting to 50% of what you have vested. Interest rates are usually prime plus 1.3% and your interest payments go back into your plan. In essence you are borrowing money from yourself and then paying yourself back.

While this trick may not earn as much as leaving the account untouched, it beats taking out a bank loan to pay for home improvements, medical expenses, or your children's education.

SWINDLES

♦ You worked long hours for your money so don't lose it the fast way: through an investment swindle. Swindlers manage to separate over $10 billion a year from their victims, victims who are probably not much different from you. The way investment swindles work and how to keep your money from helping clever crooks retire is beyond the scope of this book, but you can educate yourself by obtaining a free booklet entitled *Investment Swindles: How They Work and How To Avoid Them*. Order booklet 548X from the Consumer Information Center-X, P.O. Box 100, Pueblo, CO 81002.

Some basics to remember, even if you don't order the pamphlet:

- If it sounds too good to be true, it probably is.

- If a salesman glosses over the risk, says there is no risk, or gets aggressive when you discuss risk, be suspicious.

- Most swindles will list reasons why you must act immediately. Urgency is important to swindles; they don't want you to think or check with a regulatory agency.

- Ask lots of questions: Where did you get my name? What are the risks? Do you have a brochure explaining the investment that I can study at my leisure? Can you explain this proposal to my attorney (or banker, investment advisor, etc.)? What industry and government regulatory agencies oversee the salesman's company (tell them you want to check the company's standing with these agencies—and then do so before investing)?

- If a salesman seems unwilling to answer questions but tries to keep you answering questions (questions that seek to elicit a "yes" response) you may have problems. Same goes if a salesman takes an aggressive approach toward the questions posed. Reputable firms encourage you to gather information and ask questions.

Batteries

"Batteries not included." You see these words often—too often. Everything from the emergency flashlight in the car to the pencil sharpener on the desk runs off batteries—children's toys, personal stereos, cameras, portable tape recorders, even computers. Today, Americans own over a billion battery-operated devices, which means McDonald's is not the only one selling billions of energy packets. Batteries compete with burgers as a multi-billion dollar business.

Every time you pay $2.99 for two measly AA batteries, you're probably aware of that. But are you aware of ways to short circuit the expense? Try the following quiz.

♦ Should you buy inexpensive general-purpose batteries, medium-priced heavy-duty batteries, or expensive alkaline cylinders?

If you're energizing a little-used device, go cheap. When buying batteries for one of your mainstays, go expensive. Alkaline batteries cost three or four times more than general-purpose batteries but they last nine or 10 times longer.

Tests conducted by *Consumer Reports* showed that alkaline batteries cost about 13¢ an hour to operate. Heavy-duty batteries cost about 26¢ per hour to operate and general-purpose batteries averaged about 35¢ per hour of operation. Which means the cheapest batteries are really the most expensive.

♦ What brand of alkaline batteries is best?

Despite what Mary Lou tells you, there is little difference between *Energizers* and any other major-brand alkaline battery. Go with the cheapest or, preferably, with what is on sale.

♦ Should you stockpile batteries when they are on sale?

Yes and no. Load up with enough to see you through the next year but not so many that they'll last through the next decade. General and heavy-duty batteries have about a 9-month shelf life. Alkalines will store nicely for a few years but their light power dims if ignored too long.

♦ Are rechargeable nickel-cadmium (nicad) batteries worth the high initial cost?

If you own an often-used device that devours batteries like teenagers devour Big Macs, rechargeables can pay for themselves in several months.

Unfortunately, nicads shine only about a third as long as alkaline batteries before blackout. Then they need recharging. Nicads also leak their charge quickly so don't let them sit in a device that sees occasional use (like the emergency flashlight in a car).

♦ Are all nicads created equal?

In the AA sizes, most nicads store about 500 milli-amps of juice. But in the C and D sizes, significant differences exist. Many manufacturers fill the extra volume with air, which doesn't generate much light.

Look for high-capacity cells in the C and D sizes. They weigh about twice as much as the Twinkie (air-filled) models. They also cost more but are worth the cost because they store nearly twice as much energy. At the time of this writing, Radio Shack is a good national outlet for high-capacity nicads.

♦ How can you minimize the use of batteries?

Many battery-driven devices can be run off standard household current if you own a suitable AC adapter (transformer). Even a device that did not come with an adapter will often accept one: Check for an adapter outlet marked with a direct current (DC) voltage rating, like "DC 6V" or "DC 9V."

At Radio Shack, fixed-voltage adapters cost about $8 while universal adapters, which can be set at many different voltage levels, cost about $13. It won't take many battery charges to recoup the cost of these adapters.

When buying, take your device to the store and ask the salesperson if the adapter has the proper tip to power it.

♦ How do you ensure the batteries you buy are fresh?

Some batteries come with built-in battery testers. These battery testers work but the packaging is expensive and it doesn't take three guesses to figure out who pays for it. A cheaper alternative is to buy batteries from an outlet like K-Mart that, due to their low prices, sees a brisk business in battery sales. Their batteries don't sit long enough to get stale.

He that does not save pennies will never have pounds.
Danish proverb

Books And Magazines

It's ironic how adverse I am to buying books and magazines: I am, after all, a writer. My condition, however, started long before my career. In college days, my bookstore hung a marquee each semester congratulating students who bought themselves into the $100 Club. In 1972, $100 purchased a skyscraper of textbooks and students thought it an honor to make the list—as if the size of their stack correlated to the size of their IQ.

Personally, I took the list as an affront to my intelligence. Books for most classes could be purchased at half price from students who wanted to make the $100 Club list again and were loading the war chest by unloading last semester's books. Also, the library held reference copies of every text book used in the college curriculum. It was easy to arm yourself for a full schedule of classes for under $40.

Then, during my last two years of college, I went a little berserk. In a rebellious mood of anti-snobbery, I tried making the $0 Club each semester. I would borrow books from fellow classmates and read a week's assignments in an evening. I would use the library reference copies. I even went so far as to avoid classes where a book was absolutely necessary, choosing instead those courses in which exams were based on the material presented in class. In retrospect the $0 Club strikes me as a moronic exercise in undermining the value of a $16,000 education. Nevertheless, it did teach me fine points for finding cheap reads.

♦ Use your local library. Your taxes pay for it and you can easily get more out of it than you put in. Books, magazines, newspapers, audio books, new books, rare

books—you can get them all here. See the *Library* chapter
for using this resource to maximum advantage.

♦ If you're a voracious reader and insist on owning
the books you read, breed familiarity with the local used-
book stores (check the *Yellow Pages* under Books—Used &
Rare). Prices are usually a fraction of new—especially if
you're buying paperbacks.

♦ Take advantage of magazine come-ons to join book
clubs. You'll see deals like "Three Books for $3" or "Buy one
book at half price and get a second book free." You can be
quite confident the advertisement is legitimate when it's in
a large, national magazine, but read the fine print to see if
there is a catch—like mandatory additional purchases.
If the club has no additional purchase requirements
(i.e., I can cancel at any time) I always take advantage of
their "loss leader" offer. If the club requires additional
purchases, I join only if the majority of books offered can't
be found elsewhere (e.g., the library or used-book stores).
Most clubs send you a monthly listing of books,
featuring a "book of the month" that you will be sent if you
don't actually refuse the offer. I hate this modus operandi
so after receiving the books from the come-on, I usually
cancel my membership.

♦ Borrow from friends. If a friend raves about a book
or you see a book of interest on his or her bookshelf, ask
to read it. Naturally, one good turn deserves another: Make
sure you return the book promptly and in good condition if
you hope to borrow again.

♦ Check the classified ads under Garage Sales or
Rummage Sales to scope out the local happenings. Typically, you'll find tables of books here with ridiculous prices:
paperbacks for a dime or a quarter, hardbacks for 50¢,
encyclopedias for $5 a set...

♦ Goodwill, St. Vincent De Paul, and other thrift
stores are other good outlets for cheap reads. Use them to
stock your book shelves with paperbacks you would like to
read (if you ever get time). When vacation rolls around or

rainy weather has you cuddled on the couch, you'll have plenty of 25¢ and 50¢ books to entice you.

♦ Undoubtedly, I'm not the only person whose psychological hang-ups and feelings of ingrained guilt stemmed from the parade of unread subscription magazines that marched across the coffee table each month. When I finally let the subscriptions expire, the guilt drained away.

Most magazines (with the exception of the weekly news, sports, and business periodicals) are not particularly time sensitive. Read them now or in six months and you get the same benefit. So why pay for such information when libraries supply it free? Every month I check out six to 10 back issues of "old" magazines—several for myself, several for my wife. If the stuff never gets read, we may feel intellectually bankrupt but at least we escape the dollar doldrums, and the deep psychological disturbances that creates.

♦ I share the subscription cost of trade magazines with other writers. The subscriptions are pricey and writers are poor, so we rely on our cunning to lower prices. The same practice can easily take place among neighbors and friends with monthly magazines—share the cost and pass around the issue.

In a parallel vein, consider swapping back issues among neighbors and friends. You know, I'll swap you my Reader's Digest for your... Rolling Stone? Well, you do have to share an interest.

One day soon I'm going to ask my neighbor if he wants to go halfsies on the daily newspaper. He reads it religiously every night, I read it every other day at best, every other week at worst. We're a perfect match. And because we already share the garbage leaving our homes (we combine trash and pay just one bill), we might as well share the garbage coming in.

♦ Most magazine readers subscribe directly with the publisher, but you can often arrange a better deal buying magazines through a middleman—which makes no sense at all.

Before renewing the subscription of your favorite magazine, check out the price difference between ordering direct and ordering from American Family Publishers (800-237-2400) and Publisher's Clearing House (516-883-5432).

♦ Postpone renewing your subscriptions as long as possible. In fact, it often pays to let your subscription expire and then to resubscribe shortly thereafter. Magazines tempt you with their low subscribers' rate to renew as soon as possible. "You wouldn't want to miss a single issue," they say, or, "You can't afford to miss a single issue." Yet if you fail to renew, more and more desperate mail campaigns come your way. It's not unusual for these campaigns to throw you a bone—a lower price than the normal renewal price.

If you know the magazine is dangling an even more enticing introductory offer to new subscribers, let your subscription expire altogether and resubscribe as a new reader later. Sometimes you even receive a free gift.

He that gets money before he gets wit will be but a short while master of it.

English proverb

Cars (Road Emergencies)

My brother and I are firm believers in the emergency value of car manuals put out by such publishers as Chilton and Haynes. Once my brother, with no more car experience than changing spark plugs, replaced the engine to his VW van in the wilds of Mexico with only his manual for advice.

My manual has saved my skin on numerous pettier occasions. One night when my station wagon suddenly started lurching and sputtering, the manual helped me diagnose the problem. I promptly isolated a bad spark plug, replaced it, and was off again. That saved me a tow and a hotel bill. Following are several other cheap tricks to help your wallet survive road emergencies.

♦ Like most ex-VW Beetle owners, I've broken down on remote roads all over the country. I own real cars now, but I still carry a vestige from the old days—a box in each car with emergency tools and supplies. Even with real cars, those supplies have saved me from several tows.

What's in the box? Besides the standard stuff (tire jack and chains) I carry a selection of second-hand tools purchased at pawn shops: standard-slot and phillips-head screwdrivers, crescent wrench, box wrenches, needle-nose pliers, standard pliers, vice grips, hacksaw blades, socket wrenches, spark plug remover, pocket knife. Then there's the duct tape, extra motor oil, water for the radiator (1/2 gallon), spare fan belt, tubeless-tire repair kit and bike pump, plastic tarp to lie on, rags, flashlight (count on problems occurring at night), baling wire, nylon cord, and first-aid supplies. Finally there's a miscellaneous selection of bolts, washers, sheet metal screws, and hose clamps.

My other vehicle—the one I have less confidence in—also packs a set of jumper cables and about 35 feet of thick rope for that day when I can't fix a problem and need a tow to the nearest service station.

♦ I'm amazed by the number of friends who don't hide a spare key on the exterior of their car. The money and time this saves on that day when (not if) you lose your keys or lock them in the car, makes it ludicrous not to have a backup handy.

No need to purchase fancy magnetic key boxes here— they are more easily located by thieves, are not waterproof, and can fall off the vehicle. Instead, locate a well-hidden spot on the chassis, clean it well, center the spare key on a strip of duct tape, and rub the tape onto the chassis.

♦ It is not terribly rare to get two flat tires at the same time. Alternately, you might have one flat and discover your spare has deflated. On one such occasion, it cost me over $50 (and hours of time) to get rolling again. Now I keep a tire pump and a tubeless-tire repair kit in the car. These envelope-sized kits, available at auto-part stores for several dollars, are like adding an extra spare tire to the trunk.

♦ Drivers of older, unreliable cars might consider calling the library and reserving the book *How To Keep your Volkswagen Alive: A Manual of Step-by-Step Procedures for the Compleat Idiot* by John Muir and Tosh Gregg. Even if you don't drive Volkswagens, the manual is full of generic information to diagnose problems and, more importantly, jury-rig solutions. Thanks to the Idiot's Manual, when the clutch rod broke on my friend's Subaru I taught him how to shift without the clutch and we drove 80 miles to the nearest dealer. When the fan belt broke on another friend's Honda late one night, tips gleaned from the Idiot's Manual helped us fashion a spare from nylon cord. Another time a friend's Datsun would not start, leaving us stranded at a mountain trailhead; I remembered a trick from the book about short-circuiting juice to the starting solenoid and it got us going again.

♦ You can avoid numerous problems by steering clear of the riffraff I hang out with, but Murphy lurks wherever you go and he usually picks on the unprepared.

Cars: Mileage

I insist on wringing every mile possible from the gasoline in my cars. Which means I've employed some unorthodox (even stupid) driving practices over time. Five years ago I was in my truck-drafting phase. Tailgating 18-wheelers helped me squeeze 30 to 32 miles out of every gallon of gas—a decided improvement over my normal 27 miles per gallon. Sucking wheel also gave me turbo-power; my gutless VW sped behind the monsters a good five to 10 miles per hour faster than normal.

Bad brakes ended the practice. After nearly plastering the front of my fragile bug to the rear of several trucks, I decided I was being fuel smart but fender foolish. So I moved along to other tactics. Some, like coasting steep downgrades or mountain passes in neutral, are not legal, but in this chapter I've listed the legitimate ways of making your gas go the extra mile.

In 1990, Joe Average spent about $707 to fuel his gas guzzler (assuming he drove 13,000 miles in a car delivering about 26.5 mpg). The good news is that you can easily trim that yearly total by over 15% ($106) through proper car maintenance and good driving habits. And anyone in the market for a new car may be able to slash his or her annual gas bills by as much as 50% ($353). Here's how.

♦ Checked your tire pressure lately? Over 50% of American cars suffer from saggy tires. Under-inflation can increase a tire's rolling resistance (and hence its gas consumption) by 5%. That same rolling resistance ultimately shortens the life of your tires and engine.

That is a hat trick of reasons to check tire pressure monthly. Why so often? For every 10 degree Fahrenheit rise or fall in temperature, your tire pressure rises or falls one-pound per square inch.

♦ Check tires when they are cold and keep them inflated to the figures recommended in your owner's manual (between 30 and 34 psi for most cars).
For more information about tire mileage, safety, and pressure, request a free copy of the *Consumer Tire Guide* from the Tire Industry Safety Council, P.O. Box 1801, Washington, D.C. 20013.

♦ If you don't own radial tires, switch over next time you buy. Compared to bias-ply tires, radials deliver an extra mile per gallon and last longer. They cost more, but save you money in the long haul.

♦ The Environmental Protection Agency (EPA) reports that you will save gas by turning off the engine if your car will be idling more than a minute.

♦ Consider this interesting fact of physics: When you double your speed, you nearly quadruple your air resistance. That explains why a car getting 28 miles per gallon at 55 mph drops to 22 miles per gallon at 65 mph.
Besides saving dollars, statistics prove you're much safer driving at 55 mph—highway fatalities have increased by 20% a year on rural interstates that increased the speed limit from 55 to 65 mph.

♦ Not using the roof rack? Remove it. I monitor my mileage carefully and consistently average one or two miles per gallon less when the car racks go on. Amazing what two bars do to a car's aerodynamics.

♦ Keep the front end of your car aligned. The cost of alignments (especially from a shop offering a special) is low and can pay for itself in saved gas and reduced tire wear.

♦ Even if a car runs adequately, worn plugs, clogged air filters, and aging electrical components can increase fuel consumption by over 10%. Save gas and extend engine life with a good yearly tune-up. Change the air filter, fuel filter, spark plugs, distributor cap and rotor; check the condition of the spark plug cables and change them if they are old; in old-style cars check the timing as well as the gas/air mixture of the carburetor. A mechanical idiot armed with a manual from an auto-parts store can perform most of this work and avoid paying a professional.

♦ Putting the pedal to the metal between city intersections may impress members of the opposite sex but it also robs you of the money needed to take them out. It wastes gas, places unneeded strain on the transmission, and wears the brakes. Work your car gently up the gears and keep glancing ahead at the next traffic light. If it turns red, save your gas (and brake linings) by easing off the accelerator and letting the car decelerate on its own.

Experts recommend you drive as though eggs were taped to your gas and brake pedals. Work the pedals lightly, as if trying to keep from crushing the shells.

♦ If your car has cruise control, use it. On the highway, cruise control is considerably more efficient than the average driver who speeds above, then coasts below, the speed limit. Cruise control is also handy for ticket prevention —most new cars cruise so smoothly it's easy to awake from a daydream with the State Patrol on your tail.

Car owners without cruise control should concentrate on maintaining steady pressure on the gas pedal. Sprinting forward, then easing up, speeds up gas consumption.

♦ Advertising has convinced many drivers to buy gas with more octane than they need. Premium gas does not deliver additional power or improved mileage, so get the cheapest gas that keeps your car from pinging (knocking) when it is working hard. Most cars in this country were designed to run on regular unleaded gas (87 octane). Interestingly, although only 10% of today's cars need a mid-level or premium gas (89 and 91 octane), a third of all car owners buy premium gas.

Look up your vehicle's octane requirements in the owner's manual. Save yourself some money if you've been using Bordeaux to water a beast designed for Gallo.

♦ What happens if your car is designed for regular unleaded gas but pings when you use it? Octane levels in many states are not inspected and your local station may be selling mislabeled gas—visit a few other stations. If pinging persists, your car may simply need more octane now—these things happen with age—so try a mid-grade gas or feed the beast with a half-and-half brew (half regular, half premium).

♦ If 4/40 air conditioning (4 windows down at 40 mph) can keep you fairly comfortable, keep the car's air conditioner off. Air conditioners require additional horsepower to run and increase your gas consumption by 7% to 10%.

At freeway speed, however, opening the windows disrupts the aerodynamics of the car. Above 45 mph, it's more efficient to use the air conditioner.

Buying a new or used car? A light-colored vehicle with tinted windows reduces the need for an air-conditioner.

♦ Idling your car for several minutes before driving is not a good use of gas and, depending on how your automatic choke is set, may not even be good for the car. Instead, turn on the car and go. But drive slow and easy for several minutes while the engine warms up.

♦ A cold engine burns twice as much gas as a warm one, so run all of your driving errands at the same time to take advantage of your warmed-up engine.

♦ On downhills, let gravity help. Ease up on the gas.

♦ Drafting trucks (at a distance of four or five car lengths) doesn't make for scenic driving but it will improve your mileage by as much as 15%. Even if this isn't one of your standard ploys, remember its value when you suddenly notice your fuel gauge lying in the red zone and the nearest service station is 20 miles away. Try a few Hail Marys, too.

♦ Come springtime, take off the snow tires as soon as possible. They wear out faster than normal tires *and* deliver poorer mileage.

♦ New-car buyers should know the merits of manual transmissions. Manual transmissions are not only more reliable (fewer repair bills), they save gas, too. In some cases a four-speed manual transmission will deliver 6.5 miles per gallon more than the same car outfitted as a three-speed automatic.

♦ New-car shoppers should get the *Gas Mileage Guide* published by the Department of Energy (free from the Consumer Information Center, Pueblo, CO 81009). It lists fuel-economy figures, derived from the EPA's test, for all new cars. It contains charts so you can quickly compare the annual costs of fueling different cars—say, one delivering 35 mpg to another giving 28 mpg.

The guide also helps you see the range in performance between similar-sized cars. Some sports cars (Corvettes) get 24 mpg while others (Lamborghini Countach) deliver a scant 10 mpg. Among the subcompacts, the Audi 80 Quattro delivers 24 mpg on the highway compared to the Nissan Sentra at 36 mpg. In the mid-size cars, the BMW 7351 logs 21 mpg compared to the Pontiac Grand Prix at 30 mpg.

The guide can save you thousands of future dollars. For example, if you need a commuting car, the guide might help you pick a Honda Civic CRX HF (52 miles per gallon) over a subcompact like the Ford Mustang (27 mpg). To drive 100,000 miles the Mustang will cost you $4444 for gas (assuming gas costs $1.20 per gallon); the Civic costs only $2307. This saving of $2137 is worth considering before you give your heart to that thirsty Mustang.

Money once gone never returns.
                                        American proverb

Money is round; it rolls away from you.
                                        Yiddish proverb

Cars (Buying New)

The old cliche says, "You are what you drive." Sexy, rich, sporty, brash, conservative, pragmatic, adventurous...no matter how you think of yourself, you can find a car to fit the image. The salesman who sold you the car, however, knows what you really are. And, if you are like eight out of 10 new-car buyers who paid much too much for a car, he knows you as a sucker.

Buying a car is like few other purchases because it's a negotiating game. Car dealers cloak the true value of their products. They create high sticker prices, tack on overpriced dealer add-ons, razzle dazzle you with misinformation, and hope you'll lay down your credit card without a fight. Many people do. And they waste money big time.

Other people haggle to get the price chopped. Then they buy thinking they really showed the salesmen a thing or two about driving a tough bargain—never suspecting that their wallet was vacuumed.

For most of us, a car is a huge investment and is overshadowed only by what we spend on our house and spouse. It's a $10,000, a $30,000, maybe even an $80,000 expense. It's an expense that keeps us chained to our jobs; one where we can ill afford to line the dealer's pocket.

♦ Recognize from the start that you're in unfamiliar territory—that salesmen call upon dozens of ploys to make you overpay. Take everything they tell you with a carton of salt and don't believe that because your salesman is an amiable fellow that he'll give you a deal. He'll make you think he is working with you to secure a good price from his boss. But your salesman shares in the spoils of any extra money you pay. If he extracts an extra $1500 to

$2000 on the car, fluffy dealer options, extended warranties, etc., (not uncommon) he may earn an extra $500. Not bad for a few hours of honest work.

Also be aware that the purchase price of your new car is only one way to get nailed. High financing charges, unnecessary dealer add-ons, low payment on your trade-in...the battlefield is loaded with mines.

♦ Ignorance is your greatest enemy in buying a car. If you don't understand the process, the games played, the true cost of a car, the margins dealers will accept, what is and is not acceptable behavior on your part, the true value of the car you intend to trade in, which dealer add-ons you should not purchase, and the bank rate for financing (if you intend to finance with the dealer), then the likelihood of negotiating a good deal is slim. Although you're unlikely to "beat" a salesman at his game, information is your offense and defense in getting a fair deal.

That means research on your part. The hours spent researching can earn you thousands of dollars in savings. This chapter is one source of information but other sources will inform you in greater detail than I can. Check the library or bookstore for books like *How to Buy Your Car for Rock Bottom Prices* by Leslie Sachs. Sachs, who was once a car salesman, gives you an insider's look at the games salesmen play, the money they can exact, and how much you should pay for your car. The yearly New Car issue (April) of *Consumer Reports* usually runs excellent articles on bargaining effectively for a new car and reports on how the new cars stack up. The American Automobile Association (AAA) publishes a valuable book to pilot you through the process, entitled *AAA Car Buyer's Handbook* (purchase it at any AAA office). Consumer Guide's yearly *Car Comparisons* and *The Complete Car Cost Guide* are two more excellent resources you'll find at most libraries.

♦ Other vital rules of the game:
- Look at several cars you could live with and see what different dealers will settle for. Depending on what's hot on the market and what's not, some of these vehicles will be better deals than others. Sell your soul to one car and you sacrifice much of your negotiating edge.
- Negotiate one point at a time—the price of the car, then the dealer add-ons you want eliminated, then the trade-in value of a used car, then financing. Let the negotiations on all these points intermingle and you'll mangle the deal in your confusion.
- Be ready to walk. If you don't like the way you're treated or think that you're not being offered a fair deal, leave. It is one of your greatest weapons and, ironically, you may not get the best deal unless you're willing to walk away from it. Unless a salesperson believes you will walk away, he will keep his "final offer" high.
- Keep the negotiations cordial. Be friendly rather than abrasive, combative, or condescending.

♦ Even if you have your heart set on a particular vehicle, remember that many cars have twins. General Motors offers many of the same cars as Chevrolets, Buicks, Pontiacs, or Oldsmobiles. Chrysler often clones its cars as Dodges and Plymouths. The Geo Prism is essentially a Toyota Corolla built in the States, while the Ford Probe and Mazda MX-6 are twins. The annual car issue of *Consumer Reports* tells you which automobiles are twins. Visit the dealers selling your twin to see what deals they are offering.

♦ Tests conducted by the National Highway Traffic Safety Administration (NHTSA) show that new cars outfitted with air bags greatly reduce injury and death in head-on collisions. Interestingly, many inexpensive cars that did not test particularly well without air bags rivaled the head-on safety figures of much more expensive cars when outfitted with air bags. In a rough manner of speaking, buying air bags is a cheap way of owning a Volvo.

Note: The NHTSA figures show only how cars perform in the most serious accidents (head-on collisions) but say nothing about how cars compare if sideswiped, rolled, or rear ended.

♦ When is the best time to buy a new car? Winter— when the multitudes are financially strapped preparing for or recovering from Christmas and salesmen are hungry. The summer doldrums, caused by people waiting for next year's cars to hit the showroom, is another time when high supply and low demand works to your benefit. Be it winter or summer, the end of the month (especially on weekdays when few people shop) is a good time to visit the dealership. Salesmen may have their month-end quotas in mind and may be more cooperative.

Having said all this, informed buyers can normally negotiate a good price anytime, so shop when you have the time to become informed.

♦ When you look at cars, you'll laugh at how often the dealers just happen to have a "today-only" special on the very car you're viewing. Don't bite if you're not ready. Any price you're offered today will be available tomorrow.

The "today-only" special is a trick to make you buy now, and it works.

♦ What is a good price for a car? Work up from dealer's invoice price to determine your target price. *Full* invoice price tells what a dealer paid for the car and includes the cost of freight and shipping, making it about $450 more than *base* invoice price (which does not include shipping).

According to the book *How to Buy Your Car for Rock Bottom Prices*, the minimum price for a persistent negotiator can be as little as $150 over full invoice price or $600 to $650 over base invoice price. Why so little? Surely a dealer can't survive making a mere $150 per car sold. Unbeknownst to most people, dealers typically receive a hidden 3% rebate from the manufacturer after selling the car. On a $10,000 car, that is another $300 made.

According to *Consumer Reports*, the amount you should expect to pay over the full invoice price depends on the make of car. You may have no negotiating power on cars like the *Mazda Miata*, which are in high demand. But as a rule, the magazine says you should be able to land cars that are in good supply for 2% to 4% over the full invoice price.

Meanwhile, the annual issue of Consumer Guide's *Car Comparisons* and *The Complete Car Cost Guide* report dealer costs and a target figure to shoot for. This figure takes into account the car's popularity.

♦ There are many ways to obtain dealer cost on a car. Call AAA's *Auto Pricing Service* at 900-776-4AAA (they charge you by the length of the call: $1 for the first minute, $1.95 for each additional minute). Write *Consumer Reports Auto Price Service* for a cost printout of the car you want ($11 for the first model of car, $10 for the second, and $7 for each additional car). Or visit the library and look up dealer costs in either *Edmund's New Car Prices*, Consumer Guide's *Car Comparisons*, or *The Complete Car Cost Guide*.

♦ Many dealers will tack an advertisement allowance or "pack" onto the cost of your car. Negotiate it away. Advertising is a cost of business and paying the dealer a few percentage points over his cost compensates him adequately for advertising.

♦ Dealers use the tremendously successful trick of adding their own options and policies to the factory sticker-price. They may print these dealer add-ons on an official sheet and post it on the car, making it look like you must purchase rust proofing, fabric protection, processing fees, insurance, extended service contracts, anti-theft protection. Cross them all off and subtract the figures from the cost of the car. Why?

Rustproofing or undercoating is basically a fraud: Cars are rustproofed at the factory and, except in areas that go very heavy on the wintertime salt, don't need extra protection. What the dealer gets here is primarily profit.

Dealer prep and/or glaze and fabric protection amounts to a can of *Scotchguard* sprayed on the upholstery and a wax job. Not much for the $200 it might cost.

Processing fees can be printed on an invoice as if they were a mandatory fee. They rarely are. Eliminate them from the vehicle's cost.

Need accident, life, theft insurance? Fine. Get them elsewhere and you'll land better policies at lower costs.

Extended warranties and service contracts offered by the dealer seem like a good idea but consumer magazines and books consistently advise against them. Extended warranties possess more holes than a sponge and dealers are incredibly adept at finding the holes that shelter them from paying. Documents filed in a lawsuit against Nissan in 1988 revealed dealers paid back only 16.5% on the extended warranty packages that sold for $795. That means the dealers were sponging off huge profits. Rather than buying an extended warranty, buy a car with a good manufacturer's warranty and/or one with a history of needing few repairs.

♦ Factory-installed options are good buys, but think twice about any option the dealer wants to add—stereo, sunroof, etc. Specialty shops do better work and charge half the price.

♦ After negotiating on the new car, your resistance to the procedure may have faltered when it comes to dickering over what your trade-in is worth. You may figure, "I got a good price on the car; I can give a little on the trade-in." Don't. You deserve what the vehicle is worth. Before buying a new car, check the Blue-Book value of your old one, take it around to used-car lots for their offers, check the classified ads to determine what your year and model of car fetches when sold privately. Use this information to get what your car is worth.

♦ A car bought at a low price, but with a high financing charge is still a bum deal. You can spend thousands of extra dollars over the life of a loan in interest payments. If you're going to finance the car, check whether the manufacturer is offering low financing rates on the car you want. Also, call around for the going rate at banks and credit unions and have these quotes in hand when you shop for a car. If you arrange your financing with the dealer, you don't want to pay more than 1% over bank rate. Preferably you want the dealer to match bank rates.

Be sure to check the dealer's math when you are quoted a monthly payment—they sometimes miscalculate and, mysteriously, those miscalculations rarely work out in your favor.

To help you, come to the dealership armed with either auto-financing tables or amortization tables (available at bookstores and the reference section of libraries) and a pocket calculator. While your salesman visits the financing department to determine your monthly payment, calculate the amount yourself. If you use amortization tables, your figure may not exactly match the dealer's, but it should be darn close.

♦ Pay cash for a vehicle when possible. If you can't, finance for the shortest term you can afford: the shorter the term (and the lower the rate) the less you pay in interest.

♦ Don't tell a dealer, "I can afford a $300 monthly payment." Tell him what you can afford and he'll gladly increase the interest rate or lengthen the terms until it exactly matches what you can afford. Either way you lose.

In the privacy of home, figure out what you can afford, but don't reveal your secret at the dealership. Dicker for the lowest rate you can get.

♦ Before signing a final agreement, check it with a magnifying glass. The boys who write up the final agreement often make mistakes. Sometimes the agreed upon price gets listed incorrectly, or extras you crossed off get added back in, or a higher financing charge than the one you settled upon gets used. Give that contract Gestapo treatment.

♦ Even if you do sign, the agreement is not binding *until* you drive the car off the lot. Until that time, the dealer must refund your deposit and return a trade-in should you back out.

Therefore, you don't want to take a new car home until it is prepared as promised with all the accessories and until all the financing details are settled. If it is late and the salesman tells you to take the car home and return tomorrow to finish the details (finalize financing rates, add accessories, etc.), say "no." Tell him you want everything completed now—that the car doesn't go home until you work out the details. Tell him also that if the car doesn't go home with you now, you'll be checking out cars at other dealers. You've got a nervous salesman and a big lever for negotiating when the car remains with the dealer. Take the vehicle home and that lever becomes a toothpick.

♦ When you do take a new car home, give it a long and thorough test drive. Take the car back immediately if you detect a major problem. The courts have upheld demands for a refund when the car was returned within the first few days.

♦ At some dealerships you must play the game if you want a deal. You can't just walk in, tell them you know their dealer cost, and say you'll buy the car for $X, thank you. You need to have patience and let them play their ploys. Salesmen may be unwilling to lower the price until they've deployed their arsenal of tricks—from trying to befriend you to letting the manager bully you. They won't acquiesce until you've unarmed their deadliest weapons.

You can either play hardball with these guys or pack up early in the game and take a hike, looking for a dealer who is more forthright.

♦ The urge to own a car now, today, pronto, works strongly against you in negotiating a car deal. If the salesman perceives you are emotionally hooked (that you've got to have this car and you've gotta have it today) he's not going to come down to his lowest price. It is only when he knows you're detached enough to walk that he'll keep dropping the price.

Sometimes you just have to get up and leave. Do it slowly, look around longer, give the salesman time to restart the negotiation. He knows if you leave he's unlikely to see you again. And if he has invested time in you, he won't let you go if he can make a sale at some price.

What if he doesn't rise to the bait, what if he lets you walk out the door? Worry not. What he offered today will be available to you tomorrow. You just need to call back, and say you needed time to consider his offer and that you'll take it now.

♦ If the car or options you want are not available, you'll probably be told it will cost more to place a special order. Don't do so without a fight. Dealers rent their cars from the manufacturer. Each day the car remains unsold, the dealer must pay interest on the vehicle. Placing a special order means that the dealer makes a sale without footing the daily interest charge to inventory that vehicle— he makes a sale with less overhead. Should you pay more for this?

♦ If you lack the stomach or time for the car-purchasing game, use the services of a reputable automotive consulting and purchasing firm like *AutoAdviser* (800-326-1976 or 206-323-1976). A good service can help you decide what you want in your new car—be that safety, fuel economy, reliability, sportiness, size—and then recommend the best-rated cars that meet your criteria and budget.

After you settle on a car model, a good service will contact local dealers and negotiate the best price. The service knows dealer cost for the car and options you settle on and should guarantee you the lowest price going (their guarantee should stipulate a refund of their fee if it is not the lowest).

A friend of mine who just bought a Ford Taurus from *AutoAdviser* paid less than dealer invoice price. Not bad for the $300 flat fee he paid—particularly when he confessed that it seemed reasonable to him to pay $1000 over dealer price.

AutoAdviser operates nationally and AAA recommends it to members who need buying or consulting services.

♦ Besides getting the right price for your car, don't overlook the importance of getting the right car. The true cost of a car can be determined only if you know how quickly it will depreciate, the amount of gas it will guzzle, the cost of insuring it (very different from car to car), and how often it will need repairs. An importrant part of your library research is to determine which cars you can afford to own.

Toward this end, study the *Gas Mileage Guide*—it lists the EPA's fuel economy estimates for all new cars. Order the booklet (free) from the Consumer Information Center, Pueblo, CO 81009. Also pay close attention to the frequency-of-repair records published in *Consumer Reports* and Consumer Guide's publications.

The best single resource for determining what it will cost to own a particular vehicle is *The Complete Car Cost Guide* (order it from IntelliChoice, Inc., 800-227-2665). This book evaluates depreciation, gas consumption, insurance costs, and frequency of repairs to derive the average five-year cost of operating each car. When you see that the five-year cost of owning a Honda Civic is $15,850 versus $19,194 for a Nissan Sentra E or that the five-year cost of a Toyota Corolla Deluxe wagon is $20,669 versus $28,585 for a Ford Taurus LX wagon, you have food for thought.

A fool may make money but it needs a wise man to spend it.

English proverb

Car Rentals

They were trying to scam me. I had bitten on the ads a car rental company was running and thought I had found a steal. Now I saw the catch: They were trying to swindle me with a $13-per-day collision-damage waiver (CDW). And the lady "helping" me was twisting my arm. "Without this," she told me, "you are responsible for any damage to the car. Someone backs into you and it could cost you $2000."

I was relenting, but the thought of paying $40 for three days of insurance needled my maw. And then an idea came to me. After excusing myself, I pulled my auto-insurance card from my wallet and called my insurance agent. Five minutes later I was back staring into the challenging eyes of Ms. Armbreaker. "Nix the collision-damage waiver," I told her.

To help you be the recipient rather than the victim of a steal, here's what you should know about renting cars.

♦ CDWs are presently a car renter's biggest thorn. Hertz recently testified before Congress that the true cost of CDWs is between $2.50 and $4.50 per day. Rental companies, in turn, often charge customers $10 to $16 a day for the coverage.

Don't want to pay no stinkin' 500% profit on a CDW? Then call your insurance agent and discuss the coverage your auto insurance offers. If your policy insures substitute vehicles (rentals qualify as such) and one of your cars is insured with a low deductible, then your collision liability on a rental may be limited to the deductible of your policy.

Unfortunately, making sweeping recommendations about what *you* should and should not do is impossible. The state in which you are insured, the state in which you are renting, the coverage offered under your auto insurance, and the stipulations placed on you by refusing an agency's CDW, all affect the decision. Ask your insurance agent about your auto insurance and inform him or her of the state in which you intend to rent. Note his general recommendations but make your final decision only after reading the company's CDW, and considering what you agree to by refusing it. There may be fees (like loss-of-use fees for each day a damaged rental car is out of commission) that your insurance would not cover.

Note: Pay for the CDW insurance when renting abroad. Your auto insurance may not cover you on foreign shores, and few other legal systems in the world work like ours. Applying American strategies of win-win penny-pinching on a foreign CDW can result in unimaginable lose-lose scenarios.

♦ If you rent regularly, a credit card offering a collision-insurance bonus on rented vehicles could prove a wise investment. Such coverage is a new benefit to the American Express Gold Card and Chase Manhattan Visa or MasterCard. Merrill Lynch, Dreyfus Corporation, Dollar Dry Dock Savings in New York and the First National Bank of Chicago are also offering collision insurance with their credit cards.

Card holders with this coverage receive compensation from the card company for damage to rented cars that was not reimbursed through personal insurance. That could be the amount of the deductible (assuming your auto insurance chips in), or the full extent of the damage (if your insurance proves as useful as a screen door on a submarine).

Considering you're likely to pay over $10 a day for a rental agency's CDWs, it won't take many days of renting to pay for an American Express Gold Card ($65/year). It takes even fewer days to pay for a Chase Manhattan Visa Card ($20/year).

♦ You won't find many hard-and-fast rules about renting cars cheaply. The low-ball company in one city may be high-end elsewhere. Even in the same city, different franchises of the same company may have as much in common as Jimmy and Billy Carter.

It definitely pays to contact a cross section of rental companies for price quotes. But get all the charges—weekly or daily rates, CDW charges, extra mileage fees, gasoline charges, and airport fees—before making your decision.

To obtain rates, use the *Yellow Pages* or call the companies' toll-free reservation lines and ask for a quote in the city you will be visiting. Phone numbers are as follows: Alamo 800-327-9633, American International 800-527-0202, Avis 800-331-1212, Budget 800-527-0700, Dollar 800-421-6878, Enterprise 800-325-8007, General 800-327-7607, Hertz 800-654-3131, National 800-227-7368, Thrifty 800-367-2277, Value 800-327-2501.

If you reserve a car, minimize the likelihood of unpleasant surprises by asking for a confirmation number and the total you will be asked to pay.

♦ Rental companies with desks in the airport (Hertz, Budget, Avis, National) are generally more expensive than off-airport renters. It costs companies *beaucoup* bucks to lease airport desk space and guess who gets to pay for that!

Off-airport carriers (Alamo, American International, Dollar, General, Snappy, Thrifty, Tropical) operate shuttles to and from their offices. It may take you a few minutes longer to reach their offices, but the minutes lost may save you up to 30% on the cost of your rental.

Off-off-airport renters, whose offices are nowhere near the airport and who don't operate shuttles, sometimes offer better deals than the off-airport carriers but in many cities they don't. The only way to find out is to call a few.

♦ Always inquire about discounts when getting price quotes. Got a card certifying you are a frequent flier, AAA member, member of the North Bend Zoo, psychopathic killer? Ask whether it merits a discount. Almost anyone can qualify for discounts of 10% to 25%—psychopathic killers usually bag even better deals.

♦ CDWs aren't the only insurance peddled by rental companies. You can get personal accident insurance (for injuries to you), personal effects coverage (for loss or damage to your belongings), or supplemental liability insurance (extra liability insurance in case of a lawsuit).

Before you rent a car you may want to ask your insurance agent whether any of this is necessary. If you're properly insured for daily life, the answer should be "no" on all counts. Injuries to you should be covered by medical and life insurance. Personal property should be protected against theft and damage through your homeowner's or renter's insurance. And liability protection should be covered under your auto insurance.

Important: Horrendous insurance complications can, and will, arise if your rental car is in an accident and the driver is not listed on the rental contract. Almost all those complications are going to cost you—maybe thousands of dollars. Moral: Additional drivers (and their license numbers) must be listed on the rental contract.

Car Repairs

Some cars suck up every dollar that floats near them—call them black holes. I once owned such a demon. Year after year it rated as a four-star vacuum cleaner. Just after I fixed the starter, the alternator died. No sooner had I replaced the alternator than the brakes began squealing. On went new brake shoes, and then the ignition coil quit. Next a fuel injector began leaking, followed by the need for a new clutch, followed by a litany of other repairs. One of my all-time cheap tricks was *giving* that cursed automobile to my brother. For about a week he thought me generous. After a month he craved to dice me into little pieces.

Had I done my homework and bought a vehicle with a maintenance-free reputation, I would never have bought that car. Had I done my homework, I could have saved myself the thousands of dollars and weeks of time spent fixing it.

Buy smart. Study the frequency-of-repair records in magazines like *Consumer Reports*. Seek out those stellar performers that consistently roll over 100,000 miles with little more attention than the routine oil change. Ditch the dogs that require a second mortgage to remain roadworthy.

This buyer's advice aside, what should you do once you've bought a car? How do you minimize the need for repairs? When repairs are needed, how do you keep costs down? How do you keep your machine from becoming a black hole?

♦ Mechanics say the most effective way to immortalize your car is to change the oil and oil filter often. Oil has a monumental job to perform: It cleanses, cools, lubricates, and seals the space between the cylinder and piston rings.

Its ability to do all these jobs diminishes with time and use. And as it soils with each mile driven, the suspended dirt grates away at the guts of your engine.

Your owner's manual probably advises an oil change every 6000 to 8000 miles or every six months (whichever comes first), but most mechanics believe an oil and filter change every 3000 miles (or three months) adds years of life to an engine. This belief is supported by a *Consumer Reports* poll in which car owners, who had logged over 100,000 miles without major repairs, shared their maintenance secrets. The majority changed their oil and oil filter more frequently than normal (every 3500 or fewer miles). In fact, it's not uncommon for cars receiving frequent oil and filter changes to hit the 250,000-mile mark.

Which oil should you use? Check your owner's manual or call the dealer for recommendations. At the very least, check the label to see that the oil meets new-car warranty requirements. Also, if your climate allows it, use 10-30 oil over 10-40—the extra viscosity gives added protection.

Regarding oil filters, don't assume that any filter that screws to your car will work. Different filters remove different-sized particles. You want your filter to eliminate the particle sizes that the manufacturer deems most damaging to your cylinders. Make sure your filter is recommended for your model of car and buy good filters (i.e., those that are mid-range or higher in price).

♦ Stockpile oil, oil filters, and air filters when they go on sale. Unopened bottles of oil don't have a shelf-life problem.

♦ Learn to change your own oil and oil filter. It's easy (consult your owner's manual), cheap, and *faster* than taking the car to a garage.

Note: Dispose of your oil responsibly (i.e., not in the trash or down the sewer). Store it in old milk bottles and occasionally deposit it at a recycling center. Call auto-part stores, city hall, or a local mechanic for the whereabouts of such a center.

♦ Change a new car's oil after the first 1000 miles to remove the sharp metal shavings that form as the engine breaks in.

♦ Tune up your vehicle every 12,000 to 15,000 miles or every year (whichever comes first). Install a new distributor cap, rotor, plugs, fuel filter, air filter, and PVC valve. With older cars, have the carburetion and timing adjusted. The cost of these tuneups is more than paid back in improved mileage and prolonged engine life.

♦ Do you save money pumping your own gas? Not if you continually ignore the other chores that go along with a full-service fill up. Chores like checking the oil. Let your car run out of oil (my mechanic tells me self-servers do this frequently) and the sage who pumps his own gas becomes a stooge.

Check the oil regularly yourself or get a full service fill-up from time to time.

♦ Besides the oil, routinely check your vehicle's other vital fluids —transmission, battery, brake, and radiator fluids. Checking the radiator fluid and the condition of the radiator hoses is particularly important: Without coolant circulating through the engine you can quickly transform a valuable engine into scrap metal. If radiator fluid is low, add a 50/50 mixture of antifreeze and water. And if the fluid looks muddy rather than lime green, change the fluid. See a mechanic if you find you're frequently adding a quart of fluid or if the fluid is often muddy.

The rubber hoses leading from the radiator to the engine (and the other engine hoses, for that matter) should not be cracked, brittle, bulging, or mushy when squeezed.

♦ In the coldest parts of the country, or when an extreme cold snap strikes, alter the mixture in your radiator to 70% antifreeze, 30% water. But don't make the mistake of pouring pure antifreeze into the radiator—undiluted ethylene glycol freezes at 8°F.

♦ Drain and replace your radiator fluid every other year. After about two years the liquid's anti-corrosion elements are spent.

♦ Keep your car under a roof, preferably in a garage. Protecting the car from the sun, moisture, and temperature fluctuations does far more than preserve the paint job; it prolongs the life of every mechanical system in the car.

Fabric car covers that drape over a car like a raincoat are a bad idea if they are not removed frequently. Moisture condenses between the car and the cover and, because the car cannot breathe, mold develops quickly.

♦ Washing the exterior of your vehicle is important to prolong its good looks and resale value, but washing the engine occasionally may be more important in prolonging the vehicle's life. Dirt and grease coating the engine trap in heat and can trigger a meltdown. Wash the engine occasionally with a high-pressure hose found at a car wash.

Spray the engine down with a degreaser. Let the degreaser sit for about 10 minutes. Then, with the car running, rinse the engine with a high-pressure water spray, being careful to keep the spray off the distributor and out of the air intake.

♦ If you own a car with automatic transmission, you may be tempted to brake with your left foot. Bad habit. Left-footed braking leads to riding the brakes which results in a trinity of evils: poor gas mileage, reduced engine life, and worn-out brakes.

♦ If your car has a stick shift, don't downshift as a standard means of braking. Downshifting uses more gas and wears out the clutch and transmission (it's cheaper to replace worn brakes than a worn clutch). With a manual transmission, you'll also prolong the life of your clutch by slipping the car into neutral and releasing the clutch when waiting at stop signs and lights.

♦ Listen to the engine and keep it in a gear where it is working comfortably. Overrevving and lugging not only waste gas, they waste engine life.

♦ Don't drive with your hand on the gear shift. It may feel good, but adds unnecessary wear to the transmission selector forks.

♦ My mechanic says the most frequent problems he sees in winter are caused by water in the gas. If your car suddenly starts to sputter and lurch, he advocates adding gas drier (like *Prestone Gas-Drier* or *Heet*) to the gas. For wintertime preventive maintenance, he recommends adding drier to the gas every few fill-ups.

I thought he owned stock in the stuff until several other mechanics also recommended the product. Gas drier is an alcohol, which binds with the water in gas and then burns its way out of your vehicle.

Other ways to minimize moisture in your gas: Keep your vehicle in a garage and your fuel tank as full as possible throughout the winter. Unfortunately, it's not uncommon to pump bad gas from the filling station into the tank, so keep a bottle of gas drier in the vehicle for first aid.

Scores of companies market a gas drier and prices fluctuate widely. Buy by price among the name brands.

♦ What about oil additives claiming to extend engine life, increase horsepower, and improve gas mileage—products like *STP*, *Slick 50*, and *Hy-per Lube*. Should you use them?

These products, when fresh, are effective lubricants. However, their honey-like viscosity keeps them glued to the inner workings of your engine. When you drain the oil, much of the additive (along with dirt sticking to it) does not drain.

My mechanic says he occasionally sees dirty deposits an inch thick coating the inner workings of engines. His advice? Save your money: Use only oil and change it often.

♦ A teaspoon of liquid detergent added to tap water makes an effective and very inexpensive solution for the automatic windshield squirter (for warm weather use only).

♦ Prolong the life of windshield wipers that are not cleaning well by sanding the wipers' edge.

♦ A car's starting problems are frequently related to corroded battery terminals. Clean the battery terminals occasionally with baking soda and then reduce the corrosion problem by smearing them with a thin coating of petroleum jelly.

♦ When an obvious problem arises, don't procrastinate fixing it. More than likely, procrastination will cause additional damage and cost you more when you finally succumb and service the vehicle.

I've often played the maybe-it-will-go-away game (several times when my brakes started rasping, once when a wheel bearing began squealing, and once when my clutch started squealing). Every time my misplaced optimism has acerbated the problem and cost me more in the end.

♦ As a rule, car dealers go for greed and charge 30% to 70% more for auto parts than auto-part stores. Many parts are available only through the dealer, so you're stuck. But make a habit of checking auto-part stores first. Don't overlook the auto-wrecking yards: They're the best deal going if you don't need a new part.

♦ Where should you take your car when it must visit the shop? The dealer, an independent mechanic, a national chain?

I'm an advocate of avoiding the dealers. Call around for what dealers charge—be it for a clutch replacement, new brake shoes, or a head-gasket job—and you'll discover they consistently charge one-and-a-half to two times more than independent mechanics.

How do they get away with highway robbery? Car owners let them. Many owners take their car to the dealer by habit: After all, that is where they took the vehicle for all its warranty checks. Later when something goes wrong, (ding) the Pavlovian response is to run to the dealer.

Many car owners also believe that only the dealer can fix their car. Not true, but it keeps the dealers busy. It also lets them fleece their faithful sheep.

For a fairer deal, sleuth out several independent mechanics in your neighborhood. How do you find good ones? Call several local auto-part stores that stock parts for your make of car. Ask for the manager or assistant manager. Tell him the type of car you own and ask if he knows a good independent mechanic who can repair it. Emphasize that price is an issue: You want good work at a reasonable price. The manager will most likely know several independent mechanics with good reputations who can work on your car.

♦ Also, the nearest office of the American Automobile Association (AAA) can tell you which repair shops in your neighborhood are AAA rated. To get an AAA rating, the shop must meet equipment specifications, employ certified mechanics, and prove on an ongoing basis that it is providing a high level of customer satisfaction.

These garages may not be the cheapest on the block but they do offer a guarantee of sorts, and guarantees are hard to come by in the car-repair business. Any dispute with an AAA-approved shop is arbitrated by AAA and the shop must abide by AAA's decision.

♦ Getting a second opinion is as valid a practice in the mechanical world as it is in the medical world. If one mechanic paints a gloomy (and expensive) picture, don't hesitate to use whatever excuse you must to exit (you've got to check your finances or schedule a time when you can give up the car). Take the vehicle to one or two other auto doctors for a diagnosis before settling on a treatment plan.

It is acceptable to ask that the price quote be written down and that the mechanic contact you if the work is to exceed the quote (put this in writing, too).

♦ Need a brake job, muffler repair, or front-end alignment? Head for the shops specializing in these jobs. They offer lower prices than the dealers and polls show they deliver better customer satisfaction to boot.

Does anyone beat Midas? Probably. Polls show that between the chain specialty shops and the independent shops, the independents delivered slightly better customer satisfaction. Their advertisements tend to be more honest, their prices are slightly lower, they rarely put on a hard sell, they are on time with their repairs, and they do the best job of fixing ongoing problems.

♦ Beat the $45-per-hour rate of the local garage by taking your car to a local high school or community college for repairs. I've used vocational auto-mechanic programs for tune-ups, clutch jobs, replacement of the push rods, and in so doing skipped labor charges—the schools typically charge for parts only.

To locate the nearest school with an auto shop, look up the high schools and community colleges in the government pages of the phone book. Call each school and ask whether the school has a vocational auto-mechanics program and whether that program repairs cars supplied by the public.

♦ Suffered a ding in the windshield? Nicks smaller than a quarter can be stopped from spawning spider legs that span (and ruin) the windshield, provided you attend to them quickly. Heat, cold, moisture, dirt bumps on the road, even turning the car all contribute in spreading the nick. Need incentive to hustle? The average replacement cost for a windshield is between $300 to $400 and can be over $600 for cars like the Chevy Lumina, Ford Taurus, Honda Prelude, or Ford Explorer.

Before doing anything else, cover the wound on both sides of the windshield with a *Scotch Tape* band-aid (duct tape works too). If you have comprehensive auto insurance, call your agent—the insurance company will probably waive the deductible to have the windshield repaired. Then get the car to a windshield-repair specialist like *Novus*, and let them fix it. Repair cost will range from $30 to $50.

Take the vehicle first to a firm specializing in repair (rather than replacement) and offering at least a year-long, money-back guarantee that the ding will not turn into a crack. The reason: Many shops that specialize in replacement advertise repairs as a bait-and-switch tactic. They bait you in with the promise of a low-cost fix, tell you the windshield is a write-off, and switch you over to a costly replacement.

Do-it-yourself kits are available from such chains as Schucks or Checker and cost between $10 and $20. Try them if you can't afford a specialty shop. There are definite tricks to the trade of windshield patching, however, and learning them on your $600 windshield could be an expensive education.

♦ To repair scratches in a car's paint, discuss the problem with the dealer: They'll have, or can order, the exact color needed for a touch-up. Clean the scratch and surrounding area thoroughly with soap and water. If there's any rust, paint the scratch with rust converter (use a very fine artist's brush). Apply the paint with a fine artist's brush or a toothpick and paint in one direction only. After several days blend the colors of the old and new paint with a polishing compound. Then wash and wax.

Often you can get satisfactory results repairing a small scratch (with much less work and expense) with a crayon. Rub the appropriate color onto the scratch, buff it, rub more crayon on, buff more... The wax not only hides the scratch, it keeps the metal from rusting.

♦ Prevent the majority of parking-lot dings to the side of your car (caused as others open their doors) by applying self-adhering trim to the side of the car (sold by the roll at auto-part stores). Form a guideline along the side of the car from a long strip of masking tape to keep the trim straight.

♦ Finally, when times are good, save money for your black hole because sure as George Bush raised taxes, you're going to have future automotive woes.

Don't laugh at another's misfortune, yours is on the horizon.
    Russian proverb

Do not rely on your present good fortune; prepare for the year when it may leave you.
    Chinese proverb

Car Tires

Wheels. They're a symbol of freedom in this country. Without them you're stuck in Dullsville, USA. The sole of the wheel is the tire, a rand of natural and synthetic rubber. An expensive rand. Pay to shoe your vehicle often and you can forget about your freedom—you'll have misappropriated your gas money. So here are some tips to keep you from becoming the Imelda Marcos of tires.

♦ When buying tires, choose radials over bias-ply. You'll pay more up front but save in the future. Radials deliver better mileage because they have less rolling resistance. More importantly, they wear 15% to 20% longer.

♦ Throughout much of the country, the use of all-season radials eliminates the need to purchase snow tires. All-season tires are the most frequently purchased tires, thus the best engineering goes into them. These tires remain soft at cold temperatures and incorporate an aggressive tread design—two features giving them reasonable traction in snow.
They don't deliver the traction of a snow-and-mud tire, but they perform well enough to winter the roads around much of the country. This saves you the initial cost of purchasing snow tires and the annual cost of mounting them.

♦ People living in climates that justify full-blown snow tires should remove those tires promptly every spring. Snow tires deliver poorer mileage and wear out faster than normal tires.

♦ The cost of a new tire is a poor indicator of quality. So is the brand name—each major manufacturer produces some very good tires and some very mediocre ones. Spend an hour in the library thumbing through consumer and automobile magazines and you'll unearth valuable tips. For example, knowledge that the Dunlop Axiom not only outperformed the Michelin XA4 but cost $60 versus $95 per tire, really helped me. Multiplying the savings by four made my pre-purchase jaunt to the library a lucrative one.

♦ To help you interpret their size and quality, all-season tires come with a lot of information printed on the sidewall. Of course, most of that information is unintelligible; I'll interpret the data cheapskates should know.

- The words "Tread wear" will be followed by a number like 100 or 300. These numbers tell, on a relative basis, how much life you can expect from the tread. Under the same driving conditions, a tire with a rating of 300 will wear three times longer than one with a rating of 100.

- The "Traction" rating ranks a tire's stopping ability on wet streets. Grade A is best, C worst.

- The code following "DOT," tells you the tire's age. For example, by looking at the last three numbers in the code "DOT XF E5 X JJX 400," any idiot knows the tire was obviously made during the 40th week of 1990. You want fresh tires, not ones that have hardened with age, so purchase those that are less than a year old.

♦ Check the pressure of your tires frequently. Under-inflation increases rolling resistance, which increases tire wear and gas consumption by as much as 5%.

Check your car manual for the recommended pressure (usually between 30 and 34 pounds per square inch—lighter cars use lower pressures).

Changes in temperature alter tire pressure, so check the tires every few weeks with an accurate gauge. Check them while they are cold: Note the tires that are low and how many pounds of pressure they require. By the time you reach a filling station, road friction will have warmed the tires. Take a new reading of the underinflated tires and add the pounds of pressure that were needed when the tire was cold to this new reading.

♦ Overinflating tires improves gas mileage; it also increases tire wear. Unfortunately, the money saved on gas is much less than that spent on rubber.

♦ Check the wear pattern of your tires every month or two (during a pit stop for gas). The pattern can warn you of a variety of problems. A tire wearing quickly in the center—but not on the edges—is overinflated, while a tire wearing on both edges—but not in the center—is underinflated. A tire with irregular and uneven wear patches is improperly balanced. If one tire is wearing on one edge, either the tire is faulty or, more likely, you have a steering or front-end alignment problem (take your car to a mechanic and have the front end checked). If both tires on the front or back are wearing on an outside or an inside edge, the toe setting needs adjustment (another job for the shop).

♦ If a tire goes flat, drive *slowly* to the nearest *safe* place to change it. The farther you drive, the higher the odds of ruining the tire. Don't, however, be dollar stupid by changing the tire in a dangerous place.

♦ Rotate your tires every 6000 to 9000 miles. The goal of rotation is to get the tires to wear—and wear out—uniformly. Check your car manual for the recommended rotation scheme.

A common misconception about radial tires is that you must not change the direction the tire turns (i.e., wheels cannot be rotated between different sides of the car). This was the accepted practice in the early 1980s but no longer holds true. New radial tires can be rotated front to back AND side to side without worry.

If your car is older and the manual recommends moving radials only from front to back, you may not be maximizing the wear on your tires. Get a free copy of the *Consumer Tire Guide* (Tire Industry Safety Council, Box 1801, Washington, DC 20013) and check out the rotation scheme for your type of vehicle. This pamphlet also offers additional information to help your tires roll the extra mile.

Cars (Used)

It won't have the distinctive smell of newness. It will have the associated worry of "Why did the previous owners sell it?" But anyone wanting a really good deal on their wheels does not buy a new car. You pay a hefty premium for the odor of a new car, for the security that there are no hidden problems—once you take that new car on a Sunday cruise, its value plummets a few grand.

New cars depreciate most rapidly. During their first year on the road they will typically lose 20% of their value. A one-year-old car, therefore, gives you low mileage, the remainder of a manufacturer's warranty, little likelihood of problems...all for the right price. An example: A basic 1991 4-door Chevy Caprice lists for about $17,000, a one-year-old 1990 Caprice goes for about $10,800. The sticker price isn't your only saving. Buy a used car and you'll pay less to insure it. And in states where the yearly licensing fee is pegged to a vehicle's worth, you'll pay less licensing it.

Buy an older used car and your risk of problems escalates, but so do the savings. I bought a VW Vanagon Camper Van several years ago that would have set me back $22,100 had I bought it new. Through the classified ads, I located a used vehicle with 60,000 miles. A single owner had put on all those miles and the car's exterior, engine, and maintenance records proved the car was in good repair. So I paid a Volkswagen mechanic to give it a thorough inspection; he gave it an all-systems-go rating. I bought the vehicle for $5300.

Because independent VW mechanics informed me that well-maintained Vanagons average 130,000 miles before requiring major engine work, I figure I bought a vehicle with over half its original life remaining for a quarter of its original price.

If you're tempted to look at used cars—and you should be—consider these money-saving tips.

♦ Small- and medium-sized sedans are often the best buys. Performance cars have probably given their best performances to the previous owners. Meanwhile, convertibles and luxury cars remain pricey even when used.

♦ Research used cars like new ones. Research ensures you'll buy into a reliable, low-maintenance car rather than a lemon. In their annual automobile issue published each spring, *Consumer Reports* publishes a list of recommended cars (in a variety of price ranges) known for their reliability. These cars are chosen after studying the frequency-of-repair information collected from 800,000 readers. Sometimes the magazine also lists cars to avoid.

Research keeps you from buying a car with a history of recalls. Call the U.S. Department of Transportation Auto Safety Hotline (800-424-9393) to determine whether a particular model of vehicle has ever been recalled and to receive a report listing the specifics of that recall.

Also, call independent mechanics who specialize in repairing the car you're considering. They'll tell you whether certain years of that model were bowsers, and whether particular accessories will bite holes in the pocket book.

♦ Before you shop for a used car, be it with a dealer or private seller, know the general value of cars you're shopping for. Study a month's worth of classified ads to learn what your dream car goes for on the private market.

In the reference area of the library, look through the *N.A.D.A. Official Used Car Guide* for the value of a particular car. At a bookstore thumb through a copy of Edmund's *Used Car Prices* or Consumer Guide's *Used Cars Rating Guide*. Or call AAA's *AutoPricing Service* (900-776-4222) and tell them the car model, year, mileage, condition, and accessories you're considering. They'll quote you the price range for such a vehicle (this is not a free call).

Without such information, it's hard to negotiate effectively and knock down an inflated figure. Equally important, you won't recognize when a bargain dangles before you.

♦ Keep in mind that the price you can negotiate for used cars oscillates with the season. Buyers who are flexible can use this to their advantage.

Camping vehicles, like the Vanagon I bought, sell briskly in the spring because people are thinking about summer fun. But I bought in late October when more people were selling (after getting their summer hurrahs) and few people buying. With supply and demand in my favor, I negotiated a good price.

November, December, January are all good months to buy. Buyers are about as scarce as heat waves in Antarctica (everyone is cash starved preparing for, or recovering from, Christmas) and sellers may be swinging at lowballs.

♦ Old cars with relatively low mileage are choice buys. Age pushes the value down, but the mileage is more representative of the vehicle's true age. A properly maintained car with 50,000 miles on it is likely to have the same kick regardless of whether it is three years old or eight. The eight-year-old car, however, will be much cheaper.

♦ You wouldn't expect it in this age of regulation, but rolling back the odometer is still a frequent (though totally illegal) practice. According to the Washington Department of Licensing, "Each year approximately three million used cars have their odometers rolled back an average of 30,000 miles."

Check that all the numbers across the odometer line up straight. Cockeyed numbers should rouse your suspicion. See if the relative condition of the car matches the odometer reading. How worn are the gas and brake pedals, how do the carpet and paint look, what shape is the upholstery in? A low-mileage car (under 30,000 miles) should not have bald tires. Nor should it have brand new tires. In either case, suspect that the odometer was disconnected or rolled back.

♦ If you are buying a car from a new-car dealership or a used-car lot, contact the previous owner of a vehicle you're tempted to buy. He or she no longer owns the car and can talk honestly about why the car was dumped and what its shortcomings are. The old owner can also give you a guestimation of the car's mileage when it was traded. This tells you whether the odometer reading is accurate.

Ask the dealer for the previous owner's name, address, and phone number. In most states the dealer, by law, must disclose this information. Call your Department of Licensing or Department of Motor Vehicles (dealer division) if you want the specifics for your state.

You can make an end run around a dealer who won't relinquish (or does not know) the last owner's name by paying the Department of Motor Vehicles or Department of Licensing to perform a title search on the car.

◆ Friends can be a good source for used cars. They are less likely to hide problems and will give you a clearer picture of a vehicle's history.

◆ Private sellers (check the classified ads of the paper) usually sell for less than dealers because they don't need to net a profit. Private sellers generally approach the transaction with more honesty and less salesmanship. And you're likely to get more informed answers to the important questions you should be asking. Questions like: Why are you selling, what repair work has the car required in the past, has the car ever been in an accident, how many people have owned the car?

The disadvantage of buying privately? Usually you buy the car "as is," without a warranty. This need not be the case, however. With savvy negotiating you can often get a seller to agree to a short (e.g., one month) warranty. That is enough time to allay fears that the seller has swept some dark secret under the floorboards. Make sure you write down and both sign the conditions of the warranty.

Ask when you respond to classified ads whether the seller is a private owner, a car dealer, or a professional car trader. Personally, I distrust dealers and traders whose ads don't specify who they are.

◆ New-car dealerships often have a used-car division where they sell late-model and low-mileage cars. You're likely to get a reliable car and warranty here, but not the best price—these guys have their overhead and profit to make.

◆ Lots specializing in used cars have more older cars and, therefore, more vehicles of questionable reliability. Stick to the dealers that have been around forever and you're less likely to get stung by a shyster.

No matter whom you buy from, promises made about the car's condition, changes to the warranty, and adjustments to the price should be written down. Verbal agreements are as binding as a politician's pledge to balance the budget.

♦ People who buy a used car from a dealer should look for the "Buyer's Guide" sticker the Federal Trade Commission requires dealers to display on the vehicle. Don't see the Buyer's Guide? Then you have motive to distrust the dealer.

The Buyer's Guide notes whether the vehicle comes with a warranty and the limits of that warranty. It advises you to request your right to have the vehicle inspected. It tells you to write any changes made to the warranty or any promises right there on the Buyer's Guide.

Make sure you receive an identical copy of the Buyer's Guide (with all the added changes) when you purchase a used car. This copy overrides any of the provisions listed in the sales contract.

♦ If you are told a vehicle is still under the original manufacturer's warranty or any dealer service contracts, double-check that these benefits can be transferred from the original owner (read the contracts). Also, have the seller put in writing that the rights are transferrable.

♦ Perhaps the most important step in lemon prevention is to inspect a used car before purchase. You're a mechanical idiot? Then rope a knowledgeable friend into examining your car. Check the radiator's condition; the color and condition of the transmission fluid; for any leaks (oil, brake fluid, radiator fluid, gas, transmission fluid); for rust on the body, chassis, or exhaust system; for clues suggesting that the vehicle was once in an accident; the condition of the front end, steering, and suspension components.

While test driving, you or your sleuth should spend a good 30 minutes checking how the engine sounds and performs at many speeds. Does it steer and corner well at all speeds, brake safely at different speeds, hold with the emergency brake on, ride smoothly, look straight as it drives toward and away from a pedestrian? What happens when the steering wheel is released: Does it stay on the road? Is the vehicle noisy? How smoothly does it shift, accelerate, and downshift? Accelerate the car quickly and look for the warning sign of blue smoke exiting the exhaust pipe. Billowy white smoke also indicates serious engine problems. Don't forget to check intangibles—like how cool you look behind the wheel.

♦ If the car is still thumb's up after the initial inspection and you want to buy it, it's time to visit a professional mechanic. This will cost you at least $60, but it is not a step to avoid unless you are a mechanical ace.

Tell the mechanic the situation: You're thinking of buying the car and want a thorough diagnostic and safety inspection. You'll want him to check the vehicle's compression, emissions, brakes, carburetion, transmission, struts, ball joints, ears, nose, and throat. Get him to prepare a report and list the cost of fixing the problems unearthed. If you want to purchase the car after the inspection, the report becomes a lever to drive the price down—you've got real figures quoting what it will cost to fix the car. Therefore, a professional inspection usually pays for itself.

♦ Don't know a reliable professional mechanic? Contact the local chapter of the American Automobile Association (AAA). They can recommend a reliable (though not necessarily the cheapest) garage in your neighborhood.

♦ Never buy a used car without seeing the ownership documents. Does the car's Vehicle Identification Number (VIN) on the driver's side of the dashboard match the VIN on the title and registration?

♦ For more information on buying used cars, read the annual Car Buying issue of *Consumer Reports*, Consumer Guide's *Used Cars Rating Guide*, and *Buying a Used Car* published by the Federal Trade Commission (send 50¢ to Consumer Information Center, P.O. Box 100, Pueblo, CO 81002).

Send a fool to market and a fool he'll return.
Dutch proverb

Christmas

Here is my prescription for an inexpensive Christmas: Celebrate its religious significance as usual but delay the commercial component (tree buying, gift giving, card writing) for about a week. Why? Because after December 25, shoppers can score on the dozens of half-price, post-Christmas sales dumping merchandise, wrapping paper, cards, seasonal candy, even trees.

Unfortunately my wife has proclaimed me a heretic, which means Scrooge McDappen has to employ other tricks to make Christmas the rich holiday it was meant to be, not the one that has us filing for bankruptcy.

♦ By December 25 you're usually so sick of shopping that visiting the post-Christmas sales sounds like a form of hari-kari. The fact remains, however, that the best time to shop for *next* Christmas is the week following *this* Christmas. Hit the sales and buy next year's wrapping paper, cards, stocking stuffers—maybe even the major gifts. Stash the loot in the attic; enjoy the reprieve until next year.

♦ Shop sales throughout the year with Christmas in mind. Store the great buys you find.

♦ Long before Christmas, discuss gift giving with members of your extended family. My two brothers, sister, and I no longer give to everyone—we draw straws and after the chaff settles, each of our families has one (and only one) family to buy for. As a result, all of us spend less time and money preparing for the December greed fest.

♦ Two years ago my siblings and I held a Christmas competition: We agreed the gifts we exchanged should all be inexpensive, and the family that gave the best presents costing the least, won. It was fun.

♦ Christmas presents needn't always be new. Save items you no longer use and give them as gifts to family members or friends who will appreciate them. Or buy used items at garage sales and auctions for young children who don't yet appreciate the difference between new and used goods. Capitalize on their naiveté while you can.

♦ An obvious money saver is to use your talents to make gifts like jams, fudge, beer, wine, photographic prints, sketches, sewn goods, needle crafts, salad dressings, floral arrangements...

The *Formula* chapter also lists several possibilities for children: finger paints, play dough, or bubble solution.

♦ For gift wrapping, make many different-sized cloth bags (with drawstring closures) from scraps of colorful fabric. Buy steeply discounted remnants at fabric stores and the cloth won't cost much.

The bags take more time and money to make the first year you use them, but they are reusable from one Christmas to the next. After two or three years, the money saved on gift wrap and the time saved wrapping pays off. From that time on, you're in the black.

♦ To decorate a tree inexpensively, make tree ornaments from gingerbread people. Before baking your gingerbread, use the end of a straw to poke a hole in the head of each character. Decorate the cookies with different-colored frosting, then hang them by a loop of ribbon tied through the hole in head.

♦ Certificates pledging your time to baby-sit, clean house, give massages, weed, chop wood, mow, cater a party, cook a meal, tune a car, take someone fishing...all make wonderful gifts.

♦ See the *Greeting Card* chapter for ideas to cut card costs, and the *Paper* and *Reuse* chapters for ideas about gift wrap.

Economy is great revenue.　　　　*English Proverb*

Clothing and Shoes

Maybe I'm not the person to give you advice about clothing. After all, I'm the guy who doesn't own a suit—I share one with my brother. We call it the "wedding suit" because we both wore it to get married and we've both worn it to the weddings of others. Now when either of us has occasion to use it (rare), we put in our reservation; if the suit happens to be in the other's possession, it gets put into a box and mailed off.

Obviously, with this kind of wardrobe, we're not part of the high-society set, we're not high rollers, we don't even make it onto the dress-for-success list. But because both my brother (a doctor) and I (a writer) are in professions where people rarely bother to dress to impress, the suit trick works for us. We're lucky: Experts calculate that the average family spends nearly 10% of its income on clothing. For a minute consider your combined family income and think about how much money that is! Don't panic. Maybe you can't pass a suit back and forth with a relative, but there are plenty of ways within your world to take a scalpel to that 10% figure.

♦ Besides being a source of information about automobiles, appliances, and food, *Consumer Reports* can help you in the clothing arena. Their reviews of suits, blazers, hosiery, etc., can unearth superior garments sporting prices you usually associate with inferior goods. Recently when I needed jeans, the magazine led me past all the advertising hype to choose a brand receiving top marks for fit, durability, and quality of construction. These jeans lacked the advertising hype that hikes the price of products like Levis; they cost me $15—about half what trendy names sell for.

♦ Buying clothing on sale and putting it in storage for later can be a risky proposition—styles may change or you may lose (or gain) weight. Nonetheless, each of us can identify some items we can safely purchase when the price is right. For me these items include socks, jeans, underwear, running shoes, T-shirts, sports clothing.

Make your own list and long before you need those items, buy your future replacements when they go on sale.

♦ The true cost of clothing is far more than the sticker price. Poor materials or workmanship mean you'll be replacing your garb often. That may be fine for children's items that will be outgrown in a season, but not for apparel that must last. Inspect items carefully for the quality. Check for tight stitching, bar tacks or double stitching at stress points, straight seams, buttons that are sewn on well, pockets that lay flat. Avoid items with loose seams, mismatched patterns, crooked collars, missing buttons, cut threads in major seams, seams that don't lay flat, inside edges that are poorly finished and that will unravel.

♦ Knowing the basic price structure of brand-name and private-label clothing is important in determining whether a sale is a buyer's feast or a fleece. The accompanying table lists various seller mark-ups. Use it to calculate the wholesale cost of the goods by taking the percentages listed off the *retail* price. Example: If a dress retails for $100, the wholesale cost was probably $40 to $50 for a brand-name dress and $20 to $40 for a private label.

Table 1: RETAIL MARKUPS		
	Item	Standard Markup*
WOMEN'S	Brand name clothing	50-55%
	Private label clothing	60-80%
	High fashion clothing	60-70%
	Brand name accessories	50-70%
	Private label accessories	50-70%
	Brand name shoes	50%
	Private label shoes	60-70%
MEN'S/BOYS'	Brand name clothing	50-55%
	Private label clothing	60-80%
CHILDREN'S	Brand name clothing	45-55%
	Private label clothing	60-70%

*Markup as a percentage of retail price.

◆ Retailers buy much of their private-label goods (merchandise ordered directly from the factory with the store's label sewn in) with "sales" in mind. Because the stores buy directly from the factory, and thereby cut out layers of middlemen, private-label merchandise is inexpensive. Stores triple, quadruple, even quintuple the wholesale cost to derive a list price that is competitive with brand-name goods. After establishing this list price, the stores "discount" their private labels for the sales they advertise. Half to two-thirds of private-label merchandise will be sold at "sale" prices. By comparison, only a quarter of brand-name clothing sells at discounted prices.

Of what importance is this information? First, be wary about buying private-label goods at list price—these prices are inflated and will probably be discounted soon. Next, don't let sale figures of 30% or 40% off whip you into a buying frenzy. The wholesale cost of a $100 private-label dress is probably $25 to $30, so if the sale price is $60 (40% off the list price) the store is still netting a hefty profit. Buy the dress at these prices if you're crazy about it and are worried that the stocks are limited, but keep in mind that the store will soon drop the price to 50% or 60% off if they need to move inventory. Even at 50% off, the store will make a reasonable profit—that's not necessarily bad, it needs to stay in business. But if you continually pay too much, you may be the one filing for bankruptcy.

◆ The previous section makes no judgment about the quality of private-label goods. True, some are shoddy. But the private-labels of quality clothiers are usually well made and may even come from the same factories producing brand-name apparel.

These goods are bought inexpensively because the stores have shaved away layers of middlemen. However, the stores can't create too big a price discrepancy between their labels and the brand-name goods or they may undermine and damage their brand-name business.

Be receptive to the idea of purchasing private-labels, but recognize the dangers. Buyers lacking a critical eye for quality or ignorant of the pricing games played may fail to make a shrewd purchase.

♦ Brand-name merchandise is rarely involved in the price games surrounding private-labels, partly because consumers can price-shop different outlets to discover whose prices are hot and whose are not. The vast majority of brand-name clothes are priced at twice their wholesale cost, so a 25%- or 30%-off sale is not the smoke screen it is with private labels. Because you can accurately figure the cost of the goods, you have a much better feel for whether the offer is a good one or whether you'll do better by waiting.

♦ Patience and planning will help you buy much of your clothing on sale. The general plan of attack is to buy what you need when it is out of season and being dis-counted to make way for the next season's merchandise. Store-wide clearance sales are normally held after Independence Day, Labor Day, Christmas, and Easter.

♦ People often rush out and buy clothing when the impulse strikes. Bad idea. Add the item to a clothing master list and wait for it to come on sale over the next weeks or month. If you still "need" the item by the time a sale arises, your need is probably legitimate. But you may be surprised how often a month's wait changes the picture; items that were once absolutely necessary now seem unworthy of your money. Once again, patience pays off.

♦ Trust your gut. If it doesn't feel like you're getting a good deal, your doubts are probably well-founded. Likewise if something intangible about the item gnaws at the gut, listen: Experts say that a *third* of the clothing purchased is rarely worn because of poor choices in color, style, or size. So even if the price is right, a garment that is not worn is a waste of money.

♦ The pants of men's suits wear out years before the jackets. Men who wear suits to work each day, therefore, will get better mileage from their money purchasing a two-trouser suit. Many stores don't actually stock suits with two trousers, but if you request extra pants, arrangements can be made to accommodate you.

♦ Large, clean garbage cans with tight lids make inexpensive storage containers for seasonal clothing. They are both bug and moisture resistant. Wrap the clothing in plastic bags before it goes into the can. For more information about storing clothing see the pest subsection of the *Miscellaneous* chapter.

♦ Everyone occasionally ponders this unsolved mystery: What really happens to socks when you toss them in the washer? Somewhere between the washer's entrance and the dryer's exit lurks a serial sock killer. I can't relieve the grief, the incredible sorrow, caused when the fiend claims a member of your flock, but I can relieve the financial pain. Buy socks that are all the same color in bulk packs.

This simplifies post-wash sorting, and when a singleton appears, you can tuck it away in the sock drawer. Next time a singleton surfaces, couple it with the last widow.

Men can survive nicely with just two colors of socks: black dress socks and white athletic socks (check that the athletic socks in a bulk pack have the same-color stripes).

♦ Are your clothes really dirty when you wash them? Unnecessary washing wastes money on soap, water and power; it also wears your clothes faster. Hanging clothes in the closet so they air for a day or two between wearings lets you extend the interval between washes.

Meanwhile, clothes that are borderline for creating an olfactory embarrassment are still suitable for dirty work around home. If you intend to vacuum and dust the house, do lawn work, or exercise, don clothing that is already headed for the wash.

♦ Dryers are tough on clothes. The heat causes gradual shrinking (even preshrunk garments can contract an additional 5%) and eventually you're worrying whether it was the clothes that shrivelled or your body that swelled. Then there's the friction caused as wet clothes rub and tumble against each other. If you don't think this slowly shaves life off your clothing, ask yourself what causes all the fuzz in the lint trap. No, it's not the shredded remains of the serial sock killer's last victim.

Whenever possible, air dry your clothing. You'll cut energy costs and prolong the life of your garments. When you do use the dryer, turn dress garments inside-out to minimize the pilling on the outside.

♦ Pilling. Okay, maybe it's not quite as embarrassing as pimples but those little wads of fluff do blemish your clothing. Get rid of this unsightliness and you eliminate one reason clothes are prematurely retired. Toward this end, the properly prepared penny-pincher needs at least two weapons. For tight knits (sweatshirts), light sweaters, and shirt collars, a plain-old razor and blade can shave away the pills: Some razors work better than others and it's worth experimenting. Electric pill shavers like the Remington *Fuzz Away* ($15) also work well for these applications.

For the large pill balls on heavy sweaters and wool coats, a pill snagger works best. Try *The Sweater Stone* ($7) from The Vermont Country Store (802-362-2400).

♦ Use dental floss to sew buttons back onto clothing—it's cheap and much stronger than normal thread. Also, if you're ever at the movies and need to remove one of those tongue-aggravating popcorn husks trapped against your gum, you can strip a button and floss.

♦ The knees are the first to go—in professional athletes and jeans. Professional athletes need reparative surgery, but jeans can avoid the problem with preventive surgery. Apply iron-on patches to the inside of pant legs and you effectively double the life of the knees. This is especially useful with children's jeans.

♦ To make a matching knee-patch for the outside of children's pants, pirate the back pocket.

♦ Call the library or a bookstore and ask whether your city has a book detailing the discount shopping options in the area. In my corner of the country, a book entitled *The Greater Seattle Super Shopper* (Elliott and Fairweather Inc., P.O. Box 1524, Mercer Island, WA 98040) fills the niche; many cities including San Francisco, Chicago, New York, and Washington, DC have such guides.

These books usually cover discount outlets for food, home appliances, tools, and sporting equipment. Clothing, however, is always a main category. If your city has such a book, it probably lists the local thrift shops specializing in clothing, consignment shops, factory outlets, full-line thrift stores, low-overhead outlets with name-brand and designer labels, sample shops (where salespeople and manufacturers' representatives sell their samples), discount shoe outlets, and discount outlets for children's clothing.

♦ Look through a copy of *The Wholesale By Mail Catalog 1992* (see *Mail Order* chapter). It lists many options for getting name-brand clothing for less.

♦ To remove lint from pants, wrap a length of cellophane or masking tape around your hand, sticky side up. Wipe your pants with the tape band you've made and lint will stick to the tape.

♦ Invigorate old jeans by washing them together with new jeans. The dye running out of the new pants will help rejuvenate the geriatric set.

♦ You always wear the same face to a party, so why not wear the same clothes? It's a frugal way of dealing with the what-am-I-going-to-wear syndrome. Purchase a snappy but comfortable outfit and make it your signature garb for holiday and special-occasion parties. Have fun making a joke of your antics and soon everyone will expect to see you sporting the same outfit year after year.

DRY CLEANING

♦ A huge variable in the true cost of clothing is the cost of cleaning it. Dry cleaning downs dollars like fraternity boys guzzle booze, so check the labels of everything you buy and, as much as possible, avoid clothing with the dreaded "dry-clean-only" tag. With the endless options of clothing available on the market, you can find machine- or hand-washable items for most of your needs.

♦ Not all items with a "dry-clean-only" tag actually require dry cleaning. Some, (e.g., many silk items) can be hand-washed in cold water with a gentle detergent. Don't risk anything rare or valuable, but experiment with items that are no longer so dear to you that you're willing to finance the cleaner's vacation to Hawaii. Before washing any such item in entirety, hand-wash a hidden section of the garment as a test. After cleaning, roll up the item in a towel to extract the water, then air dry.

Silk blouses lacking a print pattern are a good bet for hand-washing. Women can save over $20 a year on each blouse they hand-wash.

♦ Don't overlook the cleaners as an outlet for clothing. Items that are dropped off and never claimed are eventually sold, often for just the price of the cleaning.

♦ Dry cleaning rates can vary tremendously and the highest price has little to do with the highest quality. Call around for rates. Also ask whether the cleaner has bulk rates for items cleaned on a per-pound basis. Often having a large load cleaned by the pound is a big-dollar saver, so get the rates and do your math. When my wife had a large load of winter woolens cleaned before the goods went into summer storage, the per-pound rate was $19 less than the per-item price. Likewise, when we had our drapes cleaned, the per-pound price of one cleaner got the job done for 50% less than what other cleaners were charging on a per-item basis.

HOSIERY

♦ Women who know the brand, model, and size of panty hose they want should try ordering it by mail—it's usually cheaper. For a bonanza savings, buy the imperfects, which are available only through the mail. The imperfects of brands like L'eggs, No Nonsense, Hanes, and Underalls sell for 30% to 50% below the regulars and usually you won't find the flaws even if you spend time searching.

To obtain these mail-order catalogs write or call: Showcase of Savings, P.O. Box 748, Rural Hall, NC 27098, 919-744-1170 (imperfects of L'eggs, Hanes, Underalls, Bali); Kayser-Roth Corporation, P.O. Box NN-1, Burlington, NC 27220, 919-229-2246 (No Nonsense); National Wholesale Company, 400 National Blvd., Lexington, NC 27294, 704-249-0211 (National brand).

♦ Women who aren't getting a minimum of eight to 10 days of use from their hose should be looking for a new brand. The longest lasting panty hose usually contain spandex, which is strong, very elastic, and prevents the knees and ankles from bagging. In fact many people wish they could get this wonder fiber transplanted around their eyes and under their chins.

♦ A new nick in hose or stockings can be kept from running by applying nail polish (uncolored) to the spot. Meanwhile, women who occasionally mortally damage their hose with a careless stab of the fingernail should consider wearing cotton gloves when slipping in and out of their second skin.

Wash hosiery in a pillow case so that it is not damaged in the machine.

♦ Singleton stockings of different colors can be dyed to make a matched pair. Soak the stockings in warm water, then transfer them into a pot of very hot, strong tea (coffee works, too). Stirring occasionally, let the stockings soak 30 to 40 minutes until the tea is cold, then rinse and air dry your "new" pair of stockings.

SHOES

♦ Alternate the shoes you wear each day. Having a day to dry and air between uses greatly extends shoe life. Along with proper airing, footwear of value should be stored with shoe trees placed inside them. Otherwise, moisture from sweat and rain will cause the shoe to bend and curl; over time the shape of the shoe will be resculpted.

♦ The best shoes generally have leather uppers and leather soles. If you live in a damp or downright wet climate, the leather soles will frequently be absorbing water, which will slowly damage the leather and reshape the shoe. Solution: Have rubber half-soles (also called zip-soles) applied to the bottom of the shoes. This costs $12 to $15 but for good shoes the added years of life you've just given the shoes justify the expense.

♦ Men and women alike need to polish their footwear if they expect it to last. Without occasional polishing, the finish dulls, scuff marks are etched into the leather, and the leather itself is exposed to the elements and cracks.

Finding the color of polish to match many women's shoes is almost impossible unless you visit a cobbler and have him mix a polish to match the shoe.

♦ Ironically, the ruin of many good shoes is not walking but driving. While working the gas and foot pedals the back of the shoe is repeatedly scraped against dirty, abrasive carpet. Eventually the back of the heel counter is irrevocably scuffed and discolored.

Because pumps and heels slip on and off quickly, women have an easy solution: Keep a pair of slip-on sneakers in the car. Wear the sneakers when driving, then slip into your unmarked, valuable shoes upon arrival.

♦ Many dress shoes, running shoes, and boots that visit cobblers each year are damaged by drying them too quickly near a furnace or fire. Heat damages wet leather and ruins the heat-sensitive glues in soles. To dry footwear, stuff the inside with wads of newspaper (get the paper down into the toes) and set the shoes in a warm room away from the heat source.

Wet running shoes and boots should not be left out in a cool, dank garage or mildew may cause damage.

♦ The tops of running shoes often spring holes where the nail of the big toe rubs against the top of the shoe. Fix such a hole (or prevent it from happening) by using a liquid-rubber compound (like *Freesole*, *Aquaseal*, *Goop*, or *Shoe Goo*). Use masking tape before applying the compound to neatly delineate where it goes. If you already have a hole, masking or duct tape on the inside of the hole creates a backing that keeps the compound from dripping through. For more information about liquid-rubber compounds, see the *Repair* chapter.

♦ Typically, heels of dress and running shoes alike take the most abuse. Save the heel and the rest of the shoe is ready to walk extra miles. With men's shoes (or women's shoes with wide heels) put plastic heel guards (about $2.50) over the spot in the heel you traditionally wear out. These protectors can be added to used shoes, but it's best to apply them when the shoe is new and the heel flat.

Sport shoes and running shoes with worn-away or collapsed heels can be repaired at very little cost with the liquid-rubber compounds mentioned in the last entry. Run a piece of masking tape around the perimeter or the worn section of the heel—this acts as a dam to keep the compound from running off the shoe before it cures. Apply the compound to the worn portion of the heel and then lay the shoe flat (sole up) or slightly tilted toward the masking-tape dam. Use enough compound so that the pool gathered behind the masking tape dam levels out the heel.

Complaining

Years ago my mother opened a can of corn and found a dead worm in the bottom. It inspired her to fire off a letter to the president of the food company and, taping the dried remains of the worm to the letter, to remark, "I see we're getting meat along with our vegetables now."

She received a lengthy letter in return, detailing the highly hygienic standards of the company. At no point did they admit that a worm could have infiltrated their impenetrable net of sterility, but they did send my mother a case of canned corn as a tacit apology.

The point? When you have a legitimate complaint, voice it. Recently, my dad took a paint sprayer, still on warranty, back to the store. He had finished painting his house but believed a part was defective. The store did not stock parts, so they sent him home with a brand new sprayer—a better model than the one he had purchased.

This advice pertains to poor service as well. Several years ago I received contemptuous treatment over the phone when I tried making a dinner reservation for eight at a popular restaurant. I was treated like a cretin for believing that a restaurant of such import could make room for eight nobodies the day before we planned to dine.

I wrote a polite letter to the manager explaining that, thanks to this treatment, there were now eight nobodies who would no longer be helping his restaurant maintain its important reputation. The manager sent me an apology and bribed me to reconsider by enclosing a $30 gift certificate. I swallowed my pride—along with some good food—and used the certificate.

A few comments about registering complaints.

♦ Yes, it is worth the time—especially with brand-name merchandise and organizations peddling high-quality services. More often than not, an organization will take fair and reasonable measures to make amends. Sometimes, they go way out of their way—the good words you pass on to friends is bankable PR for them.

♦ First step, contact the store where you bought the item and calmly explain your problem. If a salesman doesn't give you good service, move on to the store manager. Most problems are resolved at these levels.

♦ No luck at the local level? Then write a letter to the company at fault. Address your complaints to someone high enough to make the decision about what should be done. In the case of defective merchandise, send the letter to the president of the company. He or she will likely never see the letter, but it will get directed to the right person. Matters relating to poor service are usually best taken up with the manager of the establishment first.

♦ Make the letter short, listing: facts about where and when you purchased the item (or service), model and serial numbers (if relevant), nature of the problem, extenuating circumstances that have resulted. Include copies of documents, correspondence, or bills that pertain to the problem. Make copies of all letters sent—they document when and what you've done.
     Then explain what you want, too—refund, replacement, apology, a new Rolls Royce.

♦ Register complaints with a cordial, nonthreatening tone. Put yourself in the shoes of those helping you. Would you rather help a belligerent loud-mouth issuing empty threats or let him rot? It's much more fulfilling to help a polite, reasonable person who was wronged.

♦ Order a very useful guide to complaining, entitled the *Consumer's Resource Handbook*, from the Consumer Information Center (P.O. Box 100, Pueblo, CO 81002). It lists sources to help you register complaints: hundreds of customer service departments of major companies, Better Business Bureaus around the world, consumer protection offices, helpful federal agencies (is that an oxymoron?). The handbook is free but send $1 for shipping (is that a paradox?).

♦ Another useful publication to own when problems arise is *How to Write a Wrong* by the American Association of Retired Persons (AARP). It's a definitive guide for handling problems with door-to-door salesmen, mail-order firms, and normal businesses. Order it (publication #D1126) from the AARP, Consumer Affairs Section, Program Department, 1909 K Street NW, Washington, D.C. 20049.

> *Some men worship rank, some worship heroes, some worship power, some worship God, and over all these ideals they dispute -- but they all worship money.*
>
> *Mark Twain*

Computers

Computer users who have pirated software already know one popular trick to make computer ownership cheaper. They copy the software from friends, purchase a user's manual at the local bookstore, and soon they're running a $300 program for nanocents. But because the practice is illegal, it leaves you grappling with ethical questions.

What I offer below are perfectly legal methods of slashing computer costs— ones that won't have you hemming and hawing when people ask, "Where did you get your...?"

♦ Software for personal computers can be found through mail-order houses at prices well below retail outlets. Software is an ideal mail-order purchase. The diskettes and books making up the software are packaged (and shrink wrapped) for mail shipment and have nothing mechanical to break. Also, because computer users usually call the software company's technical support number when they have software problems, the need for the service a retailer will try to sell is something of a moot point.

Whenever you buy software through the mail, double-check the version you're getting. Sometimes prices are ridiculously low because a firm is moving out an earlier version.

For more information, see the *Mail-Order* chapter and appendix.

♦ In the market for an IBM-compatible machine? It's true that IBM and other major manufacturers of compatible machines (Compaq, Northgate, ALR, NEC, Dell) produce products with fewer failures, making their purchase a wise business decision (computer down-time is very costly for businesses).

Most home users, however, spend a lot of money unnecessarily for a name-brand machine. The IBM clones assembled in shops around the country can offer the same features at much lower prices. Your odds of buying a lemon may be slightly higher, but if your livelihood does not rely on your machine, it's worth the gamble.

Knowing just what you're getting is the main problem in purchasing a clone. Some firms assemble very good machines with excellent components, others cut prices by using lower quality components. If you're a neophyte, how do you know whether to move toward or away from a low-priced clone?

Ask if the machine has an FCC number (if it has one, it's probably on a sticker on the back). Then call the local office of the Federal Communications Commission and check if this is a legitimate number for the machine you're considering. Computers are not required to have an FCC number, but firms that go through the trouble and expense of acquiring a number are generally interested in building a quality product and generally use quality components.

Another strategy is to ask the vendor about the components used. Find out the manufacturer and vital specs of the system board, BIOS, disk controller, hard disk, floppy drives, video adapter, power supply, keyboard, and monitor. Next, call a technician who repairs computers and get his or her opinion about the quality of the components used and whether the machine is worth buying.

♦ When you call up an old computer file and alter it, the new information is not stored on the hard disk (or floppy) in the same location as the original data, but is tacked onto the disk where space is available. The next time you go to retrieve that file, the disk's read-write heads must travel to several locations to gather up all parts of the file. These heads are mechanical parts and the extra travel increases their wear (i.e., reduces their life).

It is economical, therefore, to periodically run a disk-optimizing program, like *Speed Disk* (part of Norton Utilities), which gathers all parts of a file and stores them together again. The result: "Mileage" on the drive's read-write heads is greatly reduced.

♦ Backing up your computer's hard drive regularly will save you much time on that fateful day when (not if) your hard disk crashes. If your computer is important for your work, time equals money. But there could be a lot more involved than just time. Restoring a crashed disk usually entails reformatting it, and reformatting erases all stored information. If you need to get that data off because you have no other backup, the process could easily cost you $500 to $1000. By comparison, the money spent on a few dozen floppy disks to back up your data look like a bargain.

For heavy computer users who have over 40 megabytes of information stored on their hard drive, it makes even a tape drive for backing up (mail-order cost of about $250) look like a steal.

♦ Computers don't like being turned on. The chance of failure at this time is high enough that many businesses never turn off their machines. Running a home computer full time makes little sense unless you use it long hours each day, but turning the machine off and on several times daily is equally nonsensical. If you step away from the computer and intend to return within three or four hours, keep it on.

When taking a break from a computer that is 'on', protect your monitor from "burn in" with a screen-saving or screen-blanking program. Alternately, dim the screen manually before walking away.

♦ Voltage spikes and surges through the power lines can fry the electronics of your computer and printer. A good surge protector is far better insurance for your machines than an extended-warranty policy.

♦ The comments about extended-warranty policies in the *Appliance* chapter also apply to personal computers.

♦ Spraying glass cleaner directly on the monitor's screen can cause damage. Spray the cleaner onto a soft, lint-free rag, then wipe the screen.

♦ There are different schools of thought about cleaning the heads of floppy drives. Many computer stores recommend cleaning them once or twice a year with a special cleaning diskette (available from computer and software stores for about $8). Other experts believe these diskettes are too abrasive and do more harm than good if used regularly. They recommend leaving the heads alone unless you experience read or write errors, at which time the cleaning diskettes can be used. If the cleaning diskette solves the problem, great. If not, get the machine serviced.

Many computer technicians clean the heads using a cheaper, safer tool: lint-free cleaning swabs purchased at electronic supply stores (these swabs are longer and thinner than *Q-Tips*). They dip the swab in isopropyl alcohol, reach through the front slot of the drive, and lightly scrub the heads. You'll need a flashlight to see the heads—look for two tooth-sized white cubes (one on the roof of the drive, one on the floor) along the centerline of the drive but behind its midpoint.

♦ Dust sucked in through the front of your floppy drive adds to the drive's wear and tear. If your drives lack a dust cover, fashion a flap from masking tape that seals the entrance slot when the drive is out of use.

Also, once or twice a year, use a vacuum cleaner set on 'Blow' (rather than 'Vacuum') to blast air through the drive and carry out the accumulated dust.

♦ Computer repairmen recommend cleaning your computer's keyboard and central processing unit (CPU) yearly to exorcise dust, dander, and hair that can damage the electronics. It's easy to save money by doing these jobs at home.

To clean the keyboard, hold it on edge (or upside down) and blast it with air from a vacuum cleaner set on "Blow."

To clean the CPU, remove the case covering the electronics. This is no big deal, even if you know zilch about what happens inside this magic box. Unplug the computer, then remove the five or six screws (in the back) that hold the case on. If you want to unplug the cords and cables, fine, just take careful notes about which cable goes where. Slide the case forward and away from the electronics. Now blow air over the electronics, (with a vacuum cleaner or canned air) to blast away the dust. Keep the vacuum's nozzle a good eight to 12 inches away from the components. If for any reason you decide to touch an electrical component, ground yourself first (on the computer's power supply) to prevent static electricity from zapping something it shouldn't.

♦ People who are not afraid to tinker can easily give their keyboard, the computer component prone to the most failure, a thorough cleaning. With the machine unplugged, expose the points of the keyboard by removing the screws on the bottom that hold the casing together (don't disconnect any wires while doing this). Blow out the dirt and dust. Then dip a *Q-tip* in isopropyl alcohol and clean the contact points of each key. Reassemble the casing in the reverse order of disassembly.

♦ Many county libraries now have computer hardware and an extensive library of big-name software that can be used at no charge. See the *Library* chapter. It's a great place to test software you have thought about purchasing.

♦ With programs becoming ever more complex and the shift toward more graphics-based programs (which uses much more memory than text-based programs), software has become a memory pig. Consequently, many computer users have found that they've outgrown their hard drives.

So what do you do, replace the hard drive with a bigger one? That's one solution, but not the cheapest option. Before taking that route, research programs that offer on-the-fly data compression. The best of these programs can effectively double or triple your hard disk space without impairing your machine's speed. With a street cost of $130 to $150, the software is half or a third the price of new hardware.

Among the best-rated compression programs are *Stacker* (Stac Electronics, 5993 Avenida Encinas, Carlsbad, CA 92008, 800-522-7822) and *SuperStor* (AddStor Inc., 3905 Bohannon Dr., Menlo Park, CA 94025, 415-688-0470). For a good overview of these programs, read the January 28, 1992 issue of *PC Magazine*.

♦ Computer users owning laser printers have a hefty expense ahead of them when their "disposable" toner cartridge needs replacing. For popular laser printers—like those made by Hewlett Packard, Canon, and Apple—new toner cartridges cost $80 to $125. New cartridges for many other machines, like the NEC printer I own, can cost $200.

But you can slash costs by recycling your "disposable" cartridge. Many companies refill old cartridges for less than half the cost of a new cartridge: Hewlett Packard cartridges can be refilled for $40 to $50 while the cartridge for my NEC printer can be refilled for $80. In the early days of refilling, the results were not always satisfactory. That's no longer true with reputable refillers—you can expect flawless performance and will usually get more pages of print from a refilled cartridge than from a new one.

Find names of local refillers in the *Yellow Pages* under Computer Supplies, Desktop Publishing, or Office Supplies. Many reputable businesses also accept empty cartridges and ship the refills by mail. Two such companies are AMS Laser Supply (430 S. 96th #9, Seattle, WA 98108, 800-289-5277 or 206-764-3344) and Laser Renew of Connecticut (55 Carmen Hill Road, New Milford, CT 06776, 800-347-4221 or 203-354-3309). Both guarantee two-day turnaround times upon receiving your cartridge.

♦ The previous information about refilling toner cartridges also applies to the "disposable" toner cartridges found in personal copy machines and fax machines. Like the cartridges for laser printers, these can be refilled for about half the price of a new purchase. AMS Laser Supply and Laser Renew of Connecticut (addresses listed in the previous paragraph) handle cartridges sent through the mail.

♦ Owners of dot matrix and daisy wheel printers may be able to slash their printing costs by re-inking their faded cloth ribbons rather than buying new ones. Re-inking entails the use of lubricated dot-matrix ink (non-lubricated inks will ruin your print head) and a machine, costing about $80, to apply ink to ribbon.

The casual computer user won't print enough to justify a re-inker, but because the replacement cost of most ribbons runs between $8 and $15, a re-inker can pay for itself after six to 10 ribbon changes. The same ribbon can be reused 50 to 100 times and the quality of the printing after re-inking is virtually as good as that of a new ribbon. The MacInker (available by mail order from the distributor: Computer Friends, 14250 NW Science Park Dr., Portland, OR 97229, 503-626-2291 or 800-547-3303) is a popular re-inker. You buy a universal cartridge base ($70) and a specialized kit ($10) to adapt the re-inker to your type of ribbon.

♦ Restuffing is another option that can lower the cost of fabric dot-matrix and daisy-wheel ribbons. Mail your ribbon cartridge to a company like Northwest Ribbon Recycling and Supplies (8175 SW Nimbus Ave., Beaverton, OR 97005, 503-641-5156). They pull the old ribbon out of the cartridge and insert a fresh ribbon.

Inexpensive ribbons, like those for the Epson MX80 printer, are cheaper to buy than restuff. But you can save 30% to 60% by restuffing medium-priced and expensive cartridges. The ribbon cartridge for the Okidata 393, for example, retails for $20 but can be restuffed for $11.

Where there is most labour there is not always most life.

Havelock Ellis

Credit Cards

You love 'em, you hate 'em. They're a godsend, they're an abomination. What would you do without them, what would you do to be rid of them?

No one would argue that there are two sides to owning credit cards. Their convenience and hidden perks offer you great freedom—until month-end when the swollen balance has you feeling the tightening of the noose. Come reckoning day you'll always get stung by the flip side of these wonderful cards. But heed the following advice and you'll see the cards as more white than black.

♦ A prime rule of Dappenomics: Carry a credit card only if you keep the minimum balance at, or very near, $0. If you can't hold to the rule, keep the devil hidden in your dresser (for emergency purposes and mail-order purchases) rather than in your wallet where it will tempt and torment you. Why? Because paying 18% to 20% interest on a monthly balance is crippling—a financial shot in the foot.

♦ Unfortunately, only a third of all credit-card users heed the prime rule. If you're part of the indentured two-thirds and have money invested elsewhere that can be freed up, pay off the balance. Why? Your yearly earnings on an investment like a $5000 certificate may be around $400. But paying 18% to 19% on a $5000 balance costs you over $900 a year. It doesn't take higher mathematics to realize this is financially unhealthy.

♦ If you can't pay off the credit card, pay what you can (not just the minimum payment). The more you pay, the lower the balance drops and the less interest you pay.

♦ Credit-card users who pay their outstanding balances each month should establish their account with a bank issuing free cards. No need to pay an annual fee of $20 for a Visa or MasterCard when you can get them free. Also, make sure your card has at least a 25-day grace period between the billing date and the payment-due date. About 6000 different banks issue credit cards and, because there is really no convincing argument to use local banks, you'll find many with no annual fee and acceptable grace periods. Among them are USAA Federal (800-922-9092), Amalgamated Bank (800-365-6464), Abbott Bank (800-999-6977) and Fidelity National Bank (800-753-2900).

♦ Two-thirds of all cardholders don't pay their bills in full and must pay finance charges on their outstanding balances. For these cardholders, finding a bank charging low interest rates is more important than finding one without an annual fee. The annual cost of carrying the average-size balance ($1600) at the average rate (18.77%) is about $300. The same balance at a rate of 10% costs you $160.

Because state laws in Arkansas prohibit banks from charging more than 10% on their cards, check out Simmons First National (501-541-1000) or Arkansas Federal Savings (800-477-3348 or 501-224-7283). Bargain rates for Visa and MasterCard can also be found at People's Bank (800-423-3273) and Ohio Savings Bank (800-356-1445).

Interestingly, some free credit cards also offer excellent interest rates. At this writing, USAA Federal (800-922-9092) gives you the best of all worlds and Amalgamated Bank (800-365-6464) also beats the total you would pay through Ohio Savings Bank.

♦ Bankcard Holders of America (560 Herndon Parkway, Suite 120, Herndon, VA 22070, 800-553-8025) publishes a frequently updated brochure listing 50 card companies offering low interest rates and no annual fee: cost is $4. Card*Trak* (800-344-7714), a monthly report of 500 bargain cards, costs $5. And "Money Scorecard" in *Money* magazine gives a monthly listing of the best half dozen bargain cards.

♦ Ironically, most credit-card owners get the worst of both worlds, high interest rates and annual fees. Currently, eight of the 10 largest credit-card issuers charge an annual fee and all of them charge high rates for financing. If your credit card is issued by American Express, AT&T, Bank of New York (Delaware), Sears, First Chicago, Bank of America, Wells Fargo, Chase Manhattan, MBNA America, or Citibank, ask what favors these card-issuers bestow on you. More than likely you're doing them the favor.

◆ If you are a card user who carries a balance from month to month and who pays the monthly minimum on time, you are a valuable customer to a card company (they're making money off you). Valuable enough that when it is time to renew the card you can probably get the annual fee waived by calling the card company and stating that because of the fee you're considering taking your business elsewhere.

Credit card companies deny publicly that they waive annual fees but insiders admit the practice is often used to save valuable customers. Squawk and you shall receive.

◆ Consumers who pay their balances in full can get interest-free loans for nearly two months if they plan big purchases carefully. Make large card purchases just after the last statement's closing date. Then, pay off the card at the end of your grace period. Time it right and you'll get to borrow money free for about 50 days.

Say you purchased a computer worth $3000. Keeping your money in a money market fund paying 6% would earn you $25 during that time.

◆ Card companies are consolidating quickly and if yours is devoured by bigger game, the terms are likely to change—probably for the worse, because the major buyers are the big 10 mentioned earlier. Research new options when you are notified of a change; then you'll be ready to ship out if you don't like the way interest rates or yearly fees shape up.

◆ Paying more for a gold card rarely justifies the expense. Few people use all of the extra enhancements and free cards can usually be found offering the specific enhancements you covet—be that collision insurance on rental cars or airline frequent-flier points.

As for getting your credit limit raised, you probably don't need to upgrade to gold. Assuming you have a reliable credit history, you can usually raise the limit of a standard card just by asking.

♦ Report lost credit cards immediately—first with a phone call and then with a letter to the card issuer reporting the card number, when you lost the card, and when you first called the company about the loss. You are not responsible for illegal charges if you report a loss before any charges are made.

And don't worry about paying for credit-card insurance limiting your liability in case of loss or theft: Your maximum liability in these instances is $50. Such theft (and loss) protection is a strong incentive to carry a credit card instead of large quantities of cash.

♦ Another important form of protection offered by credit cards is a safeguard called a chargeback. Chargebacks can protect you from shabby or faulty merchandise, mail-order disputes, custom orders that are wrong, unsatisfactory service (e.g., lost luggage, unsatisfactory car repair), and billing errors. The muscle power of the chargeback is so significant that you should charge all large expenditures to your card—just in case you encounter problems and the vendor refuses to make things right.

The first step with any problem is to try resolving it with the vendor. If this fails, *write* to the customer service department of your card company (within 60 days of receiving the statement with the disputed charge) and give them your name, address, facts related to the dispute, and results from contacting the vendor. Tell the card company you are requesting a chargeback under the rules of the Fair Credit Billing Act and that you will be withholding the specified amount on your next bill. (Note: Inform your card issuer in writing *before* you withhold payment.)

American Express uses a different procedure for chargebacks. Call 800-528-4800 and they will note the details of the dispute over the phone.

Your card company will freeze that particular charge (and any associated interest) until they make a ruling.

By the letter of the law, the chargeback rule applies only to purchases greater than $50, less than two months old, and made within 100 miles of home. In practice, many card companies are quite lenient and entertain chargeback requests well outside of these parameters.

If you've already paid for the disputed product or service, most card companies will still investigate a legitimate grievance and deduct the full amount of your withholding from a later statement. This is a large boost to consumer rights, since the card companies are obligated to withhold only the unpaid amount still owed the vendor.

What are your odds of winning a chargeback dispute? Excellent if the facts and law are behind you, but you may need persistence. If the facts (though not necessarily the law) are with you, your success depends heavily on the attitude of your card company. You can hope that yours gives the benefit of the doubt to the cardholder.

♦ Billing errors with your card company are handled similarly. Notify your card company in writing (within 60 days of the disputed statement), listing the charges you believe to be erroneous. Then withhold payment for those charges until the card company makes a ruling and notifies you accordingly.

♦ Some people find it worthwhile to own two cards: A no-fee card for items you will pay off and a low-interest one for purchases you intend to finance. Sole proprietors should consider a third card for business purposes. That's all you need. Ignore department store credit cards in favor of major credit cards. This keeps you from running up more debt; saves you time (don't have to pay as many bills); and saves you from sending checks, envelopes, and stamps to many different department stores. Furthermore, the financing charges of department stores is usually in the 18% to 21% range, so if you get one of the low-interest major cards mentioned earlier, you'll want to use it. Finally, in the event of a chargeback dispute, you'll have more clout working with a major card company.

♦ Using your Visa or MasterCard for a cash advance sounds great in theory; in reality, this "service" must have been concocted by Shylock himself. You get no grace period on these advances—you start paying interest immediately. And the interest applied to cash advances can be even higher than the astronomic rate applied to purchases. Finally, some card issuers sock you with a service charge— a charge that can be as high as 5% of the money borrowed. If you need cash, use your debit card.

♦ If a store adds a surcharge to your bill for paying with a credit card, refuse to pay it. Credit card companies like American Express, Visa, and MasterCard do not allow vendors to add a surcharge to credit-card purchases.

♦ When traveling abroad, pay as many bills as possible with your credit card. Card companies, being large financial institutions, extract a better exchange rate than you can as an individual. That means you save. Plus, the card companies don't charge you the transaction fee that banks often lay on you when you exchange dollars in a foreign bank.

Dates

It's worthwhile considering Machiavellian principles in the dating game. This sounds ominous, I know, but hear me out. Many of Machiavelli's principles revolve around the premise that a privilege once given cannot be taken away: Give citizens the right to vote and you can't return to a dictatorship, improve the public's standard of living and they won't stand for the rag times of old.

Give a date a dozen roses once and a simple carnation later will precipitate disappointment. Dine at Maxim's on a first date and McDonald's is spoiled forever. See what I mean? Start a relationship with precedents you can sustain. And don't worry if you're broke. You can nurture high romance as a low-roller. In fact, if you don't flaunt money, you can rest assured that the affection that flourishes is for you, not your bankroll. That in itself may convince the affluent to set frugal precedents.

This chapter approaches dating from the traditional point of view (man pays), but women wanting the lead role will learn from these tips and strategies, too.

♦ While most people habitually spend money dating (movies, dinners, theater, amusement parks) there's no dearth of activities that require little or no money.

Jocks have many such options for dates—tennis, hikes, walks or jogs in the park, bike rides, swimming, croquet. Auctions are a fun and inexpensive date—if you can refrain from bidding on the Porsche. In the same vein, flea markets, bazaars, rummage sales make for a fun afternoon of treasure hunting.

♦ Need a high-brow, but cheap, date? Spend an afternoon visiting several local art galleries. Use the *Yellow Pages* (look under Art Galleries or Art) to contact the local galleries. Ask to be placed on the mailing list announcing their gallery openings. At these openings you can view good art, hobnob with interesting people, and gawk at eccentrics who often prove to be more interesting than the art.

Poetry readings provide another high-brow possibility for a date. If you like poetry, great. If your idea of quality literature is a romance novel, poetry readings are still fun for the experience and their rubbernecking value. Call the larger bookstores in your area and ask them to put you on their special events mailing list. Libraries are also likely to sponsor readings at certain times of the year, so keep tabs of their monthly (or quarterly) programs.

♦ Get a book of constellations from the library and arrange a starry-night date to identify constellations. Bring a thermos of hot chocolate.

♦ Take advantage of free tours in the area. Brewery tours, wine-tasting tours, even factory tours can be interesting, depending on your date's interests.

♦ If you have a steady, take classes in subjects of mutual interest—drawing, canoeing, wine-making, music, volleyball, dancing... See the *Entertainment* chapter for tips on scoping out cheap courses around the community.

♦ Once you know a person's interests, you have a gateway to new cheap dates. Is she interested in architecture? Ask her to give you a tour of the city and teach you what she knows about the buildings. Does she have musical interests? Find out what music festivals the city and park departments are sponsoring. Books her thing? Go to the rare-book stores together and browse. With a little creativity, you can find ways to convert personal interests into cheap dates.

♦ Romance is the flattering and caring attention given a person, combined with the artful delivery of that attention. It is at the heart of what most women desire from dating and, in truth, has little to do with money. Sure, boxes of chocolates and candlelight restaurant dinners ring of romance, but the creative cheapskate can kindle a romantic fire on a dime-store budget. How?

1. When she's not looking, leave a loving note in a woman's purse.

2. Write her a poem: It can be original or copied. You'll find a lifetime supply of poetry at the library. If you are at a loss for words to copy, try something from Shakespeare's sonnets or Kahlil Gibran's *The Prophet*. Or ask a librarian to suggest several romantic poems.

3. Give your date or steady frequent but sincere compliments about the qualities you admire—her good nature, positive outlook, sense of humor, intelligence, sparkling eyes.

4. Pick her up and deliver her to a candlelight dinner at your house.

5. Send frequent special occasion cards. They are considerably cheaper than flowers and words can pack more punch than mute flowers.
6. Bring dinner and candles to her apartment and cook dinner.
7. Bake brownies or cookies and deliver them to her at work.
8. Send wish-you-were-here postcards when you travel.
9. Make her things—carvings, necklaces from shells, origami flowers. If the stuff is tacky, laugh over its tackiness: The thought will still be appreciated.
10. Use any musical talents you have and, when the mood is right, put on a serenade.
11. During summer, take evening walks and talk.

♦ If you want to give flowers and are desperately broke, you can always plan a midnight visit to the community cemetery to see what the day's mourners have dropped off. Leave your ethics at home and have the sense not to confess from whence the flowers came.

Scrupulous flower-givers should remember what I said about precedents. A dozen roses is flashy, but a single rose is elegant and wins nearly as many points for thoughtfulness. It is also a precedent you can afford to maintain.

Large supermarkets selling flowers and bouquets are usually a cheap bet—prices here are generally lower than at a retail florist. If you do need a large order of flowers, check the Yellow Pages under *Flowers—Wholesale* and call a few local wholesalers. Some wholesalers don't sell to the public, others will allow you to make cash purchases—purchases that will cost you half or a third of what a retail florist charges.

I can get 24 long-stemmed roses from a nearby wholesaler for $23 (less than a dollar a rose). Meanwhile, the retail outlets charge $37 to $47 for 12 roses ($3 to $4 per rose), depending on the season. Same goes for medium-stemmed roses: I can buy two dozen roses from a wholesaler for $15 or one dozen roses from a retailer for $25 to $30. Orchids, bought in bunches of five or 10 from a wholesaler, cost only a quarter of the retail charge.

To make purchased flowers last, cut the stems just before placing them in a vase of warm water. Adding nourishment to the water is also recommended. Mix

Floralife (available from a florist) in the warm water or, because *Floralife* is predominantly glucose, stir in one or two teaspoons of sugar per quart of water used.

♦ On a rainy day, bring over a basket with the food and drink for an indoor picnic. Spread the blanket indoors and pretend.

♦ Find additional tips for planning cheap dates in the *Entertainment* and *Restaurant* chapters.

* * * * * *

Death

Contemplating your demise is both emotionally distressing and financially worthwhile. The money saved may not help *you* where you're headed, but it will help your survivors. And you'll want your loved ones, not an undertaker (oops, the word now is funeral director) or Uncle Sam, to inherit the bulk of your fortune.

There is another excellent reason to plan for your death immediately—a reason related to the immutable laws of Mr. Murphy. The fickle finger of Fate, Murphy says, is most likely to mold the future we are least prepared for. Get yourself ready for the Big Sleep, and Fate may spite you by preserving you 'til the wrinkled age of 99.

So while you may call the following tips "death planning," I call them "life insurance."

FUNERALS, CEMETERIES, CREMATORIES

Vendors of cemetery goods usually deal with families in crisis—bereaved survivors who must make a quick decision about a costly process and are in no state of mind to comparison shop. Many vendors are honest and will help families make wise decisions. Unfortunately, many are also quite happy to make a quick buck off grieving or guilt-ridden survivors.

The goods and services you require when a family member dies depend on many factors including religious beliefs, cultural customs, and economics. Consequently, some of the following tips won't fit your belief structure. Those that do, however, can make a huge difference when the inevitable arrives.

◆ The average cost of a funeral (over $3000) and burial (over $2000) make death one of the larger expenditures a family faces. An easy way to drive prices down is to make your own arrangements. Use the luxury of time to comparison shop for goods and services you want instead of giving the onus to a grieving relative who will feel guilty cutting financial corners.

You may not care if you're buried in a cardboard box or an orange crate but, to a spouse or relative, penny-pinching may smack of disrespect. So make your own plans for the end. If you are married, make your plans with your spouse.

◆ Shop for funeral goods and services like you would a washing machine—look around. By law, funeral directors must have price lists of their goods and services, though cemeteries don't. In 1988 the American Association for Retired Persons (AARP) reported, "a task force in Phoenix found that the same traditional funeral (a hardwood casket, transportation of the body, memorial observances, and the funeral director's charges) cost as little as $1100 and as much as $4500 at different homes in that city."

Some homes have the prestige to get away with high prices. Others exact outrageous profits because they can get away with it, because people don't comparison shop.

Compare the *total* costs at the homes you check. Funerals are a combination of goods (caskets and outer burial containers) and services (transportation, use of the facilities, care of the body, services of the funeral director).

◆ Most people purchase mid-range products. In the case of caskets, a top-end box may run $5000 while the low-end option may cost $650—which leaves a large mid-range. Interestingly, funeral directors know that by introducing the average buyer to the high-end casket first, Mr. Average will settle for a casket costing half as much ($2500). By introducing the average buyer to the low-end product first, Mr. Average will buy a casket costing twice as much ($1300). Through subtle salesmanship, the funeral director has wrung an extra $1200 from the average person.

Fortunately, you're not average and you'll recognize this trick. Right? I'm not just talking about caskets, either; the technique works for selling cars, stereos, refrigerators.

♦ Be ready for the "show-how-much-you-care" sales pitch used to upgrade survivors to more costly goods and services. Ridiculous. Expressing the depth of your love must be done while a person lives.

♦ Few people can notice the difference in a basic 20-gauge steel casket and an 18-gauge steel casket (especially if the casket is closed). The 18-gauge casket, being thicker steel, however, costs many hundreds of dollars more.

♦ A traditional funeral entails holding the body for the service, a casket, embalming (not always necessary), and a sizeable price tag. Increasing numbers of people are now opting for immediate burial or for direct cremation of the body. The survivors often organize a memorial service later (without the body present).

Different funeral homes offering the same basic package (moving the body to the funeral parlor and later to the cemetery, holding the body for a day or more, a low-cost container, payment to the funeral director) will charge prices as low as $500 and as high as $1400. An outer burial container (required by many cemeteries), a plot, and other cemetery charges will be additional.

Direct cremations at different funeral homes offering the same services (moving the body to the parlor and later to the crematory, holding the body for a day or more, payment of the funeral director, delivery of the cremains) can cost between $500 and $1550. Containers for transporting the body may be extra.

♦ In many states you can make cremation plans directly—without a funeral director acting as a middle-man—to reduce costs. Call the listings in the *Yellow Pages* under "Cremation Services" and "Crematories."

♦ If a body is to be cremated after a traditional funeral, don't buy a casket, rent it. After the funeral, have the body transferred and cremated in an alternative container. Because a vendor may want the profit derived from selling a casket, he may hint that caskets are required for cremation. Not true. Crematories do want the body delivered in a combustible container, but there are much cheaper options than a casket.

♦ Over 150 nonprofit memorial societies around the U.S. and Canada help members obtain a dignified funeral (or cremation) at an affordable price. These societies negotiate lower prices with a local funeral home and offer members several "package deals." In Seattle, $10 makes you a lifetime member of the People's Memorial Association (2366 Eastlake E, Seattle, WA 98102, 206-325-0489). Upon death your survivors can choose one of three plans: cremation for $447 (includes pickup of the body and delivery of the remains), direct burial for $565 (does not include cemetery charges), and a traditional funeral for $690 (includes a minimum cloth-covered casket but no cemetery charges). These prices are very low for the Seattle market.

Members of a memorial society have reciprocal agreements with other societies. If they move, they become members of the closest society. If they die while traveling, the nearest society will handle their body.

To get the name and the address of the memorial society closest to you, send a self-addressed stamped business envelope to Continental Association of Funeral and Memorial Societies, 6900 Lost Lake Road, Egg Harbor, WI, 54209 or call 414-868-3136.

♦ In 43 states, families, friends, or religious groups can handle all death arrangements without "hiring" a funeral director. You can transport the deceased yourself to the cemetery or crematory (after you've attended to the necessary paperwork). The process saves a considerable sum of money. Equally important, families who care for their dead say that personal involvement in the process has a healing power that is absent in the clinical atmosphere of a funeral home.

In earlier days, families and friends routinely cared for their own dead, meaning there is nothing new or unusual about the process. The present system of using a funeral director is really the new kid on the block.

The book *Caring for Your Own Dead* by Lisa Carlson (Upper Access Book Publishers, P.O. Box 457, Hinesburg,

VT 05461, 800-356-9315) explains the benefits of doing it yourself. It also details the legal requirements for each state, describes how to obtain permits and fill out death certificates, and explains cremation and burial procedures. Mail-order cost is $14.95.

♦ Donate your body to science and, abra cadaver, funeral and burial expenses disappear. Most state universities with medical research and training schools operate a willed-body program. Programs differ but most of them work like this: upon death, the university picks up the body (no charge for local pick up); later, when the research is completed, the university cremates and buries the body in one of its plots or, if the survivors wish, returns the remains to the family.

For more information about these programs, call the nearest university with a medical school and ask for their body-donation program. The book *Caring For Your Own Dead* (mentioned earlier) lists the medical schools around the country (addresses and phone numbers included) with such programs.

Note: Not all members of a willed-body program will be accepted when they die. Infectious diseases, trauma, and obesity are among the reasons bodies may be rejected. Better work out a contingency plan.

♦ If you are part of your region's organ donation program (as opposed to a full-body donation program) you do not avoid funeral expenses. After the organs and tissues have been recovered, the family still must make arrangements for the body.

♦ Fees for cemetery goods and services (grave site, marker, care of grave site, etc.) are separate from funeral home expenses and can easily add over $2000 to the cost of death. Visit (or call) several cemeteries to compare costs.

♦ Most cemeteries require a liner or a vault to cover the casket. Both keep the earth from sagging around the grave site as the casket deteriorates. Funeral directors may steer you toward vaults, which are more expensive, saying they retard the deterioration of the body. Retard, yes: prevent no. And because the body is going to decompose no matter what, opt for a less expensive liner.

♦ Most veterans, as well as their spouses and minor children, qualify for free burial in a national cemetery. Additional benefits to veterans include a grave marker and perpetual care of the site. Any Veteran Administration office can supply more details.

♦ Pre-planning funeral goods and services is one matter, pre-paying is quite another. The funeral industry has myriad "pre-need" plans designed for pre-paying funeral costs. Most people should avoid pre-need plans. Some plans are not safe and you may lose money if you move (and want to cancel your plan) or if the funeral home dies before you do. Other pre-need plans are trust funds or savings plans that trap your money into low-yield investment plans.

If the concept of budgeting for your funeral is compelling, the AARP recommends you consider establishing your own *Totten Trust*. These trusts are safe—establish them with a bank and you are insured by the FDIC. The trusts are also portable and you'll net a higher return on your money than with most other plans.

♦ For more information about these topics, order the following Product Reports from the AARP (1909 K Street, N.W. Washington, DC 20049): *Funeral Goods and Services, Pre-Paying Your Funeral?, Cemetery Goods and Services.*

Additional materials to help you plan a dignified funeral at affordable prices, prepare a durable power of attorney, donate your body or organs, and learn the wholesale costs of caskets are available through Continental Association of Funeral and Memorial Societies (6900 Lost Lake Road, Egg Harbor, WI 54209, 414-868-3136).

DISABILITY

♦ People plan better for death than for disability—perhaps because death is inevitable while disability is only possible. Still, a bad roll of the dice—an accident on the highway or at work—could instantly transport any one of us from the driver's seat to the vegetable bin. Suddenly, we may need family or friends to tend our affairs.

Cheery, eh? It can get uglier still. If disaster struck and you hadn't filled out the proper paperwork, even your spouse could lack the legal power to handle your affairs, sell jointly held property to pay expenses, make decisions in your business matters, or tap into your pension accounts to pay mounting bills.

Relatives working in your behalf would need to ask the courts to appoint a guardian and conservator—a process that could take months, cost dearly, and create endless frustrations.

The solution? Prepare for horrible possibilities while you are healthy: Have a lawyer draft an inexpensive document called a *durable power of attorney.* This empowers an appointee to make decisions (legal, medical, and financial) in your behalf. Everyone over age 18 should have this document prepared because who knows when a car hurtling down the highway will sway across the center line and forever change your future?

♦ Fill-in-the-blank forms assigning durable power of attorney to an appointee are better than nothing, but, should you become disabled, the homemade job could easily become a false economy. An attorney specializing in estate matters will list powers and address tax issues the average person will omit using a standardized form.

♦ To pull the plug or not to pull the plug? That is the question behind a *living will* (or directive to physicians).

If two physicians agree you have an incurable injury or a terminal illness, and that life-sustaining procedures are artificially prolonging the moment of death, what would you have them do? Sign a living will and you opt to pull the plug (i.e., withhold or withdraw life-sustaining procedures).

The topic is an emotionally charged one brimming with moral and religious arguments. Nonetheless, most people don't want to be kept alive artificially against their will. They argue that they have a right to die with dignity and without bankrupting their survivors (artificially sustaining a person's life can easily cost $2000 per day).

If you are such a believer, make out a living will and give a copy to both the executor of your estate and your doctor. Books in the library will likely have forms for living wills you can copy. Alternately, get forms from Continental

Association of Funeral and Memorial Societies (mentioned earlier) or Choice in Dying (250 West 57th Street, New York, NY 10107, 212-246-6962).

WILLS AND LIVING TRUSTS

♦ Doesn't matter if you're young or old: If you want your possessions, property, and money passed on to family and friends when you die, prepare a will or living trust. Why? So your affairs are handled in an orderly fashion; property is distributed to family and friends according to your wishes; and inconvenience, expenses, and taxes are all minimized.

Unfortunately, a high percentage of people never draft a good will. Younger people, who still believe themselves immortal, are especially unprepared for death. But they should be prepared, especially if they are married or have children.

Without a will or living trust, state law controls what happens to your estate. The intent (or even the legality) of a poorly drafted document can be contested. Either way, the government or the lawyers may have a feeding frenzy at the expense of the people you care about.

♦ Many books encourage you to write your own will. For a couple with uncomplicated assets and the wish to make a spouse the beneficiary of the entire estate, a do-it-yourself document may suffice.

But the claims made by books that anyone can write his or her own will are half truths. After writing our wills, my wife reports anyone can do it, just like anyone can rebuild an engine. Unfortunately, most people lack the time to learn the intricacies of federal estate tax, state taxes, and of substitutes and complements to wills (joint tenancy, community-property agreements, revocable living trusts).

Most people are better off hiring an attorney who specializes in estate planning.

♦ Of course if you let a lawyer work on your estate for more than a few hours, there may be no estate left to pass on. Get organized before your meeting and you'll minimize the charges. Foster Pepper & Shefelman, a Northwestern law firm that is well-respected for their

estate-planning specialty, recommend that clients answer the following questions before visiting a lawyer.
- What is the net value of your estate?
- Will you leave your estate to someone (spouse) with no strings attached?
- Who will administer your estate (list backups)?
- What items of personal property will you leave to specific people?
- What will you leave to charity?
- Do you want to avoid probate?
- Are your financial records comprehensive and accessible to your personal representative?
- Do you want a personal statement in your will?
- Are you donating your organs for research or transplantation?
- In the event of terminal illness, should life-support procedures be terminated?
- Who should manage your affairs in the event of incapacitation?
- Who should inherit your estate if your entire immediate family dies in a common disaster?
- Should property left to children be kept in a common fund or in separate funds for each child?
- At what age should children receive their inheritance outright?
- Who is the trustee (and backup trustee) of your children's trust?
- Who is the guardian (and backup guardian) of your minor children?

♦ Revocable living trusts have received oceans of ink lately as *the* salvation from the evils of probate (partially true) and as a way of reducing estate taxes (false). Consumers who believe the savings of a living trust will total thousands of dollars are routinely being sold packages costing $750 to $1500.

That's not necessarily bad. If your state probate fees are based on a percentage of the value of the estate or if the state probate laws require frequent intervention of the court to approve sales of property or payment of debt for the estate, then the cost of probate may be much higher than the cost of avoiding it through a revocable living trust.

In states where the probate laws have been simplified and streamlined, however, the cost of establishing a revocable living trust usually exceeds the cost of probate.

Living trusts are not only expensive to establish, they are also comparatively difficult to maintain because all past and future assets must be titled to the trust. Meanwhile, the trusts won't reduce or eliminate estate taxes, as many people mistakenly believe (avoiding probate and avoiding taxes are entirely different issues).

Revocable living trusts are not the only way to avoid probate. For many people, the problem can be solved simply and cheaply through other devices like joint tenancy (with the right of survivorship) or community-property agreements.

The moral? Don't jump blindly onto the living-trust bandwagon. Many unscrupulous salesmen are peddling a product many buyers don't need. Find a good, reputable estate-planning lawyer (through friends, insurance agents, or the *Martindale-Hubbell Law Directory* at the library) and put stock in his or her opinion of the tools which will best serve you.

◆ Shopping for legal services is not terribly different from shopping for a carpenter—call several firms and get price quotes for the services you require. Firms with a specialty in estate planning or probate practice should be able to give you accurate bids for matters discussed in this chapter.

As with carpenters, the most expensive quote does not ensure the best work nor does the cheapest quote guarantee shoddy work. Law practices specializing in an area of expertise can often streamline work and offer you a better price. Other firms may offer lower prices because they use less expensive paralegals to handle the routine chores of a procedure.

Men are divided between those who are as thrifty as if they would live forever, and those who are as extravagant as if they were going to die tomorrow.
Aristotle

Dental Tips

I once believed my dentist genuinely enjoyed my visits. His smile upon my arrival, I thought, meant he enjoyed my quick wit and insightful perceptions. It took my quick wit many years to conclude that my perceptions got little notice when they were bottled up behind a rubber dam. Which made me reevaluate my position. Now I think that smile was a Pavlovian response to the sound of a mental cash register. "Dappen's back," he was thinking. "There *will be* money for this month's Ferrari payment."

During my teen-age years, I was reckless with my mouth. I was on the dental dole of my parents' insurance. The dentist represented a few hours of pain every six months, but he never struck the truly sensitive nerve of my wallet. That changed with the severing of the parental strings. Here is what I've learned about keeping my mouth clean now that the golden years are over.

♦ Dentists and hygienists are always giving us flack about plaque and harping on us to brush and floss. It's good advice. Plaque, a sticky film of bacteria and salivary components adhering to teeth, is the major cause of cavities and gum disease and its cumulative effects account for the loss of teeth in 35% of all senior citizens. Plaque also hardens into tartar, a crusty coating over the teeth that contributes to gum disease and loss of teeth. Control disease-producing plaque and you'll prevent (even eliminate) most dental problems. The good news: Prevention is cheap and will spare you horrendous dental bills later in life. The bad news: Brushing, flossing, and frequent professional cleanings (twice yearly) are still the most effective weapons.

◆ If you're going to brush, do it right. Proper brushing will save your teeth and gums from unwanted problems that could cost megabucks later (gum surgery, for example, can run upwards of $12,000).

Here is a recap of what you've heard umpteen times but are probably not doing. Place the brush at a 45-degree angle at the intersection of the tooth and gum. Gently vibrate the brush in small circles, cleaning one or two teeth at a time. The goal is not to polish the flat surfaces of your ivories but to thoroughly clean the boundary between the gum and each tooth. Finish your brushing with a gentle scrubbing of the chewing surfaces.

The gumlines alongside molars and the backs of teeth need just as much attention as the smile surfaces. Devote at least three or four minutes to the job.

Brush twice a day if possible, but if you do it just once, brush at night: Oust the army of bacteria before giving them the evening to dig in.

Use small, soft-bristled toothbrushes. Giant brushes won't speed up the dreaded deed and they are not as effective at scouring the little grottos sheltering plaque. Meanwhile, hard bristles damage your gums.

◆ Brandish your toothbrush with a pencil-style grip rather than a racket-style grip. Foreign research shows that the pencil grip gets teeth as clean but causes less gum damage—apparently this grip promotes a vibrating motion more than a stroking one.

◆ A good hand brushing can be just as effective as an electric brushing but the average person does a much better job with a good electric brush. Forsake the old-style electric brushes, in which the entire brush vibrates, and purchase the new style (*Interplak, Superbrush, Rota-Dent*) in which the stem remains stationary while the bristles rotate. These brushes work like the ones used by dental hygienists and, according to research, remove as much as 98% of the plaque (most people using a brush only eliminate 50%). They're not cheap ($70 to $100) but hygienists attest there is a tremendous difference in the quality of cleaning they see between clients using the new electric brushes and those brushing by hand. Moreover, electric brushes stimulate and tighten up the gums.

According to hygienists, the benefits of these brushes far outweigh the cost.

♦ Choose any fluoride toothpaste approved by the American Dental Association (ADA), an independent body that rigorously tests the products it approves. Products that don't sport the ADA's seal (most generics don't) may have an inactive fluoride, may use coarse abrasives, or may not have been tested by the ADA.

As for the hoopla about pastes with tartar control, few people need to pay extra for it. Any paste that scrubs away plaque—as they all do—will control the development of new tartar deposits for the vast majority of people.

♦ Buy a good brand of toothpaste, but don't waste it. Advertisements showing the brush smothered with toothpaste cunningly encourage overconsumption—if manufacturers train you to use three times more paste than necessary, you'll buy three times more product. A little dab (a third the length of the brush) will do ya.

♦ An inexpensive toothpaste substitute that dentists endorse is plain old baking soda. Wet the brush and dab it in the powder. The cost is a fraction of what you'll pay for toothpaste—which makes up for the taste being many times worse. Adding a teaspoon of shredded orange rind or several drops of mint extract improves the flavor.

Personally, I use a small jar to store a wet paste of baking soda and *Act* fluoride mouthwash. The mouthwash improves flavor and adds fluoride to my powder.

♦ If your local water lacks fluoride, drink teas. Black tea delivers more fluoride than fluoridated water.

♦ Flossing is equally important to brushing because it cleans between the teeth below the gumline—places where a brush can't reach. For the long-term health of your mouth, it's just as important as brushing. Do it daily.

As with brushing, do it right. Use a gentle sawing motion while moving the floss in the gap between the teeth. At the gumline, bend the floss into a "C" and cup one tooth while continuing the back and forth motion. Curve the floss around the other tooth and floss it in kind. Go slow and scrape the teeth at and below the gumlines without abusing the gums. Spend about four minutes each night flossing.

♦ Wax, unwaxed, flavored, tape, generic...which floss is best? For most people it doesn't matter, although people with widely-spaced teeth may prefer tapes while those with tightly packed ivories may opt for waxed string. Most store brands are sound investments that cost about half as much as a brand name. If you happen upon one store brand that frays easily, try another.

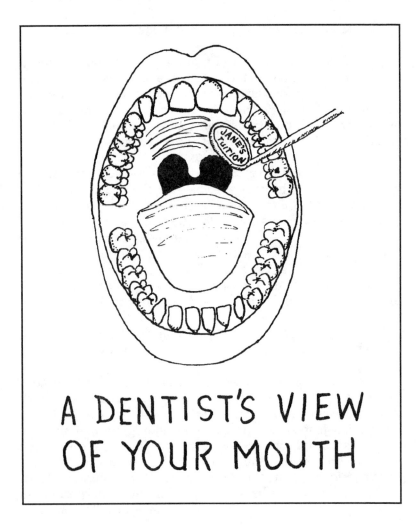

A DENTIST'S VIEW OF YOUR MOUTH

♦ Use disclosing tablets (available at drugstores) periodically to check family members' effectiveness at brushing and flossing. The dye in the tablets stains any plaque remaining on the teeth after cleaning. Check the gumline, spaces between teeth, molars, and backs of teeth closely. Hone your brushing and flossing to snuff these bacterial havens and you'll reduce cavities and gum disease.

♦ A cheaper substitute for disclosing tablets is red food coloring. Spread petroleum jelly on your lips (keeps your lips from turning Dracula red), then add seven or eight drops of red food color to 1/2 teaspoon of water. Swish the solution around for 60 seconds, then check for plaque.

♦ See your dentist or hygienist for professional cleanings at least twice a year (people with diagnosed gum problems will need three or four cleanings a year). Even with proper brushing and flossing, you won't remove all the plaque encrusting your teeth at and below the gumline. That spells future trouble unless you scrape it off regularly. Professional cleanings are cheap medicine compared to treating future gum disease and tooth loss. An added bonus: Most dental policies pick up the tab.

♦ College and university dental hygiene programs are excellent places to get teeth cleaned. The community college near me charges $25 per routine cleaning while hygienists at dental practices charge $45 to $50. Use the blue pages of the phone book to determine if your local university or community college has a dental hygiene clinic.

♦ Most cleanings with a hygienist include a quick examination with the dentist. Unfortunately, the five minutes he or she spends on the once-over of your mouth costs you $18 to $20. If you don't have dental insurance and have no unusual problems, paying the dentist to inspect your mouth twice a year is overkill. Save yourself $20 every other visit and request a cleaning only.

♦ When a dentist does examine your mouth, he should use a periodontal probe to check the pockets between your gums and teeth. These pockets hold bacteria and the larger they become, the more likely you are to need expensive dental work later. Not all dentists probe your pockets, so you should routinely ask whether you have any pockets and what their depths are. Pocket depth of 3 millimeters or less is fine. At 4mm or 5mm, you can reverse their ill effects by improving your flossing and brushing. At 6mm, you've got the potential for serious trouble and should be getting your teeth cleaned professionally four times a year.

If your pockets are enlarging, the *Interplak* toothbrush can help tighten up the gums and reduce pocket size.

♦ Finish meals and snacks by rinsing your mouth with water. It's fast, it's easy, it washes out substantial quantities of bacteria and food, and it's free.

♦ *Listerine* was once the only over-the-counter mouthwash claiming to fight plaque and gingivitis (inflammation of the gums) that carried the ADA seal. Non-partial studies showed it reduced plaque buildup by 22% and gingivitis by 28%.

Now the private label firms supplying the *Listerine*-like mouthwashes for K-Mart, Wal-Mart, Walgrens, Kroger, Target, and Topco have the ADA seal, too. These competitors often sell their wares at half the price of *Listerine*.

Do you need these mouthwashes? Not if you're conscientious about brushing and flossing. If you're delinquent, however, post-meal swishing is better than nothing.

♦ You'll get the same health benefits from commercial mouthwashes by using about a third of the recommended amount. Use just enough to swish around. A bigger gulp simply sends a larger quantity down the drain.

♦ The damage sugar inflicts on teeth is not a function of how much you consume but of how long you expose the teeth. Encouraging children to orgy on Halloween candy is better for their teeth than rationing. Dole out candy over the course of weeks and each candy session resupplies bacteria with the fuels they need.

By the same token, a big candy bar devoured in bites does less damage than a little sucking candy that continually coats the teeth with a sugary film.

◆ Don't let infants and toddlers take bottles to bed. Milk and juices that pool around the teeth create an idyllic environment for bacteria to attack teeth. Baby bottle mouth causes cavities in the front teeth—expensive for you, painful to children, and difficult for the dentist (imagine trying to give screaming toddlers Novocaine shots and fillings).

Sometimes decay even results in having teeth pulled prematurely, which contributes to malocclusions (bad bites).

◆ Fluoride, a mineral that combines with and strengthens tooth enamel, has decreased cavities in children by nearly 40%. The best way to get fluoride is through drinking water, but if your water lacks fluoride, talk to your doctor or dentist about fluoride drops or tablets. It is especially important for children to get fluoride when the permanent teeth are forming (before the age of 6).

◆ The importance of fluoride for adults is controversial, but according to a 1988 study published in the *Journal of the American Dental Association*, fluoridated toothpastes do reduce cavities in adults. Still, the vast majority of dentists do not give fluoride treatments to adults living in municipalities where the water is not fluoridated. Dentists who give adults such treatments (the ones where your teeth soak in a sappy-tasting gel) are generally believed to be milking their clients.

As for fluoridated mouthwashes, don't worry about them unless your dentist or hygienist advocates their use.

◆ Sealants, a plastic material used to cap the top of children's molars, reduce cavities in children by as much as 80%. Sealants protect the permanent molars from bacteria and decay by filling macroscopic and microscopic pits and crevices that trap food and bacteria. For children, whose teeth are considerably softer than adults', sealants are a tremendous preventive weapon against cavities.

Have the first four permanent molars sealed when they come in (around age 6) and the second four permanent molars sealed after they emerge (around age 12). Cost runs $30 to $50 per tooth—a bargain considering that the initial cost of each cavity will be at least twice that amount. Furthermore, any cavity will need refilling later in life, making its actual cost considerably higher.

♦ A hygienist friend tells me that children's teeth get X-rayed yearly with little thought as to whether the X-rays are needed and whether you can afford the $30 expense. Children with a history of little tooth decay don't need yearly X-rays. Stop the habit by printing this message across your children's charts: "No X-rays unless confirmed by parent."

This message can also stop the unnecessary X-raying of baby teeth. With baby teeth, problems that require attention before the tooth falls out are generally visible without film. A better time to take a child's first X-rays is around age 6 after the first permanent molars emerge.

♦ Adults who have had little decay from year to year don't need X-rays very often either—once every two or three years will suffice.

♦ Some dentists have capitalized big time off of patient's paranoia over the mercury in amalgam fillings and have made much money replacing amalgam fillings with plastic ones. Non-partial studies do not support the premise that amalgams represent a health hazard. Meanwhile, it is well-known that plastic fillings don't hold up well on the chewing surfaces of teeth. Consequently, people who are having their amalgams replaced with plastics are getting ripped off twice.

If your dentist suggests you have all your amalgams replaced, definitely get a second opinion.

♦ Malocclusions (bad bites) usually occur at the time the permanent teeth come in—between the ages of 6 and 12. Besides the genetic factor, thumb-sucking and early loss of primary teeth can play a significant role. Orthodontics are an expensive proposition that no one suffers gladly so eliminate the environmental factors working against you. If your child is a thumb-sucker, break the habit around age 5—the product *Stop Zit* (available at most drug stores) works well for breaking the habit (paint it on the thumb, its bitter taste does not wash off easily). Bedtime bottles that can result in baby bottle mouth should be stopped immediately because premature loss of primary teeth will impact the spacing of the permanent teeth.

Your child will have tantrums as you break their habits. But the crying now ain't nothing compared to the years of moaning a teenager with braces can heap on you.

♦ Low-income and fixed-income families should check out the dental services available through their county's public health services. Many counties around the country offer extensive dental care (both preventive and restorative) and charge on a sliding-fee, according to a client's ability to pay. To investigate the opportunities here, look up "Health District" or "Health Services" in the county listings of the phone book.

♦ If your local university has a dentistry school, it probably needs patients for student practice. Sound ominous? It shouldn't. Procedures performed by students are overseen by faculty. You get expert care and the advantage of all the new advances in the field. Unlike private dental practices, in which corners are cut to increase production (the more mouths a private dentist sees in a day, the more money he makes), you can be sure the work at a dental school will be done slowly and by the book. This, in fact, is the main drawback: It takes time to do meticulous work and have it inspected every step of the way, so you'll be in the dentist's chair much longer. The payback? Dental work for about half what private practitioners charge.

The phone book will include the dentistry school under the university listings.

♦ I think my parents erred by sheltering me from dental bills as a kid. They should have required that I help pay for the cavities I incurred: It was my responsibility to clean my teeth and I should have suffered part of the financial burden when I blew it. Had the payment for my transgressions affected my piggy bank, I would have paid more attention.

Set up a fee schedule for your kids. Incorporate bonuses for perfect checkups. See if it helps. Even if your kids fail to cooperate, you still win—now they're helping share the burden.

Desperate Times

You think you've got it bad, that you'll never reach your financial goals, never own your own home? Be thankful you're not living in Tokyo where residents are now taking out 100-year mortgages. No joke. With one-bedroom apartments selling for $650,000, many families can afford housing only by putting the financial yoke on themselves, their children, and perhaps on their grandchildren.

Think about qualifying for such a loan. Does the bank use a psychic to decide whether your children and grandchildren can make future payments? Or do they conduct personality tests to determine whether you've got a Gestapo personality that can horsewhip the next generation into paying their dues?

In perspective, maybe things aren't so bad for you. But if times are tough, what you need more than the knowledge of other miserable company is the knowledge of how to surmount the financial pit. Following are some tricks offering you just that know-how. Some may seem dire—kind of like a 100-year mortgage—but sometimes it takes drastic measures to surmount desperate times.

♦ If you overextended yourself with a large house during the spend-spend years of the 1980s, downscaling to a smaller house could give you the financial breathing room needed to start accumulating savings. A house with just one less bedroom could drop your yearly housing costs by thousands of dollars. Example: a family putting their equity and appreciation from a four-bedroom into a three-bedroom house of equal age and quality could decrease the size of their mortgage nearly $40,000. Once the reduced house payments, taxes, and upkeep are added, they may realize a savings of $3000 to $4000 dollars a year.

Many variables affect whether this strategy would work for you (or be worth the hassle and heartache involved in a move). But if getting through each week is a walk along a financial tightrope, the strategy is worth serious consideration.

♦ With a flat or falling housing market plaguing the country and interest rates so low, the temptation for home buyers is to buy a bigger house than they could normally afford. Think hard before taking such a step. The housing market is expected to appreciate by only 5% through the decade—a rate that is only slightly higher than inflation. Unless you'll be rooted in your home for the long term, hopes of a quick rebound, and thus a hefty profit when you sell, are unfounded.

Also, consider that throughout much of the country, property taxes have been rocketing skyward and are likely to fly into orbit. Buying too much house may subject you to tax burdens you can't afford. Finally, your utility and maintenance bills will be proportionately higher in a larger house.

Buying more house than you absolutely need can make the difference between living on the edge and building your savings.

♦ If your life is a sprint on a treadmill that leads no closer to your financial goals, consider this drastic measure: move somewhere with a lower cost of living. The cost of living in the most and least expensive parts of the country varies by 90%, yet salaries rarely fluctuate more than 25%. The Economic Research Institute states that professionals moving from Los Angeles to Atlanta could expect a 13% drop in earnings *and* a 50% drop in the cost of living. The difference in purchasing power means a person who was unable to afford a home in California might buy one on Day 1 in Georgia.

Atlanta may not be your idea of Shangri-la but the example applies to hundreds of towns and cities around the country; some of those places may be perfect for you.

♦ Other ways to axe huge expenditures from your budget are scattered throughout this book. For the most significant money savers, see the *Insurance* chapter about health maintenance organizations versus traditional policies, *Children* chapter about public versus private education, and the various car chapters about buying new and used automobiles.

* * * * * *

Entitainment

As long as an enamored public tolerates the inflated earnings of entertainers and sports heroes, mainstream entertainment will forever cost dearly. The millions Madonna gleans to jiggle while she jingles or Costner collects to set hearts throbbing come straight out of our savings. Fortunately for those of us with shallow pockets, a tremendous amount of free or very inexpensive entertainment hides in the shadow of the limelight. This chapter illuminates opportunities you may be missing. And, if you're insistent about staying in touch with the mainstream—about keeping abreast of Madonna—this chapter helps you control the damage.

♦ Currently, a first-run movie in Seattle costs $6.50—all for the privilege of having basketball players sit in front of you and gossips grab the seats behind. Admittedly, there are pictures that videos don't do justice to (even when you sit two feet from the television)—so here's how to get the big-screen effect on a small budget.

- Take advantage of matinees. You'll pay half the price and get twice the elbow room.

- Watch your movies at multi-plex theaters. Few multi-plex theaters usher you out the door when your feature ends, so you can wander from one movie to the next. Make an evening of it and watch two or three films for the price of one. If you are ushered out the door, don't patronize that theater again, find one with more relaxed attitudes.

- In most cities you'll find discount theaters featuring films that are neither fish nor fowl (i.e., neither first run nor in video). Because films reach this no-man's-land so quickly and because discount theaters give you the big-screen effect at a nominal cost (about $2 a person), it pays to be a few months behind the times.

- Movie theaters glean much of their profit through food and drink. Popcorn costing you 30¢ to make runs $3.50 at the theater. A quarter's worth of pop rings up at $2. Bring your own refreshments and escape the scalping. Theaters don't encourage these practices (lost revenue) so be inconspicuous: Carry the contraband in a small day pack or a woman's tote bag.

♦ Most performing-arts theaters use last-minute ploys to unload unsold seats. Those ploys translate into discounts for you. Some theaters, like the A.C.T. Theater in Seattle, sell half-price tickets at the box office on show day—you can call the box office and make the purchase with a credit card. Others, like the Seattle Repertory Theater, sell "rush tickets" about 15 minutes before show time and those tickets still on the rack go for half price. Rush tickets may be unavailable for the Friday or Saturday showings of a popular play, but if you call the box office, they'll tell you which evenings have seats available.

Other theaters offer discount days or showings: You can see a show for half-price during a matinee, or during a specified weekday evening. Then there are student and senior citizen discounts, which are typically 25% to 50% off normal prices.

Because each theater will have its own policies and programs, call them all and ask each how to obtain discounted tickets for their productions. Ask if they sponsor discounted showings, sell half-price tickets on show day, or sell rush tickets. If they sell rush tickets, ask which nights you're sure to score seats.

♦ Ushers at plays watch the production free. Some theaters have long lists of groupies wanting to usher, others may be in need of your services. Call the administrative offices of your local theaters for the scoop.

♦ In a dozen major cities around the country you can buy half-price tickets for any of the major performing-arts theaters on show day from a half-price ticket broker. In Seattle, Ticket/Ticket coordinates the half-price sales for all shows in the city (plays, concerts, ballet, opera, lectures). New York City, Boston, Washington D.C., Pittsburgh, Chicago, Montreal, Toronto, Denver, San Diego, San Francisco, and Portland are among the other cities using a centralized half-price ticket broker. The name of the broker varies from city to city; contact the city tourist office or a performing-arts theater for the broker's name and number.

◆ Don't overlook community theaters. In large cities the quality of the productions is usually high while the ticket price is low compared to professional theaters. Community theater around Seattle costs $7 to $10 a seat compared to $17 to $35 for professional theater.

A city's semi-professional theaters also offer the opportunity to see excellent quality productions at mid-range prices. Use the tricks listed above (rush tickets, half-price ticket brokers) and you'll see professional-quality performing arts at movie-theater prices.

Your city and county arts commission (listed in the government pages of the phone book) are the best sources for listings of community, semi-professional and professional theaters. Or if you know one community or semi-professional theater, their administrators can tell you the names of others.

◆ If the cost of theater is beyond your budget, invite friends over for the reading of a work in which you each play a part. You'll have an evening of culture and laughs.

◆ Colleges, universities, and community colleges all sponsor a host of events (lectures, concerts, movies, performances, dances), many of which are free or very inexpensive—even for the public. At private and community colleges, the student activities office, public events office, or communication center is most likely to coordinate the events. Call and ask to be placed on their mailing list.

Keeping track of a large university's activities is tougher because no single office monitors all events. Call the offices mentioned above and get onto the mailing lists they maintain. Call the university box office and the athletic department for the sports schedules. Call the university paper and ask what day of the week they publish the most comprehensive listing of events. Finally, ask whether a weekly or monthly publication informs university employees about campus news and events. At many universities, this is the best centralized source of information: Call the publication and ask about subscribing.

♦ Enrolling in an accredited course at a local university or community college (most offer night classes) is an inexpensive road to student privileges. Why bother? Because a student I.D. card gets you into the gym free, which by itself is cheaper than joining a health club. You also get free use of the library; free entrance into many university-sponsored events; cheap rates at university movies, productions, and sporting events; possibly even health-services benefits. And then there are the discounts you'll reap on movies, plays, and concerts around town.

If you want the benefits but not the homework, some people drop their course after they've obtained the student I.D. (don't quote me on this practice). I recommend enrolling in a class you will enjoy; view the course as another form of entertainment.

♦ Universities and community colleges also offer non-credit, continuing-education courses. These courses span a galaxy of interests—from avant-garde art to zithers. Enrolling in these classes won't earn you a student I.D. card, but they can both enlighten and entertain you for a ridiculously low cost.

♦ Local clubs catering to your special interests can pack your calendar with activities and social functions for a low, low price.

Scope out the clubs in your area by looking under "Clubs" in the Yellow Pages or calling the Chamber of Commerce. In my town, a bedroom community of Seattle, the Chamber's list includes a coin club, stamp club, several garden clubs, opera club, music and art club, rock and gem club, 4-H Club, Boy Scouts, Girl Scouts, and Campfire Boys and Girls.

Also, call the retail shops stocking supplies for your hobbies. By calling local outdoor-equipment stores, I unearthed contacts and phone numbers for a climbing club, orienteering club, bicycling club, hiking club, and canoeing and kayaking club. Computer shops will plug you into computer clubs, photography stores will expose you to photo clubs, craft stores can point out the needlecraft clubs...

Finally, use the library to locate clubs. Call the reference desk and ask them where you can locate the nearest chapter of the club for orphaned twins, or one-armed sky divers, or left-handed sumo wrestlers. You'll be amazed by what they unearth.

♦ The library itself is another entertainment possibility. It sponsors a roster of events: lectures, slideshows, readings, speakers, kid's programs. Get in the habit of picking up the calendar of events when you visit.

♦ Join (or form) a book club. The extra reading will have you spending less money on movies and less time with the television. You might even decide to cut the cable (television), which will defang one of the wallet leeches. Call the library about local book clubs or ask friends whether they would like to form one.

♦ Entertainment books with discount coupons for theaters, restaurants, recreational facilities, and hotels are a good buy if you would be frequenting several of the haunts anyway. If, however, they lure you to places you wouldn't normally visit, they are a false economy. You may do better scrapping the book and using your local newspaper. Thumb through the Friday and Sunday entertainment sections of the paper; you'll find enough free entertainment or low-cost entertainment to make the coupon books superfluous. See the *Hotel* chapter for more about this topic.

♦ Dinner parties are an expensive way to entertain friends. If you want the social rewards without the pecuniary penalties, host potlucks. Or invite friends over for weekend brunches where you can serve a savory yet inexpensive cuisine of egg dishes, waffles, pancakes...

♦ Sports enthusiasts can watch cheap, live action by tracking the local university (college) teams. The area's minor league or farm teams are inexpensive and fun to watch—call the sports department of your newspaper and ask them which minor league teams play in the area and how to keep tabs of their schedules.

◆ The local community centers financed by the city have been good sources of cheap entertainment for my wife and me because they offer a diverse curriculum of inexpensive classes and activities. We have taken their dance classes and have used their wood shop to build some of our living room furniture.

◆ Flip through the government pages of the telephone book and you'll uncover a rich deposit of resources and facilities for your entertainment. Under *City* listings you may find: zoos, golf courses, swimming pools, community centers, parks, aquariums, dance studios, theaters, boating centers, libraries, and art commissions. Under *County* numbers: libraries, parks, educational services. Under *State* listings, look up the parks. And under *Public Schools*, study the different departments of the local colleges and universities.

Call the numbers which arouse your curiosity. Find out what they do and ask to be placed on the mailing list for their schedule of events.

Jan and I get the schedule of events from the pools, libraries, zoo, aquarium, theaters, and local parks.

Most people spend most of their days doing what they do not want to do in order to earn the right, at times, to do what they may desire.

John Mason Brown

Fitness

Longer life, better looks, more vigorous sex, improved self-image, elevated energy, arrested aging, and increased happiness have all been flaunted as the benefits of exercise. About the only claim proselytizers avoid making is that it will make you rich. In fact, with Jane Fonda vying to sell you her newest video, health clubs hounding you to join, and Nike ads telling you to "Just Do It" (with their $100 shoes), exercise can make you very poor.

Financial pain, however, is completely unnecessary to reap the health gains of exercise. Recent studies, like an important one from the Institute of Aerobics Research in Dallas, show that sedentary people have higher mortality rates. But men and women alike who incorporate low-intensity exercise (like 30 to 60 minute walks) into their daily regime sharply reduce their death rates. The death rates of low-intensity exercisers is only slightly higher than those of hard-core runners logging 40 miles a week.

How do you reap these benefits? Get off the couch each day and walk to the store, climb stairs, garden, chop wood, rake leaves, shovel snow, push the vacuum. Do them all at a vigorous pace and you can make the chores of living your daily workout. Do something physical daily and shoot to burn *at least* 1100 calories a week (see Table 1).

For many, however, low-intensity workouts are not enough to transform their bods into the turbo-charged fitness machines they hope to become, and so begins a more rigorous regime aimed at strengthening the cardiovascular system.

Table 1: CALORIES USED	
Activity	Calories/hour
Brisk walking	320
Turbo housecleaning	320
Rigorous gardening	330
Raking leaves	405
Mowing	450
Steady-paced bicycling	405
Stair climbing	420
Stair climbing (fast)	510

Everyone knows the regime as *aerobics* and for maximum benefit, the American College of Sports Medicine (ACSM) recommends three to five aerobic workouts each week. To score maximum benefit, the session should keep your heart pumping within its "target rate" for 15 to 60 minutes. To calculate your target rate: subtract your age from 220 to obtain your maximum heart rate (MHR). Multiply the MHR by .6 and then by .8. Now exercise at an exertion level that keeps your per-minute heart rate between these two figures.

If you are 40 years old, for example, your MHR is 180. Exercise so that your per-minute heart rate is between 108 and 144. If you're aerobically fit, work out in the higher end of the range. Use the lower end of the range if you're just starting a fitness program or are quite fatigued from yesterday's activities.

Okay, so there, distilled on one page, you have the vital information explaining the whys and hows of exercise—information that fitness books spend chapters developing and delivering. Now I am going to explain how you can get your necessary exercise cheaply.

♦ As explained earlier, any steady movement that maintains your target heart rate will keep you aerobically fit. The options include jogging, bicycling, shadow-boxing, home aerobics, dancing, super-charged wood chopping, running stairs, pushing a toddler in a stroller, speed mowing, chasing your children around the yard, swimming, continuous calisthenics, turbo-vacuuming. The aerobic workouts from these free activities are just as good as those involving the use of a Stair Master at a health club.

♦ If the distances are right and your employer has a shower, run or bicycle to work. You score a hat trick of benefits: low-cost exercise, reduced commuting bills, and lower utility bills (take a shower on the company).

♦ The ACSM also recommends that healthy adults incorporate strength-training into their weekly regime. At least twice a week, do repetitions of 10 different exercises that tax the body's major muscle groups (each muscle group should be very fatigued after eight to 12 repetitions of a specific exercise).

You don't need the YMCA's $2000 Nautilus machines for this. Pull-ups, push-ups, sit-ups, squat thrusts, knee bends (not too deep), and other calisthenics employing the body's weight for resistance work just fine.

♦ Free weights, like barbells, are also excellent for strength-training but are quite expensive. Make your own 8-pound weights by filling gallon milk (or bleach) bottles with water or sand. Use a bottle in each hand for arm raises, twirls and pumps (if 8 pounds is too heavy, use 1/2 gallon bleach bottles instead). For bench presses, curls, shoulder presses, upright rows, and squats, make a barbell by sliding a 1-inch dowel (or broom stick) through the handles of several milk bottles. A 5- to 6-foot dowel will easily handle five or six bottles (40 to 50 pounds).

Would-be Arnold Schwarzeneggers need heavier weights to build bulk, but for most of us, pumping 50 pounds of milk bottles is remarkably effective strength-training.

♦ Pumping rubber is another inexpensive alternative to pumping iron. Products like the *Lifeline Gym* and *Pumping Rubber Xercise Kit* are made from a length of heavy-gauge rubber tubing and have a handle attached to each end. These products, which weigh under 2 pounds and occupy less room in a house than a dictionary, can compete with a Universal Gym in their ability to exercise all the major muscle groups in the body. The *Lifeline Gym* is so effective that a long list of professional athletes, astronauts, mountain climbers, and military personnel use it to build muscle and maintain stamina.

The *Lifeline Gym* is quicker and easier to use than free weights, does not clutter up the basement or garage, travels with you on business trips, *and*, at $60, costs a fraction of what weights cost. For information, contact Lifeline International, 1421 South Park Street, Madison, WI 53715, 800-553-6653 or 608-251-4778.

The *Pumping Rubber Xercise Kit* costs about $20 and works well for exercising the entire body, although it lacks several useful accessories found with the *Lifeline Gym*. For information, contact SPRI Products, 507 North Wolf Road, Wheeling, IL 60090, 800-222-774 or 708-537-7876.

◆ Kids often exercise without warming up. With age, however, you'll discover cold starts tear muscles and ligaments. These ailments then lead to pain medication and doctors' visits.

The usual recommendation is to stretch before exercising, but stretching cold muscles improperly can also cause injury, so stretch slowly and gently. A growing number of experts recommend you warm up simply by jogging in place, riding a stationary bicycle, or starting your workout at a slow pace for the first five to 10 minutes. Once you've broken a sweat, gradually increase the pace.

In cold weather, warm up inside.

◆ A quick (and potentially dangerous) drop in blood pressure occurs if you stop suddenly after rigorous exercise. Finish your workout as you started, at a slow pace. Over the course of a few minutes, gradually downshift from high to low speed. Gentle post-exercise stretches are also good for your muscles.

◆ People who take their exercise seriously often believe they need to consume more protein. Not true. The average American consumes twice the recommended daily allowance for protein and adding more protein to the diet only wastes money (protein is the most expensive part of the food bill). What the body needs during exercise is carbohydrates.

◆ Contrary to what manufacturers tell you, water is the best drink for athletes because it is absorbed faster than any other fluid. Only after two to three hours of rigorous exercise do sports drinks that replace electrolytes or supply carbohydrates make any sense at all. Then these drinks help supply energy, but so would a banana.

Studies have failed to show one sports drink superior to the rest. If you use them, buy by price.

◆ Own a decent bike? In winter you can use it inside as a stationary exercise bike with a training stand like the *Blackburn Trakstand* or the *Nashbar Folding Trainer* (available from Bike Nashbar, see mail-order appendix). The cost (about $120 and $100 respectively) is small compared to the $500-plus you'll spend on a good stationary exercise bike. These training stands also solve the wintertime dilemma of where to store the bike.

♦ Joining a health club is a wise financial decision only if you use it at least two or three times a week. To get your money's worth, consider these pointers:
- Choose a club that is within a 10- or 15-minute drive.
- Before joining, visit the club at the different times you're likely to use it (get a one-day pass). A club that is crowded when you will be visiting is of little value to you.
- Talk to other club members when you visit. What do they like and dislike about this club?
- Health clubs are very diversified and many offer a wide range of courses. Find a club with a schedule of classes and activities you want to take.
- Check the equipment. It should be up-to-date, well-maintained, and in abundant supply. No use joining a club that doesn't maintain or have enough equipment. Also, check the cleanliness of the sauna, steam room, showers, and hot tub.
- Avoid lifetime memberships: You can't predict the club's solvency next month, much less next year.
- Some clubs have, or will include at your insistence, a stipulation that your fee will be refunded if you decide to quit. Without such a provision, try the club for a month before signing on for a year or more. Avoid clubs that aren't confident enough in their product to give you some kind of "try-it-you'll-like-it" option.
- A club that will extend your membership to compensate for travel, injury, or illness can save you substantial money each year.

♦ Finally, if you are a long-time slouch, get a medical check-up before starting an exercise program. This is especially true if you are at risk of heart disease, have other health problems, are overweight, or are over 45.

Food

"When fools go to market, peddlers make money."
—Dutch Proverb
"When a fool goes shopping, the storekeepers rejoice."
—Yiddish Proverb

In 1989, the *Statistical Abstract of the United States* reported the *average* couple spent $9.14 per day ($3338 per year) on groceries. My wife and I were feeling smug: Our yearly grocery bill totaled $2975, a good dollar per day less than average. Felt smug, that is, until we compared figures with my parents, who paid less still *and* who ate steak when we ate hamburger. It dawned on me then that I was among the fools who kept the storekeepers rubbing their plump hands in delight.

Which got me thinking—just how much could I pare down my food bills? Could I cut them in half and still eat as well? Probably. In theory, by sticking religiously to the commandments of smart shopping that follow, I could. In practice, not all the commandments made sense for my lifestyle, so I ignored some and employed those that were fast but effective. The results? My food bills dropped about 30%, a savings of a $1000 per year. Not bad for a fool.

♦ COMMANDMENT 1: SHOP AND EAT THE SALES.
Using the newspaper ads to shop the weekly grocery specials, you can chop your food bills a good 25%.

Most people browse the sales and add items to the grocery list that complement the menus they have already planned. Big mistake. Use the weekly specials to maximum advantage by planning your menus around them. Scour the ads from the store (or stores) you shop and put together the week's menus. Turkey breasts, bone-in ham, lean hamburger, and round roast on sale? Use these for the week's dinners. Check the pantry and freezer for foods to complement these meats, then scan the sales for additional vegetables and starches to round out your meals.

The same approach works for lunch. After noting what refrigerator and freezer foods should be used, plan the additional lunches needed around the cold cuts, cheeses, sandwich spreads, and soups found on sale. Buy vegetables, fruits, and snacks on special to complement the main fare. Ditto for breakfast.

Planning the weekly menus in this fashion takes no extra time. I find it faster than my old method of browsing the recipe box because I don't have to deliberate over what to make; the specials lead me to quick decisions.

My dad, who is the chef of his roost, shops the specials and visits two or three stores weekly for their sale items. This gives him more diversity in what he serves; it also allows him to stock his pantry with a wider array of sale items. I rarely have time to shop multiple stores so my selection is reduced. Nevertheless, I can buy 80% of the food needed for the coming week from the specials.

♦ COMMANDMENT 2: STOCK UP ON SALE ITEMS.

When the price is right, stock up—buy enough to last you until the next sale.

This is especially valid for items with long shelf lives, like canned and dry goods. Freezer space will dictate whether you use this strategy with meats, breads, frozen drinks, desserts, and vegetables.

The goal is to *never* pay full price again. No one achieves that goal, but the more you stock up when the price plummets, the less you'll need when the price rises.

Pantry space is important toward this end. You may lack a kitchen pantry, but you can make space elsewhere—in other closets, on top of cupboards, in the basement, in the garage, in the space beneath stairs, under beds, by inserting more shelves in the existing cupboards, under sinks, on shelves above the washer and dryer...

It's easier to play the game successfully with a standalone freezer. Meat consumes about a third of the food budget, so a freezer lets you stock up on protein at prices you can stomach. But that is only part of the benefit. When cheese, flour, bread, candy, vegetables, even milk, are offered at loss-leader prices—you can really score.

♦ COMMANDMENT 3: STICK TO THE GAME PLAN.
Supermarkets are selling machines: The aroma from the bakery is meant to instigate a feeding frenzy, exhibits of food at the front of the aisle are designed to tempt you, staples like eggs and milk are purposely placed in the rear of the store so that you will pass hundreds of other appealing products en route to them, impulse items are placed by the register where they are difficult to resist.

Before you even step into the supermarket, food companies and manufacturers have spent some $6 billion a year on advertising to weaken your resistance. With all this working against you, studies have shown that shoppers, most of whom make two-thirds of their buying decisions in the store, often spend twice what they anticipated.

Your defense? Arrive at the store with a grocery list and stick to it. Don't succumb to impulse buying. Remain flexible only to the extent that you will consider the unadvertised specials you find. Add these to your purchases or substitute them for other items on your list. Otherwise, stick rigidly to the list.

A related defensive tactic used by a friend is to shop once—and only once—per week. The tactic reduces your exposure time to the impulsive temptations of the super-market, and thus the likelihood that your resistance will crack. It also forces you to budget food efficiently during the week. If one night you scarf down the extra pieces of chicken you intended to use later as leftovers, you may be fasting the next night.

♦ COMMANDMENT 4: KNOW A GOOD PRICE.
This is not a skill you'll develop overnight but one you should work on every time you shop. Why bother? Because 15% to 20% of the items highlighted in the specials are listed at normal prices. You don't want to buy these "specials" under the illusion that you've scored a deal.

In some stores, items placed on exhibit at the end of the aisles are not always on sale—you need to recognize the impostors from the real McCoys. At other stores, you'll also see yellow price-reduction signs on hundreds of items.

Unless you know prices, you can't identify the good pitches from the sucker balls. The pitches to swing at are those giving you a discount of 25% or higher. Now we're talking about some money.

I keep a master list of some 150 items I buy frequently and I mark sale prices on it. Next time I see the item on sale, I can check my list if I need to verify how good the offer is. You needn't be this compulsive: Just don't shop like a zombie. Keep your brain turned on, pay attention to prices, and after four or five months you'll develop a sense for good deals.

♦ COMMANDMENT 5: BUY STORE BRANDS.

In most supermarkets you'll find goods under three different labels: national labels (brand names), house labels (store brands), and economy labels.

National brands are the most expensive because they are heavily advertised. Consider a box of cereal: About 30% of the cost covers the food while 15% of the cost represents gross profits. The remaining 50% of the cost covers advertising, promotional games, coupons, and glitzy packaging. Much of this advertising and packaging brainwashes us into thinking we pay more because we are getting a higher-quality product. In truth, we pay an extra 15 to 20% solely to offset the advertising costs spent baiting us.

Store or house brands are typically of the same quality as the national brands. In fact, the same plants packaging brand-name foods often package the store brands for major grocers like Safeway, Albertson's, A&P, Kroger, Grand Union. Stories abound of store employees opening cases of their house-brand foods and finding packages of name-brand product mixed inside. In many food-processing plants and canneries, the identical fruits and vegetables go into bags with different labels and different price tags.

With canned soups, stews, chili, etc., national brands have their own patented recipes. Therefore, store brands may taste different, but the foodstuffs are of equal quality.

The benefit of store brands? The store, with a built-in market for its label, spends much less on advertising and can offer you a product of equal quality for 15% to 20% less. Studies show that it is even cheaper to buy store brands than to purchase national brands with cents-off coupons. Unless you use your cents-off coupons in combination with sale prices (a valid practice but one requiring considerable time and organization), store brands save you time and money.

Economy brands usually have a name identifying them as a discounted product—Scotch Brand (Safeway), Cost Cutter (Kroger), Basics (Grand Union). Such brands often cost 20% to 40% less than national brands but they can be lower-quality or irregularly sized goods. The food is safe and healthy—it must meet FDA standards and regulations—but the aesthetics or texture may not equal the standards of house or national brands. If you are unsure whether a label qualifies as an economy or a store brand, ask a store employee.

◆ COMMANDMENT 6: SHOP DIFFERENT STORES.
Instead of pricing all their merchandise with a flat markup of 20%, grocers use a variable-price system to mark each item individually. Their goal: Lure you inside with

their discounted specials and then quietly make a profit on the items that have been marked up. Shoppers who buy many non-sale items, therefore, give back to the store the discounts that lured them in.

Stores use variable pricing to their advantage in other ways. They keep a selection of visible staples at very low prices, often well below what competitors charge. They'll sell other staples at a mid-range price. Then they mark up less frequently purchased merchandise, merchandise buyers are unlikely to know the value of. Stores can make you believe their prices are lower than average when, across the board, they are mid-range or high-end.

By paying attention to prices (Commandment 4) you can beat the supermarkets at their own game. Shop several different stores to learn which staples each discounts. The local Safeway may discount mayonnaise, frozen orange juice, cheddar cheese, and flour, while the local Super Saver may offer excellent prices on cheese, milk, hamburger, sugar, bread, and canned soups. Consequently, the next time you are in Safeway purchasing the specials for the week, stock up on their discounted staples. Same goes for the Super Saver when the specials take you there. Milk each store for its bargains and ignore the offerings designed to milk you.

An axiom to this commandment: Don't play supermarket games. Games encourage you to shop faithfully at one store. Collecting trading stamps or receipts to claim prizes is sinful for the same reason. Shop at one store only and you become the victim rather than the master of variable-pricing.

A second axiom: Don't buy non-food items at the grocery store. You'll usually find pharmacy, cosmetic, school, and auto supplies at better prices elsewhere.

♦ COMMANDMENT 7: JOIN MEMBERSHIP WAREHOUSES.

If you have a membership warehouse near you (Costco, Pace), join. These membership warehouses sell food at wholesale prices and in bulk, meaning they can take a big bite out of your food budget. A staff member of *The Seattle Times* who compared her savings buying food from these warehouses versus the grocery store, determined she earned her family $60 every two weeks. Her yearly saving of $1560, made the membership fee (about $30) look cheap.

There are several dangers to shopping these warehouses, however. You can't assume everything is a better price. Some staples are still cheaper at the grocery store, and sale prices at grocery stores will often score a bigger savings than the stock price at a membership warehouse. You still must know a good price when you see it.

Also, these stores can bankrupt impulse buyers. So many items look like deals that instead of walking out of the store with the $70 of groceries you needed, the cart overflows with $150 worth of goods. No problem if these are staples you are stocking for later. But if, like me, you buy five-pound bags of chocolate, three-pound bags of cookies, and jars of mixed nuts on impulse, you are damaging both your budget and beltline. Go in with a list and stick to it.

Most membership warehouses are easy to join: Private business owners, government employees, school employees, hospital employees, bank and credit union employees are all eligible. Some warehouses allow anyone to join, although non-business owners sometimes pay an extra 5%.

If you are ineligible to join, shop occasionally with friends who are members. If you are feeding a large family, it may be worthwhile to get a state business license and resale number (set up a fledgling retail business). With the business license in hand, join the membership warehouse.

♦ COMMANDMENT 8: SUBSTITUTE, EXPERIMENT.

Many people worry about following the letter of the recipe as if the slightest deviation could change their ambrosia into Alpo. Lighten up. Recipes were not brought down the mountain by Moses, they were created by people who were dallying. So don't be too worried about conducting experiments of your own—or about finding a detour around an expensive ingredient. If a recipe calls for one-quarter teaspoon of a spice you never use, substitute a similar spice or omit the spice. If a recipe calls for a can of peas but canned beans are on sale, try a switch. If a recipe calls for a cup of bacon when you have leftover ham in the refrigerator, use the ham.

Change too much and you might concoct something that could have been made by German rocket scientists. But don't worry about cutting costs by altering a few ingredients at a time.

There are myriad ways to substitute cheaper products you may have around home for those the recipe lists. It pays to compile your own list of substitutes and hang it inside your pantry. Following are some examples.

Per cup of buttermilk or sour cream, substitute 1 cup of milk with 1 tablespoon of vinegar or lemon juice added.

Per cup of sour cream, substitute 1 cup of plain yogurt.

Per cup of brown sugar, use a mixture made from 1 cup of white sugar and 1 tablespoon molasses.

For any kind of nut, substitute equal quantities of a cheaper nut (e.g., switch almonds for walnuts).

For mozzarella cheese, substitute equal amounts of jack cheese.

Per cup of honey, substitute 1 cup sugar plus 1/4 cup of water.

Per square of unsweetened chocolate, substitute 3 tablespoons of cocoa powder and 1 tablespoon of butter.

Per tablespoon of cornstarch (for thickening), substitute 2 tablespoons of flour.

Per teaspoon of allspice, substitute 3/4 teaspoon cinnamon, 1/8 teaspoon ground cloves, and 1/8 teaspoon nutmeg.

Per cup of cracker crumbs, substitute 1 1/4 cup of bread crumbs.

Per cup of self-rising flour, substitute 1 cup all-purpose flour plus 1 1/2 teaspoons baking powder and 1/8 teaspoon salt.

Per cup of cake flour, substitute 1 cup of all-purpose flour. Replace 2 tablespoons of the all-purpose flour with 2 tablespoons of cornstarch and sift several times.

Per cup of skim milk (for cooking), substitute 1/3 cup of instant dry milk (nonfat) and water to make 1 cup.

For the non-dairy creamers used in coffee, substitute powdered skim milk.

For more expensive cooking wine, substitute dry table wine.

For lettuce on sandwiches, substitute celery leaves or thinly cut cucumbers if there is a price advantage.

◆ COMMANDMENT 9: BUY DATED GOODS.

As a culture, Americans are incredibly spoiled. Bread turns a day old, we call it stale; meat sits in a cooler for a few days, we think it rancid; dairy goods pass the "sell-by" date on the label, we call them poisonous. We are so paranoid about our food that stores are hard pressed to rid themselves of aging goods—unless they slash the price. Stores may still have difficulty selling it, which explains why tons of perishables (fruits, vegetables, dairy products, baked goods) get trashed every day. Before it gets trashed, however, you can often net a steal.

Beef sitting under fluorescent lights for a few days is often steeply discounted because it develops a green patina; it is still perfectly safe and perfectly delicious. Day-old bread may have lost its downy softness but is probably still fresher than the bread in your pantry that you've eaten without complaint. Dairy goods, if kept refrigerated, will keep long past the "sell by" date printed on the label. Vegetables that look shoddy will still be excellent for cooking if used promptly. Aging fruit will still be sumptuous for fruit salads or baking.

Ask a store employee to show you the different areas in the store housing dated goods and unadvertised specials. Check those areas whenever you're in the store and you'll unearth many treasures over time.

♦ COMMANDMENT 10: BUY BY UNIT PRICING.
Consumers frequently hear the advice, "Buy in bulk." It is so ingrained that we reach for the largest bottle of ketchup, the largest carton of paper towels, the largest cylinder of frozen orange juice without thinking. As a rule, bulk buying saves money, but there are many exceptions to the rule—toilet paper that is cheaper by the roll than in cartons of six, 8-ounce cans of tomato sauce that cost less than half the cost of 16-ounce cans, 12-ounce cylinders of frozen orange juice that are twice as cheap as 16-ounce cylinders.

Rather than grabbing the biggest pack, check the store's tags and buy the size with the lowest unit pricing (price per ounce).

♦ COMMANDMENT 11: COUPON LAST.
Believe what the shopping experts show you on television and you believe that with coupons and rebates you can buy the entire grocery store and get money back.

Only in your dreams. In reality, coupons and rebates can save you money, but they have major pitfalls, too.

For starters, these practices are time consuming: The average devotee spends about eight hours a week for a 25% to 30% savings (people who are short on time can achieve the same savings much faster by shopping the sales). Coupons and rebates also encourage impulse buying: Studies show couponers are more likely to buy things they don't need just to use the coupon. Finally, cents-off coupons for brand-name goods won't save you money unless you combine their punch with a sale (otherwise, it's cheaper to buy store brands).

All this said, if you enjoy couponing as a hobby and employ them wisely (use them on sale items and resist impulse buying), you'll definitely spend less bread buying your bacon.

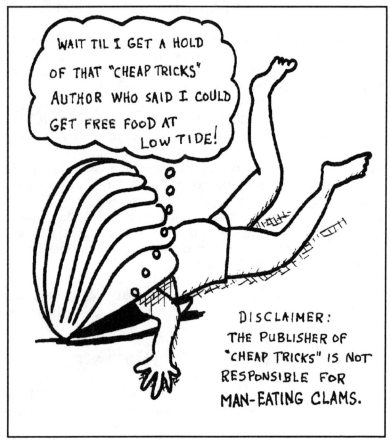

Food Tips

Local construction work had dried up and I knew Philo ached for cash, especially when he dropped by my house just in time for lunch. Over a sandwich—make that several sandwiches for Philo—he mentioned his financial straits, told me if more work failed to surface he might sell his car for food money. I couldn't help him find a job, but I told him to hang onto the car, that I was going to initiate him into the great fraternity of "urban farmers."

We drove to the rear of my local grocery store and after a few surreptitious glances I hopped from the car, scampered up the side of the metal dumpster, and dropped inside. Two minutes later I rolled out with unopened packages of maple bars, apple fritters, bread, and whole-wheat rolls. I also carried out pounds of produce: carrots, potatoes, heads of lettuce, apples, oranges, and grapes. The goods lacked the freshness of those inside the store, but here was several day's worth of food, all of it perfectly edible, all of it absolutely free.

I offered Philo an apple fritter, but he gagged on his pride. I told him it was perfectly safe, that I was living proof. "But you're deranged, " he rebutted. So I told him the Community for Creative Nonviolence had served members of Congress a meal of crab quiche, fresh fruit, vegetable salad, yogurt, cold cuts, cheese, and raspberry shortcake and that all of it had come from the dumpsters of grocery stores.

The implication: Food good enough for senators was good enough for him. To Philo this simply explained the government's shortcomings, "Garbage in, garbage out," he replied.

I should have given Philo the conventional course on squeezing food from pennies. I should have given him the scores of suggestions I am about to bestow on you. In combination, these suggestions create a more dignified way to eat without selling the farm—or the car.

TRIMMING FAT FROM THE MEAT BUDGET

♦ Americans spend a third of their food budget on meat, partly because meat is expensive and partly because the average American eats 50% more meat than the Recommended Daily Dietary Allowance (RDA). Casseroles, stews, and soups will slash your meat expenses without slighting the daily requirement for protein.

♦ When you prepare meat as a stand alone dish, serve small portions. Let your family fill up on noodles, potatoes, rice, and salads—all of which are cheap.

♦ Once mayonnaise, onions, celery, and spices are added to tuna in salads and casseroles, the taste difference between expensive white tuna and cheaper chunk tuna is undetectable.

♦ A *Consumer Reports'* test of over 35 brands of pork bacon found few consistent taste differences among the brands. The magazine recommended buying by price. Because different brands have different percentages of fats, the uncooked cost of bacon varies from the cooked cost. Nonetheless, the cheapest uncooked bacon is usually the best buy.

♦ Frying thin strips of ham is more economical than frying bacon. It's also healthier.

♦ Paying more for brand-name chicken is folly. Pick your label by the per-pound price. Then pick a package with plump thighs and breasts.

♦ Prepare stir-fry meals and you'll use about half as much meat as the standard American dinner.

♦ Boneless chicken or turkey breast can be substituted for veal scaloppine or cutlets. The taste and the savings are both favorable.

MORE WITH LESS

♦ Next to meat, nothing bruises the food budget like snacks. Candies, chips, cookies, and flavored crackers can cost you a pound of flesh. The wisest trick is to keep these foods out of the house. When munchmania strikes, rely on these cheaper snacks: popcorn, peanut butter or jam on toast, peanut butter and jelly sandwiches, pretzels, graham crackers, microwaved strips of potatoes, ginger snaps, brownies made from a mix, popsicles made from frozen juice, yogurt, raisins, seasonal fruit, peanut butter on saltines or celery.

The $15 Popcorn Pumper (air popper) we bought years ago is a treasured budget saver in our home. A few times a year I buy 12-pound bags of unpopped corn at our membership warehouse for $2.75. Often each week I prepare a big bowl of popcorn at lunch: cost—including margarine and electricity—is under a dime. Then I spend the afternoon raiding the bowl. It doesn't help me get any work done, but it saves me from devouring a dollar's worth of expensive snacks.

If you are a chocaholic and my list of substitutes doesn't cut it, replenish the candy reserves after holidays like Easter, Halloween, Valentine's Day, and Christmas. Leftover candy is deeply discounted after holidays. Fill the drawers and freezer with enough dope to last until the next post-holiday sale.

♦ Candy junkies wishing to diminish the strain their addiction places on both the budget and beltline should store candy bars in the freezer. When the DTs hit, you have to wait awhile for your treat to thaw, which reduces the amount of candy you'll consume each day.

♦ Ingredients for casseroles, stews, and soups needn't always be of the highest quality. Economy-brand vegetables are often irregularly sized, but does that matter in a casserole? Might as well save 20% to 40% by buying an economy brand over a store or national brand.

♦ Avoid "gourmet" popcorn. Many national and store brands taste as good at half the price. Experiment with "normal" brands and find one you like.

♦ Dry cereals are inflated: with air and in price. Hot cereals are a double bonus, supplying more food for less money.

♦ To make milkshakes without ice cream, place 2 cups of skim or 2% milk in the freezer for 70 to 90 minutes (time is temperature dependent). Pull out the milk when ice crystals have turned it into a slurry, add the desired fruit and flavoring, then blend (or shake). You're left with an inexpensive, tasty milkshake.

♦ Ten ounces of frozen vegetables equals the vegetable contents of a 16-ounce can (cans are heavy with water). Keep that ratio in mind when deciding whether canned or frozen vegetables are the better buy.

♦ Buying non-fat dry milk in bulk is much cheaper than buying fresh milk. Adults raised on fresh milk are not wild about powdered milk, but if you serve powdered milk to kids, they might learn to like it as well as the real McCow.

To make powdered milk more palatable to adults, mix it half and half with whole or 2% milk. Alternately, add a little vanilla extract to the mixture. Also, chilling the mixed milk for a day improves its flavor.

♦ Beating a ripe banana and an egg white together makes an inexpensive substitute for whipped cream.

♦ Oatmeal can substitute for nuts in cookie recipes.

♦ When finished with a jar of pickles, cut cucumber rounds and soak them in the same brine. After a day or two they make an excellent side dish to complement lunch or supper. You can use the brine several times before you've sapped it of its strength.

If you're not fond of cucumbers—or they are out of season—soak carrots, celery, or tomatoes in the brine.

♦ Eggs are sized extra large, large, medium, or small and per dozen weigh 27 ounces, 24 ounces, 21 ounces, or 18 ounces respectively. If you find a price difference of 10% or less between two sizes, buy the larger size.

♦ Potatoes are among the most important foods in the world. A seven-ounce, unskinned baked potato supplies over 200 calories, iron, potassium, B vitamins, a little protein, a lot of fiber, and about half the RDA for vitamin C. Considering the price—about 20¢ a pound—this ordinary tuber is quite extraordinary.
Eat lots of them. If you cook them without oil and do not slather them with butter, they aren't fattening. To get the maximum nutritional value, eat the skin.

♦ To compare the real cost of different fresh fruits, consider how much of the product is useable. Who says you can't compare apples and oranges? Tacking on an additional 20% to the cost of oranges compensates for the weight of its peel. Add 30% to the cost of bananas, melons, and pineapples when comparing their cost to fruits like grapes, peaches, or pears.

♦ Taste tests of fruit juices show that many people prefer frozen concentrates to bottled juices. Because concentrates are cheaper, bottle fanatics should hold their own taste test to decide whether to make the big switch.

♦ To wring more juice out of citrus fruits (oranges, lemons, limes) soak them in hot water for several minutes before squeezing them.

♦ Throw away less of your asparagus by shaving the bottom third of the stalk with a potato peeler. Strip away the tough fibrous sheath until you reach the soft interior. Then steam as normal.

♦ Make mini pizzas by cutting English muffins in half and sprinkling them with toppings. Place them on a cookie sheet and bake at 375°F.

♦ Health foods are often isolated in a separate section of the store because they are expensive. Separating them discourages comparison shopping. Many foods found in the other aisles are equally healthy and considerably cheaper.

♦ The fad for drinking spritzers, soda water, and bottled water is commendable. It has reduced many people's tendencies to booze it up when dining out, and it's not often that you hear about swerving Perrier drinkers killing innocent motorists.

The problem arises only if you think these bottled waters are healthier than the water welling forth from the municipal water system. Non-partial organizations testing bottled waters have found little or no reason to recommend them over the tap water supplied by public systems in 97% of the country. For the vast majority of people, bottled water is a bottled waste of money. If your water is not the best tasting, bottle it yourself with a few slices of lemon and keep it chilled. Also, if the water is heavily chlorinated, letting it sit in an open pitcher for several hours allows much of the chlorine to escape.

USING LEFTOVERS AND OLD FOOD

♦ Store soup makings in a jar kept in the freezer. Leftover vegetables, spare scraps of cheese or meat, leaves off celery stalks, extra salad makings, lettuce and cabbage scraps, uneaten pasta or potatoes, and/or excess spaghetti sauce can all be frozen in the jar and dumped into the next batch of soup.

♦ Leftover or overripe fruit can be frozen. Slice large pieces of fruit, take bananas out of their peel. Some of this fruit (apples, berries, peaches, bananas) can be mashed into pancake or waffle batter. Alternately, make fruit drinks by blending the frozen fruit with cold water, powdered milk, and sugar.

♦ Aging fruit can also be oven dried and eaten later as a snack. Slice pears and apples into 1/4-inch slices, peaches into 1/2-inch slices. Slice bananas into quarters along the long axis. Lay the fruit on cake-cooling racks and set it in the oven until it reaches the desired dryness (between 12 and 24 hours).

The pilot light of gas ovens provides enough heat for drying, while a lightbulb (you'll need to run an extension cord through the oven door) converts an electric oven into a drier. The oven temperature should be between 110° and 160° F (130° is ideal) so if you own an oven thermometer you can experiment with different bulbs to find the wattage that provides the perfect temperature (usually 75 watts). If you find yourself drying often, build several drying racks (wood frames with fiberglass screen-door mesh stretched over them). Make the racks stackable, allowing 1 1/2 to 2 inches of air space between each.

♦ Freeze aging (and sagging) vegetables. Dice carrots, celery, onions, lettuce, cabbage, and green peppers and use them later for soup. If you spread the vegetables and freeze them on a cookie sheet before clumping them all in a bag, they won't freeze into one solid mass.

♦ Air-dry old bread and crusts for several days. Then roll or blend the bread into crumbs. Store the crumbs in a jar for later use.

♦ If you make several pots of coffee each day, don't dispose of the old grounds. Pour the new grounds over the top of them and you can leach additional flavor out of the old maids. This reduces the new grounds needed by a quarter to a third.

♦ Invigorate dried-out cake (including fruit cake) by poking holes in the top and spreading a thin layer of frozen orange juice concentrate over the top. As the concentrate melts it will absorb into the cake.

♦ To remove mold from a block of cheese with a minimum of waste, use a potato peeler instead of a knife.

♦ Hardened cheese can be mashed with mayonnaise to make a cheese spread.

♦ Sprinkle old, dry rolls with water, wrap them in foil, and pop them in the oven for a few minutes.

♦ Pour leftover gravy and meat juices into ice cube trays and freeze them. When you need instant gravy or stocks for soup, use the cubes. Just be careful not to pop one of these into your booze.

♦ Revitalize soggy cereal by spreading it on a cookie sheet and baking it for three or four minutes at 250° F. Dry out stale potato chips in the same way by putting them under the broiler for a short while. Watch them closely or you may alchemize chips into Crispy Critters.

♦ Save the carcasses, necks, and gizzards of chickens for making soup stock. Save bones from roasts and steaks for the same purpose.

♦ Save leftover dinner wine for future cooking needs by pouring a little vegetable oil into the bottle. The oil floats and seals out the air that can turn wine to vinegar.
Alternately, pour the wine into the smallest jar possible (to minimize the amount of entrapped air) and cover with an air-tight lid.

♦ Thinly sliced leftover meatloaf makes excellent sandwiches.

♦ Save or freeze stale bread and use it for making French toast. Many chefs believe that French toast made from stale bread is superior to that made from fresh bread.

♦ Slice stale donuts in half (bagel style) and dip them in egg. Fry them like French toast.

♦ Leftover hamburger and hot dog buns make excellent dinner rolls. Spread butter, garlic powder, and parmesan cheese over the top, then bake for several minutes.

♦ Don't refreeze melted ice cream: Refrigerate it and pour it over cereal.

♦ Cut stale cake into half-inch slices and pop them into the toaster for a novelty snack. Trim off the icing first.

MAKING FOOD LAST

♦ Get rid of the plastic tabs that come with bread—they don't seal the bag well, and contribute toward stale bread. Instead, suck or squeeze air out of the bag, then tie the end of the bag into a loose knot. Don't cinch the knot.

♦ Use jars to store snack mixes, pretzels, nuts, etc. The goods stay fresher than those stored in plastic bags.

♦ Mushrooms last longer if stored in paper bags rather than plastic bags.

♦ Celery and lettuce both last longer if wrapped in a paper towel before being stored in a plastic bag. Alternately, store them in paper bags.

♦ Parsley stored in a sealed jar will keep well. Parsley also freezes well.

♦ An apple slice or celery stalk stored with your bread keeps the bread fresher.

♦ Once bananas reach their desired ripeness, place them in the refrigerator. The skin will blacken but this won't hamper the fruit's taste.

♦ To prevent berries from molding, refrigerate them and don't wash them until you're ready to serve them.

♦ Keep dried fruit in the refrigerator or, if space allows, in the freezer.

♦ A no-cook, no-trouble method of preserving vegetables: Wash 'em, slice 'em, and pack 'em in a clean jar. Then add a dill brine made from 1 part white vinegar, 2 parts water and sprigs of dill according to your taste. Tomatoes, cabbages, cauliflowers, peppers, cucumbers all keep well this way. Refrigerate.

Buy vegetables in bulk when they are cheap and preserve some of them this way.

♦ Air trapped in the plastic bags storing bread, meat, cheese, or leftovers, shortens the life of your food. I laughed when my dad showed me this trick, but after trying it I'm impressed. It's fast, effective, and eliminates expensive machinery for vacuum packing your food. Put your food in a holeless plastic bag. Gather the plastic at the neck of the bag as though you were going to blow it up with air. Instead of blowing air in, however, suck air out: Your lungs make an excellent vacuum pump. You will see the plastic shrink in tight around the food. Finally, tie off the bag in a loose knot that you can easily untie.

If storing food in a zip-lock bag, seal the bag from the two ends and leave a half-inch in the center unsealed. Push in on the unsealed segment so it puckers into a circle, then suck out the excess air and seal the bag.

FREEZING AND REFRIGERATION

♦ Proper packaging is important for successful freezing. Use moisture-proof packaging and squeeze (or suck) all the air out. The plastic bags inside cereal boxes make excellent freezer bags.

♦ Frozen foods have a longer shelf life when kept at the right temperature. Beef will keep for about 13 months at 0° F, but only five months at 10° F. Check the temperature of your freezer with a thermometer: It should be between -5° and 0° F.

For a complete freezing guide, order a copy of *Freezing Fish and Meat in the Home* from the U.S. Department of Agriculture, Washington, DC 20250.

♦ Use a thermometer to set your refrigerator temperature at 37° F. Just like the freezer, foods kept at warmer temperatures spoil faster.

♦ Buy green peppers on sale, wash and dice. Spread the pieces on a cookie sheet and freeze. Once frozen, pour the pieces into a plastic bag. Take what you need out of the bag to complement your cooking needs.

This trick works when freezing most vegetables used for cooking—celery, onions, carrots.

♦ Flour keeps well in the freezer—mice and insects have cold feet raiding these stocks. If you have freezer space, stock up when flour is on sale.

♦ When fresh fruits are on sale, prepare fillings for several pies. Use cellophane or aluminum foil to line a pie tin and fill the tin with fruit. Wrap the fruit in the liner and freeze it. Next time you want a pie, pop your frozen fruit into a pie shell and slide the works into the oven.

♦ Milk freezes for up to three months so don't hesitate to put it into cold storage when stores offer it at loss-leader prices. After thawing, shake it well. Its appearance and taste may be slightly altered, but it's nutritive value remains the same.

MAKE YOUR OWN

♦ To make cheap, fat-free French fries, cut potatoes into half-inch-thick strips and soak the strips in water for at least two hours. Bake the strips at 400° F on a greased cookie sheet for 35 to 40 minutes. Don't let the French fries touch—last time that happened we ended up with the film *Night of the Killer Potato.*

♦ Store-bought frozen pancakes (waffles, too) are mostly expensive air. Next time you make pancakes or waffles from scratch, prepare a double batch and freeze the cakes you don't eat. When you want instant pancakes, reheat several of them in the microwave or toaster.

Note: When freezing your pancakes (waffles), put a layer of cellophane or waxpaper between each one so they don't weld together.

♦ To make yogurt, the only specialized equipment needed is a candy thermometer. Heat a quart of skim or whole milk to 170° to 180° F for three or four minutes. Let the milk cool to 110° F and stir in 1 teaspoon of yogurt culture or a heaping teaspoon of plain active yogurt. Pour the milk into a jar with a good lid and swaddle the bottle in a blanket or winter coat. After 24 hours the yogurt should be pudding-thick in consistency. Refrigerate.

♦ Biscuit mix for pancakes, biscuits, waffles, etc. is simple to make. To 10 cups of flour, add 1/3 cup baking powder, 1 1/2 cups nonfat dry milk, 1 2/3 cups shortening, 2 teaspoons salt. Sift the dry ingredients together, then cut in the shortening in spoonfuls until you have a mixture the consistency of cornmeal. Cost is about half the store price.

♦ Several easy-to-make salad dressings cut the cost of store-made brands by 60% to 70%. To make blue cheese dressing: Mix 2 ounces crumbled blue cheese, 1/2 teaspoon salt, and 1/4 teaspoon pepper in 1 1/2 cups mayonnaise. Stir well and store in a wide-mouth jar. Refrigerated shelf life: three to six months.

For Italian dressing: Mix 2 cups of vegetable oil; 1 cup of wine vinegar; 1/3 cup of grated onion; 1 teaspoon each of oregano, basil and celery seed; and sugar to taste (1/8 to 1/4 cup). Refrigerated shelf life: six months.

♦ Snack mixes and trail mixes are so easy to make it's silly to spend top dollar for pre-mixed varieties. The standard ratio for trail mix: equal parts raisins, nuts (most any kind), and chocolate chips or *M&Ms*. If desired, add or substitute coconut, mixed nuts, or other dried fruit.

For snack mix, stir together equal parts of pretzels, corn chips, and *Cheetos* crackers. Add peanuts and/or cereal (*Cheerios* or Chex cereals) if they appeal to your taste.

♦ Although the flavored noodle mixes on the market are supposedly a convenience item, they don't save you any time over making unflavored noodles and adding your own spices. Put together the spices while the noodles are cooking. Or make spice mixtures in quantity and then sprinkle what you need over pasta.

For a basic cheese sauce: Mix 1 cup instant nonfat milk; 3 tablespoons grated Romano, Parmesan, or cheddar cheese; 1/3 cup dried onions (minced); 1 tablespoon garlic powder; 1/2 teaspoon salt; and 1/4 teaspoon pepper. To use: Combine 1/4 cup of the mixture with 1/4 cup milk and 2 tablespoons butter and pour over drained noodles. Kept in a jar, this mixture keeps in the pantry for four months.

♦ The above advice also applies to rice mixes, most of which save you little time yet cost three or four times more than making your own spiced rice. Add the desired spices and other flavoring (e.g., bouillon cubes) to the rice. Cook the rice as instructed on the package (usually 2 cups of water per cup of raw rice) with a tablespoon of margarine.

♦ Detailing hundreds of inexpensive recipes that would control your food budget is beyond the scope of this book—it is a book unto itself. Browse your cookbooks for inexpensive recipes or visit the library and scan cookbooks geared toward budget-conscious chefs.

The book, *Thrifty Meals for Two: Making Food Dollars Count,* is worth ordering. It gives you two weeks' recipes of inexpensive but healthy meals (breakfasts, lunches, dinners, and snacks). Order it (item #122X) from the Consumer Information Center-X (P.O. Box 100, Pueblo, CO 81002). Send $2.50 for the book plus $1.00 for handling.

ENERGY-SAVING COOKING

♦ If a recipe calls for several strips of bacon, cook the entire package. Roll what you don't use in a paper towel, wrap it in cellophane, and freeze it. The next time you want bacon, unroll what you need from the paper towels.

♦ Accelerate the cooking of brussels sprouts by cutting an "X" in the bottom of each.

♦ Pour freshly made coffee into a thermos after brewing it. This lets you turn off the coffee maker. More importantly, it keeps the coffee much fresher and prevents you from discarding the last few cups.

♦ To make pasta, bring salted water to a boil, add pasta, then turn off the heat. Pasta will be perfectly cooked in 12 to 15 minutes.

♦ Reduce the baking time of potatoes by 15 minutes by impaling them, lengthwise, with a clean nail. Leave the nail in while you bake.

Alternately, cut the potatoes in half and bake them, cut-side down, on a lightly greased cookie sheet.

♦ Make hamburger patties with a nickel-sized hole in the center. The hole allows them to cook faster and more uniformly. Such patties can also be frozen and then cooked without defrosting.

♦ Meat loaf zapped in the microwave is much cheaper to cook. Place your meat loaf in a glass baking dish and pack the meat loaf against the edges of the baking dish, leaving a doughnut-like hole in the center. Cook on high for a minimum of 10 minutes.

FOOD AT WORK

♦ Don't buy coffee out of a machine. Carry in a thermos with your own poison—be that regular or Irish coffee. If your office has a microwave, keep a stock of tea bags, instant coffee, instant hot chocolate at the office. Heat the water and add what you will.

Same goes for snacks. Buy candy bars, potato chips, or cookies on sale from the grocery store, then tote them in on a daily basis. These two tips will save you over a dollar a day—and a dollar a day keeps repoman away.

♦ Brown bag it a few times a week. A sandwich, apple, can of pop, and several snacks will cost you about $1.25. Comparable food at an eatery will set you back at least $4.50. Two meals a week from the brown bag puts an extra $325 a year into the fiscal grab bag.

♦ Most major cities have books similar to *Seattle's Cheap Eats.* Call the library or a local bookstore to get the book and note the "Chez Cheaps" near work.

FOOD FOR THOUGHT

♦ Eating cheap is almost synonymous to healthy eating. Beans, potatoes, bananas, oranges, apples, grains, rice, carrots, oats, flour, additional fruits and vegetables— they all cost under 50¢ a pound. In fact, you probably can't name an unhealthy food costing under 60¢ or 70¢ a pound.

Not all good foods are cheap (dairy products, nuts, fish, breads) but very few people in this country who shop smart need to resort to "urban farming."

Formulas

Shopping 25 years ago was noticeably simpler than it is today. That was before the age of specialization, before we had a cleaner for every household object, a wax for every make of car, and a cosmetic for every body part.

Some of today's products are better mousetraps. Commercial copper cleaner *does* work better than the old-fashioned mixture of vinegar and salt. But if you own little copper, why buy an expensive cleaner when a nickel's worth of vinegar can polish off the job?

Meanwhile, many "specialized" products packing the shelves of stores are not special at all. Formerly, I worked for a mail-order company that sold an ordinary liquid detergent as a "specially formulated" cleaner of waterproof fabrics. We repackaged the detergent, hyped it as if a team of rocket scientists had invented the stuff, and peddled it for a special price (four times what it was worth). Later, we discovered the same detergent cleaned silk, so we printed new bottles, advertised it as one of the world's great silk cleaners, and sold it—again for an outrageous price.

The recipes and formulas that follow will help you avoid paying such outrageous prices. These formulas arm you with inexpensive substitutes for many not-so-special products. And they are easy to make: You'll spend less time making these products than brewing your morning coffee.

Store the concoctions that follow in nice bottles purchased at a hardware store or in ones you've saved (cheaper). Label your bottles well. For convenience, write the recipe on the label; then you can whip up a new batch whenever the bottle runs dry. If you're recycling old bottles, remove or cover the old label and clearly mark the bottle as poison—you don't want to confuse a child who will recognize the shape of milk and pop bottles.

CLEANERS

♦ **WARNING:** Treat any of the following cleansers containing ammonia carefully. Without proper ventilation, ammonia can irritate the eyes and lungs. Also, don't mix ammonia with bleach or commercial cleansers because the interaction can form dangerous fumes.

♦ **All-purpose cleaner.** To 14 cups warm water, add 1 cup washing soda (available at some grocery stores) and 1 cup ammonia (either sudsing or non-sudsing). Fill a spray bottle with the cleaner and apply it (full strength) to spot jobs on tile, counters, metal, porcelain... For large jobs (floors, walls), use 3/4 cup cleaner per bucket of warm water. Costs about 50¢ to make versus $12 for a gallon of name-brand cleaner.

For a milder (no ammonia) all-purpose cleaner, add 2 teaspoons borax and 1 tablespoon of liquid detergent to 1 quart of warm water. Store in a spray bottle and apply directly to surfaces.

♦ **Automatic dishwasher detergent.** Mix 3 cups borax, 3 cups washing soda, and 1/8 cup powdered laundry detergent. For most types of water, this blend gives reasonable results. If you have the ingredients, try it.

♦ **Barrier cream.** Before working on cars or other greasy machines, spray shaving cream on your hands and rub them well. Hands will clean much easier afterward.

♦ **Bleach for synthetic and delicate clothing.** For a medium-sized load, mix 1/4 cup of 3% hydrogen peroxide and your laundry detergent into the wash water. Add clothes and let them soak 15 to 30 minutes before running the machine.

♦ **Bug off.** Remove dead bugs from the front of the car by sponging on a paste made from 1/2 cup baking soda and 1 pint water. Let the paste sit for at least five minutes before *gently* wiping off the bugs.

♦ **Car-wash solution.** To a gallon hot water, add 1/2 cup liquid detergent and 1/4 cup baking soda. To wash cars, use a cup of this solution per pail of warm water. Alternately, add 1 cup kerosene to a bucket of warm water and use this mixture to wipe down the car. Even if the car is filthy, you won't have to wet the car first or rinse the car afterward. Plus, you don't need to wax the car—when it rains, water will bead up.

♦ **Decal remover.** Coat in vegetable oil. Let it soak five or ten minutes, then rub it off.

♦ **Diaper and soiled clothing presoak.** Toss clothes in washer and cover with water. Add 1/2 cup baking soda and 1/4 cup ammonia per gallon of water used. Soak items several hours before filling the machine with cold water, agitating, and spinning. Now wash as usual.

♦ **Diaper wipes and towelettes.** With a serrated knife, saw a normal roll of paper towels into two half-sized rolls. Pull the cardboard core from the center and place one of the mini rolls in a coffee can. Feed the center sheet of the roll through an X cut in the can's plastic lid.

Mix 1 to 1 1/2 teaspoons liquid dishwashing detergent with about 1 1/2 cups water and pour the solution over the towels (exact quantities of water vary according to the type of towels used).

Note: To make the exterior of the can more attractive and to keep the interior from rusting, paint the can first.

♦ **Disinfectant spray.** In a spray bottle, mix 1/2 cup chlorine bleach with 3 1/2 cups water. Costs about a dime versus $5 for a name-brand spray.

♦ **Drain cleaners.** As preventive medicine, occasionally pour 1/4 cup baking soda and 1/2 cup vinegar down the drain. Close the drain until the fizzing stops, then flush with a gallon boiling water.

If the drain clogs, dissolve 1 pound washing soda in 3 gallons boiling water and pour the solution down the drain. The solution will sometimes dissolve the clot by itself, but using it in tandem with a plunger or plumber's snake increases the likelihood of success.

♦ **Dry Cleaner.** Cornstarch makes a good dry cleaner. Rub the cornstarch into stuffed animals, let it stand for half an hour or more, then brush it off.

♦ **Gem cleaner.** Tooth brushes and paste will keep more than just your teeth pearly, they'll keep your gem stones glittering, too.

♦ **Grease cutter.** For really dirty work clothes, add 1/2 cup of ammonia to the wash water.

♦ **Leaf polish.** To 1 quart warm water, add 2 teaspoons soap flakes (shred the remains of bar soap) and 1 teaspoon wheat germ. Very dusty plants should be showered first. Then dampen a cloth with leaf polish and gently wipe leaves. Costs about 10¢ versus $10 for a comparable quantity of brand-name product.

♦ **Liquid soap** (general-purpose body and hand soap). A good way to use the soap scraps out of the bathrooms. Grate 1 cup hard soap, add 6 cups boiling water, and stir until the soap dissolves. Let solution cool completely, then stir. Pour some into a liquid soap pump bottle and the remainder into a storage container.

♦ **Oven cleaner.** Relatively clean ovens: Scrub with baking soda. Filthy ovens: Turn oven on for 15 minutes (low setting), then turn off and place a bowl of ammonia on the top shelf and a pot of boiling water on the lower shelf. Keep the oven door closed overnight and the steam and ammonia will loosen the grime. Next day, open the oven and let the vapors vent. Pour the remainder of the ammonia into a gallon of hot water and use the mixture to scrub the oven. Make sure the ventilation is good.

♦ **Poor man's self-cleaning oven.** Simplify the job of cleaning a regular oven. Dissolve 1/2 ounce of baking soda in a cup of warm water. Wipe the interior of a clean oven with the solution; next time you clean, the muck will scale off faster. Reapply after every cleaning.

♦ **Scouring powder.** Sprinkle baking powder or borax on the surface to be scrubbed. Alternately, you can mix 1 part soap flakes and 2 parts baking soda. Sprinkle on stains or dirty surfaces and scrub with a wet rag.

♦ **Silk cleaner.** Hand wash silk with shampoo or dishwashing detergent.

♦ **Silk flower cleaner.** Put flowers in a paper bag with salt and shake.

♦ **Sink cleaner.** Whiten porcelain sinks in the bathroom or kitchen by covering them with paper towels saturated with bleach. Let the towels sit for several hours. It's cheap and takes no elbow grease—just what we lazy housekeepers love hearing.

Another approach: Plug the sink and pour in enough bleach to cover the bottom. Fill the sink with water and let it soak overnight.

♦ **Spray and wash laundry spray.** To 8 cups water, add 1/2 cup white vinegar, 1/2 cup ammonia, 1/4 cup baking soda, and 3 tablespoons liquid dishwashing detergent. Spray solution onto soiled sections of clothing several minutes before laundering.

♦ **Tile, grout, and porcelain cleaner.** To 14 cups warm water, add 1 cup baking soda, 1 cup ammonia, 1/2 cup white vinegar. Spray directly on tile or grout and scrub. Or simply spray a mixture made from 1 part bleach and 3 parts water onto tile and scrub. Some name-brand tile cleaners are little more than bleach disguised with perfume and a coloring agent; the disguise sells for 25 times more than pouring your own bleach (generic) and water into a spray bottle.

♦ **Toilet bowl cleaner.** Use an all-purpose cleaner. Or pour 1/8 cup chlorine bleach into the toilet bowl and let sit for half an hour. Return and swirl the bowl with a brush before flushing.

♦ **Vinyl cleaner.** Sprinkle baking soda onto a damp rag and wipe.

♦ **Wall cleaner.** To 15 cups warm water, add 1/2 cup borax, 1 tablespoon dishwashing detergent, 2 tablespoons ammonia. For large jobs, add 1 cup cleaner to 1/2 bucket of water and wipe walls with a soft cloth. For spot cleaning, spray on undiluted. About 30 times cheaper than commercial cleaners.

♦ **Window and glass cleaners.** For lightly soiled windows, warm water is all you need. Try it—it works and it's free. For heavily soiled windows, mix 1/2 cup ammonia (sudsy preferred), 1 pint 70% isopropyl alcohol, and 1 heaping teaspoon liquid dishwashing detergent to 13 cups warm water. Use it just like a commercial window cleaner; it costs about 15 times less but has the same ingredients.

♦ **Windshield-washer solution.** Combine 1 quart isopropyl (rubbing) alcohol with 2 cups water and 2 tablespoons liquid detergent. If you live in a very frigid climate, use only 1 cup water.

♦ **Wool and delicate-clothing soap.** No need to buy a special product, use the same liquid detergent you'd normally use for hand washing dishes. Use 1 teaspoon detergent per quart of water.

CHILDREN'S ITEMS

♦ **Finger paints.** Mix 1/4 cup cornstarch with 2 cups cold water and boil mixture until it thickens. Pour into suitable containers, then mix in food colors.

♦ **Play dough.** Mix 2 1/2 cups flour, 1/2 cup salt, 1 tablespoon alum, and 1 package Kool-Aid (unsweetened packet). Add 2 cups boiling water and 3 tablespoons vegetable oil. Mix the works together, then dump out the resulting dough on the counter and knead in an additional cup of flour. Add additional flour if the dough is still too sticky. Store the dough in an airtight container at room temperature and it will last many months.

♦ **Bubble solution.** Add 2/3 cup clear dishwashing detergent (e.g., *Dawn*) and 1 tablespoon glycerine (from a drugstore) to 15 cups warm water.

DEODORIZERS (and odorizers)

♦ **Disgusting body odor.** Rover really reeking? Give him a bath with several cups of tomato juice mixed into the water. The juice neutralizes a whole spectrum of gamy smells.

Tomato juice diluted in bath water works on more than pets. If your "bo" has a B.O. problem, express your love with a case of tomato juice. Hospital nurses have reported that a 15-minute tomato-juice soak works miracles on patients whose odors would offend Rover.

♦ **Gamy garbage disposals.** Run orange, lemon, or grapefruit peels through the disposal. Or sprinkle in about 1/4 cup baking soda, and run.

♦ **Open houses.** Envelop the house in fresh fragrances by sprinkling cinnamon on a sheet of aluminum foil and baking with the oven door open. Or, add a tablespoon of coffee grounds or sweet herbs to a pot of boiling water.

♦ **Putrid pets.** Don't want to give them a bath? Rub baking soda into their coats, then brush it off.

♦ **Stinking sinks.** Plug the sink and pour in about a gallon of water and 1/4 cup bleach. Wash the sink and then let the water drain out slowly. The bleach water will attack odors emanating from the drain.

♦ **Malodorous bathrooms.** If you have no children living with you, keep a packet of matches on the toilet. To mask unpleasant smells: Light a match, let it burn a few seconds, blow it out, and let it smoke. Once the smoke stops, toss the match in the toilet—it's no cheap trick if, in the aftermath, you burn down the house.

♦ **Repugnant refrigerators.** Place a box of baking soda (opened), a dish of charcoal briquettes, or a lemon half in the back of the refrigerator. Replace every few months.

♦ **Pungent plastic containers.** Fill them with crumpled newspaper and cover, or wash them with baking soda and water.

♦ **Reeking rooms.** Leave an uncovered dish of ammonia or vinegar in the room overnight. The same remedy applies if smoke or paint odors overpower a room.

♦ **Fragrant clothing.** Scent drawers and closets with unwrapped bars of soap.

♦ **Fetid carpets and cars.** Sprinkle baking soda on the carpet before vacuuming. Sprinkling a powder made from 1 cup borax and 2 cups cornmeal will also work. Both methods work best if you let the powders sit for at least an hour before vacuuming.

Soda water, or baking soda on a damp handkerchief, will eliminate localized carpet odors caused by urine, vomit, or spilled milk. Some people dab the area first with vinegar before the soda treatment.

♦ **Smelly sponges.** Wash in the dishwasher or soak in bleach overnight.

♦ **Mordant shoes.** Place crumpled newspaper in shoes. Or sprinkle in a little baking powder (wipe out the powder with a rag before wearing).

♦ **Caustic cutting boards.** Rub salt over wooden cutting boards. Eliminates most smells and stains.

♦ **Loathsome laundry.** To eliminate perspiration odors, dab the area with white vinegar just before laundering. Or wipe the underarms, collars, etc., with hair shampoo about 30 minutes before laundering.

♦ **Foul air.** Make a spray deodorant by adding 1 cup baking soda, 1 tablespoon scent (vanilla extract, pine oil, lemon extract), and 1/4 cup ammonia to 15 cups warm water. Keep some in a spray bottle with an atomizer. Don't spray over wooden furniture. Cost: 50¢ versus about $20 for same amount of name-brand spray.

♦ **Trenchant trash cans.** Pour 1/2 cup baking soda in the bottom of the cans.

MISCELLANEOUS

♦ **Dust spray.** Out of dusting spray? Horrors. Would you believe that a rag that is just ever so slightly damp will hold dust to it just fine? Would you believe you can live without *Endust?*

♦ **Fabric softener sheets.** Rather than buying expensive tear-off sheets, simply pour a few capfuls of fabric softener onto a folded washcloth. Wring the washcloth to remove excess softener. Toss the washcloth in the dryer with wet clothes.

♦ **Fire extinguisher** (dry). Pour 6 pounds fine sand into a pail and mix in two pounds baking soda. Keep the container in the shop or garage for emergencies -- sprinkle or pour the mixture onto oil, grease, and petroleum fires.

♦ **Lens cleaner for cameras.** Mix 6 parts isopropyl alcohol with 1 part water. You can also use the window and glass cleaner mentioned previously in this chapter.

♦ **Penetrating oils** (for rust). Hydrogen peroxide and kerosene both work as penetrating oils if allowed to sit on frozen bolts. You can also free rusted bolts by pouring carbonated beverages on them. Let the carbonation work awhile before loosening. Makes you wonder what our stomachs are made of.

♦ **Starch spray.** To 2 cups warm water, add 4 teaspoons cornstarch and about 1/4 teaspoon cologne (optional). Stir or shake well. Store in a spray bottle. Rinse the nozzle after use to prevent clogging (tape a pin to the bottle in case you get an occasional clog).

♦ **Static Electricity Eliminator.** Mix 1 cup fabric softener with 2 quarts water. Spray carpets where you want to kill static electricity (like those around a home computer) until they are damp. After the carpet dries, it will remain static-free for several months.

♦ **Tape recorder head cleaner.** Dab a cotton swab in isopropyl alcohol, then rub the heads.

♦ **Wallpaper remover.** Combine equal parts of white vinegar and hot water. Roll or sponge the solution on and wet the wallpaper thoroughly. Apply twice and the paper will pull off in sheets.

♦ **Weed killer and weed prevention.** Mix 1 pound of salt in a gallon of boiling water and pour the solution on weeds along walkways. Sprinkling borax in cracks along walkways in the early spring will help prevent weeds from sprouting in unwanted places.

COSMETICS and PERSONAL HYGIENE

♦ **Baby oil**. Mix 1 cup mineral oil with two or three drops of perfume or cologne.

♦ **Chapstick**. Bet you didn't know that you've always got a personal supply of chapstick on hand and that it's absolutely free. Rub your index finger over the exterior of your nose and it will absorb some of the skin's natural oils. Now rub your finger over your lips to give them a dose of the best lip oil available.

♦ **Cleansing cream**. Undiluted vegetable oil doubles as an excellent makeup remover. Wash with soap and water after using.

♦ **Deodorant**. In a spray bottle, combine 1 pint warm water, 2 tablespoons alum (from the drugstore) and a little cologne (or aftershave). Or, over very low heat, stir equal parts of petroleum jelly, talcum powder, and baking soda into a smooth cream: Transfer into a small jar and use as a cream deodorant. Or make a powder deodorant by mixing equal parts of cornstarch and baking soda.

♦ **Disinfectant**. Hydrogen peroxide (3% solution) works well as a disinfectant: Apply directly to cuts, scrapes, punctures. Dabbed on a cotton ball, it's also effective for cleansing the oily skin of teenagers.

♦ **Eye Cream**. Some plastic surgeons recommend this to patients: Before bed, rub the odorless form of castor oil around the eyes.

♦ **Face moisturizer**. Pricey spas use this technique. Rub small amounts of petroleum jelly onto your clean, wet face. As you rub in the jelly, keep wetting your face with a little warm water. The finished effect will not feel greasy.

♦ **Hair conditioning**. Massage 1/2 cup mayonnaise into dry, unwashed hair. Add two slices of bread and you've got a disgusting sandwich, but leave the goop in your hair for 10 or 20 minutes and you've got a superb conditioner. Finish with a thorough rinsing, then shampoo.

♦ **Mousse**. Really, this is not an excuse for an early-morning nip of the bottle. The beer in the pump bottle is for your hair. After a bath or shower, towel-dry your locks, then spritz them with a thin film of beer (or pour a little beer into your palm, then rub it into you hair). Now blow-dry and style as normal. The beer helps set your hair.

Oh yeah, once your hair dries, the odor of beer vanishes, which means your colleagues won't be reporting you to AA.

♦ **Nail polish remover.** Mix 1 part water with 2 parts acetone (found at any hardware store). Add a few drops of perfume to mask the smell of the acetone.

♦ **Skin moisturizer.** At such a low cost and without a mouthful of unpronounceable chemicals you may not believe they can work, but according to dermatologists, two of the best skin moisturizers are baby oil (mineral oil) and petroleum jelly.

Dermatologists also give *Crisco* shortening top marks as a moisturizer. Just watch out if you notice your spouse licking his chops next time you moisturize.

♦ **Tooth powder.** Mix 1/4 cup baking soda with 1/4 teaspoon salt and 2 tablespoons grated, dried lemon or orange peel. Store in a jar and dab with a wet toothbrush. The taste is not super, but the price is.

PESTS

♦ **Animal repellent.** Sprinkle chili powder around the gardens and many mammals that terrorize your prize vegetables and flowers will stay clear.

♦ **Ant and cockroach killer.** Mix 2 cups borax (available at grocery stores) and 1 cup flour in a quart jar. Punch holes in jar and sprinkle the powder outdoors and around the foundation of house. Sprinkle along baseboards and door sills. Sprinkle some into jar lids left under the sink and in the cabinets.

♦ **Furniture saver.** Keep dogs from chewing the furniture or edge of rugs with a solution made from 1/4 cup clove oil, 1 tablespoon paprika, and 1 teaspoon black pepper. Sponge the solution on the furniture and rug edges being chewed. Reapply as needed.

♦ **Trash-can repellent.** Dogs, cats, raccoons, opossums will leave your garbage can alone if you spray the outside with a mist of full-strength ammonia. If your garbage is particularly ripe, spray ammonia on the inside too.

TARNISH REMOVERS

◆ **Brass, bronze, and copper.** Make a paste by adding 1 tablespoon vinegar or lemon juice to 1 tablespoon flour and 1 tablespoon salt. Rub paste gently onto brass with a cloth or very fine steel wool. Wash well in warm, soapy water and dry.

◆ **Chrome.** Use straight vinegar.

◆ **Copper.** Rub the copper with ketchup, or a mixture made from 2 tablespoons vinegar and 1 teaspoon salt. Wash with soap and warm water.

◆ **Pewter.** Make a thin paste from wood ash and water and rub on the pewter.

◆ **Silver and stainless steel.** Make a paste by mixing baking soda and lemon juice (baking soda and water works, too). Rub paste on silver with damp cloth or sponge. Rinse off in hot water and dry.

Greeting Cards

My wife can punish me for weeks if I fail to give her a card on her birthday, Valentine's Day, Mother's Day, Easter, or our anniversary. "You don't love me," she sniffles—if she speaks to me at all.

"Not true," I say, "But how does a dollar spent on a mass-produced card demonstrate love?"

"It's the thought that counts."

All this has given me occasion to ponder ways to keep us both happy. She wants proof of my *amour*, yet I hate supporting the very companies that have brainwashed her (and so many others) into thinking that a yearly toll of six or seven special-occasion cards proves devotion. That's why I latched onto a trick my sister taught me. "Photocopy the cards," she said.

My local drugstore had a copier and a rack of special-occasion cards, so I surreptitiously copied a few cards while copying other materials. What a coup, I thought. This would strike a blow against the very companies that created this unnecessary demand.

"A xeroxed card," Jan wept upon opening the envelope. "Am I so meaningless that you'll only waste a nickel on me?"

Okay, with Jan, it's more than the thought that counts—how much I spend matters. But I haven't completely caved in to the card companies. Here are my guerrilla tactics of counterattack.

♦ Copy the cards you buy. Some folks (like Jan) want the real McCoy so give them an original card. Other people (in my case, my family and several friends) will be flattered you remembered them at all and will get a laugh out of the penny-pinching antics. Give them a photocopied card.

If you cut and paste a copied image onto the front of a nice sheet of stationery and personally write the text inside, you increase the card's perceived value with only a tiny increase in cost.

♦ Pick up cards during post-holiday sales. Buy Valentine's, Easter, Mother's Day, Father's Day, and Christmas cards after the big day, and you'll get 50% to 75% off the sticker price. I've got a hidden stash of cards now, bought for a quarter each. When Jan reminds me that it's a special day (i.e., our anniversary) I act like I knew it all along, wander upstairs, rifle through the stash, and find an appropriate card.

She thinks me both thoughtful and a big spender.

♦ Be unique: Send out New Year's cards rather than Christmas cards and you can buy your cards for half-price on December 26.

♦ Make your own cards. It's easy. Pull out a nice sheet of stationery and fold it in half. Then add a poem you like, one of Billy Boy's (Shakespeare's) sonnets, a nice thought, a quote (from a book of quotes found at the library), etc.

Original cards are easy, too. Example: I'm brainstorming about Jan's birthday. Within a minute a hackneyed but suitably sappy thought pops into my head. "You're like a fine wine — you get more full-bodied with age." Then I go to my *Time* magazine, and (being careful not to cut out the picture of Elizabeth Taylor before her diet) find a svelte beauty to add to the inside of the card (where I'll add a flirtatious remark). It takes less time than going to the store and the price is right.

♦ My grandmother would use a decorative sticker (or white-out) over the signature of the cards she received. Then she reused them. I doubt that she ever sprung for a special-occasion card—not even Christmas cards.

♦ To beat the Christmas-card racket, save all the cards you receive and cut off the backs. Now you have a crop of postcards for next Christmas. You won't have to buy cards *and* you'll save on postage (postcards fly for 30% less than letters). Finally, the space restrictions of a postcard give you an excuse for not writing a treatise about the past year, meaning you can write your cards quickly.

A few tips here. Make a note of who sent you the card in the first place (pencil their initials in the corner of the postcard). This gives you the fun of sending the card back to the original sender—or helps you avoid this fate if that embarrasses you. Remember, too, that card dimensions must be under 4.25" X 6" for postcard rates. Larger cards do not require an envelope but need more postage.

◆ Convert the cards you are given for birthdays, Easter, Valentine's Day, etc. into postcards (cut off the back panel) and you'll never buy a postcard again.

◆ Make your own Christmas postcard from a family snapshot. Photographic prints (used as postcards) cost less than store-bought cards and you score the added benefit of postcard rates. Remember, too, that your friends would rather see a picture of you and your family than one of Santa stuffing a stocking.

◆ The special occasion cards you receive can be valuable if you reuse them. Convert Christmas cards into holiday place mats: Sandwich several cards that make an attractive collage between two pieces of clear, plastic contact paper. Make holiday coasters in the same way. Create jigsaw puzzles for children by gluing large cards onto cardboard and then cutting the works into assorted shapes.

Reduce the complexity in life by eliminating the needless wants of life, and the labors of life reduce themselves.

Edwin Way Teale

Half As Much

Imagine the benefits to be harvested if you cut your use of consumables in half. Products would last twice as long. You'd spend half as much money, spend less time shopping, work less, and spend more time pursuing your interests. Those interests would flourish and soon you'd be rich and famous doing what you love.

Sounds good, eh? Well, the rich and famous part is up to you, but I can help with the first part of the equation. Cutting your use of consumables is surprisingly simple if you remember a basic premise: Manufacturers routinely recommend you use more of their product than necessary. Why? To ensure the product lives up to the claims made and to increase sales. After all, the more you use the more you buy. This is not cynicism, but an acceptance of capitalism at work.

Try the following tricks and prove to yourself that half as much is sometimes twice as good.

♦ Laundry detergent. My father has sensitive skin and contracts skin rashes easily. Over the years my mother discovered that washing clothes with half the prescribed amount of laundry powder allowed clothes to rinse better and relieved my father's rashes. She also found the laundry got just as clean. Now, unless the clothes are abnormally dirty or are stained she only uses half the manufacturer's recommendations.

If your water is hard or has a high mineral content, stick to the manufacturer's recommendations. Otherwise, try this trick.

♦ Dishwashing detergent. Filling the dishwasher's detergent bin is overkill. Experiment with half that quantity and increase the amount as necessary. I don't pre-rinse my dishes (that's the dishwasher's job, right?) so I find filling the detergent bin just over the half-way mark works perfectly. If I pre-rinsed my dishes I'd use less than half a bin.

♦ Toothpaste. We're conditioned from years of TV ads to load our brushes with an inch-long bead of paste. That much toothpaste makes you froth like a rabid dog. What's more, that froth is wasted toothpaste.

Most people can cut the toothpaste used by two-thirds without impairing the job. In fact, toothpaste is almost incidental to keeping teeth clean. It's the mechanical action of brushing (and flossing) that really counts.

♦ Liquid hand soap. The liquid soap bought for washing hands is strong stuff and a little dab—one with a pea-sized circumference—will do ya. A full stroke of the bottle pump gives you three times more soap than needed.

♦ Bar soap. Smothering your hands or limbs with a heavy lather is wasteful. You could wash your entire body in a hygienic fashion with the amount of soap many people use for their hands alone. As long as the film covering your hands or limbs remains slippery, you've got enough soap for the job.

♦ Shaving cream. In college days when my brother introduced me to this trick, I burst out laughing—it's classic Dappenomics. Naturally, I still use it.

Spread a small dollop of shaving cream over half your face and shave. Instead of rinsing off the razor with water, spread the foam over the other half of your face. The whiskers in the used foam won't hinder its performance.

If you're heavy-bearded and want the foam to soften your whiskers for a minute before shaving, cover your entire face. Remember, however, that a thin layer of foam over the whiskers softens them as much as a thick, white beard of foam.

Note: Moistening whiskers with a lather of soap is cheaper than shaving cream and works nearly as well.

♦ Toilet paper. I can still recall a spanking I received as a four-year-old when the ream of TP I had used to clean myself clogged the toilet and created flood conditions in the bathroom.

After impressing my transgressions upon my fanny, my father taught me how to do the job in under 10 squares. When I go into public rest rooms and see toilets clogged with paper, I realize there are hordes of people in need of a spanking.

♦ Shampoo. Use just enough shampoo to create a thin layer of lather around the entire head. Keep in mind that lather is cleaning power that has not been used, so the thicker the layer of lather, the more shampoo you've wasted.

As for washing your hair twice with each shower, it's unnecessary. Save the shampoo, water, and time.

♦ Liquid dishwashing detergent. When handwashing dishes, use a teaspoon to measure your detergent. People who eyeball it use more than necessary. One teaspoon of *quality* detergent polishes off a load of dishes.

Note: some "bargain" detergents are a gyp because you'll use two or three times more product to get decent cleaning power.

♦ Food. My goal now is to live on half rations. Like many Americans, I eat twice what I really need, so the opportunity to save money here has me salivating. Unfortunately, so does food. Cutting back means kicking an addiction.

To beat that addiction, I'm experimenting with a theory. I think the satisfaction of eating comes from the amount of time and chewing involved. If I eat half as much food but chew it twice as long, maybe I can fool myself into thinking my diet is unchanged. Tell you later if it works.

Fortune helps him that is willing to help himself.
English proverb

Heating

Trivia question of the day: What consumes the most energy in a home? A) The water heater B) Heating and/or cooling C) The refrigerator D) A teenager's stereo?

Forget D: Music creates energy—positive for some, negative for others. Nix C: The refrigerator is only the most energy-consumptive "appliance" in the house. Disregard A: Hot water is the Avis of the household. That leaves the furnace and air conditioner as the energy drains that have you paying until it Hertz.

On the average, 50% of a family's household energy consumption goes into space heating or cooling. That equals over $450 per year for the average family. Fortunately, after reading this chapter you'll be much smarter than the average consumer.

GENERAL TIPS

♦ Modify your habits. In winter, each degree you raise the thermostat raises your heating 3%. You can put a 15% dent in your heating bill by keeping the daytime thermostat at 65 degrees Fahrenheit (instead of 70°F) and the nighttime temperature at 55° or 60°F (instead of 60° or 65°F). That's worth shivering over—or wearing an extra sweater for.

♦ A good set of long underwear will let you turn the heat down without requiring that you dress up like the Michelin Man. Polypropylene and polyester underwear hug the body and create dead air (and therefore insulation) right next to the skin where it has the most insulating value. A good set of long johns will keep you warmer than a bulky, but baggy, sweater.

Avoid wool long underwear: it's itchy. Cotton and silk get the thumbs down if you also intend to use your longjohns for skiing, hiking, hunting, or fishing—both fabrics are dangerously cold once wet.

Look for the following design features: a turtle neck or a snug crew neck to reduce the amount of body heat escaping out the top, adequate length in the sleeves and pant legs to cover wrists and ankles, long-bodied tops that tuck well below the waist, bottoms that don't creep down the hips as you walk.

Mail-order outlets for such underwear include: REI, L.L. Bean, and Campmor (see the *Mail-order Appendix*).

♦ A hot-water bottle also goes a long way in keeping the thermostat down. Place the hot bottle on your belly between a T-shirt and sweat shirt. The bottle is particularly useful when you're vegetating (e.g., reading or watching TV). If you move around the house a lot, the bottle may be inconvenient unless you sew a kangaroo pouch inside an old sweat shirt to hold the bottle.

Rewarming the bottle is far more convenient (and economical) using a microwave oven. Remove the cap, prop the bottle against the side of the microwave to keep it from leaking, and nuke it. Once hot, slip the bottle back into your kangaroo pouch for another few hours of luxury. Ahhh, it feels positively atomic.

The same bottle can preheat your bed at night.

♦ Thick comforters or electric blankets are far more economical ways to sleep warm than keeping the heat on.

♦ If you refuse to set the nighttime temperature at 55° or 60°F because you can't stand rising to a cold house, replace your thermostat with a clock thermostat. It will cost $50 to $100 and pay for itself in a year. Set the clock so the house is warmed about an hour before you get up.

♦ Air conditioning is even more expensive than heating and each degree of cooling consumes at least 5% more energy. It's no real sweat to set the thermostat from

70° to 77°F, especially once you know this will cut your utility bill 35%.

♦ Close off unused rooms and shut the heating vents. Why heat or cool, unused space? If you are currently heating an unused room, it's costing you between $30 and $50 a year. You can save another $20 to $30 over the winter by heating the core of the house during the day and closing off the bedrooms until nighttime. Because most homeowners spend little time in their basements, this is another logical space to keep unheated.

Be aware that the air ducts of forced-air central heaters often have dampers back where the ducts exit the heater. These dampers (flaps inside the ducts) can be shut to keep heat out of particular rooms and shutting the heat off here is more efficient than closing the heating vents inside the room.

♦ Turn down the heat or air conditioning when you leave the house—even if you're leaving on a short errand. You'll save energy.

♦ In many homes the chimney is the single largest source of heat loss, so when the fireplace is not in use, close the damper. Because heat rises, an open damper allows the loss of more heat than a hole in the wall twice its size. Install a glass door across the fireplace to further block heat from flying away.

♦ Turn the thermostat down to your bedtime temperature an hour or two before retiring. The house will remain a comfortable temperature for a few hours.

♦ Blankets in the TV and reading rooms will keep you comfortable while the thermostat is set lower.

♦ Hot air rises and escapes out the ceiling, so use ceiling fans in vaulted rooms to blow the warm air back down to floor level where it will warm you.

♦ Turn the heat down to 55°F when you leave for the day—or for holidays.

♦ Try heating European style by keeping the central heat in the house set to a low temperature (about 55° to 60°F) and using portable space heaters to warm those rooms where you work, eat, or read.

Also, use space heaters in the morning while preparing for work. Warming up the bathroom or kitchen with a portable heater is considerably cheaper than heating the entire house.

Good electric convection heaters (those with blowers) can be bought for around $40 and are the best bet for warming a room quickly. Radiant heaters are a good source of heat if you want to keep the spot around you warm (as you read or work) without raising the temperature of the entire room. Ceramic heaters, while safe and popular, have three strikes against them—they're pricy (around $100), distribute heat poorly, and don't regulate heat well.

♦ If you heat with oil, stock up in summer. Thanks to the laws of supply and demand, summer prices are normally lower.

KEEPING IN THE HEAT (OR COLD)

♦ A poorly insulated house can easily waste 30% to 50% of the energy poured into it, which makes an energy audit that pinpoints problems in your home's insulation worth the trouble. Utility companies (both gas and electric) often perform this service free or for a nominal fee. If your utility company does not, check under *Energy* in the Yellow Pages for a professional energy auditor. A good audit will cost around $75.

The U.S. Department of Energy now recommends that walls and floors of houses be insulated to values of R-19 (the R-value measures the resistance to heat flow: the higher the number, the greater the resistance). Ceilings should be insulated to R-30 in the Southern U.S., R-38 in the middle latitudes of the country, and R-49 in the harsher northern latitudes.

♦ Do-it-yourselfers wishing to improve the energy efficiency of an older house can most effectively add insulation in the attic and beneath floors with a crawl space below. Check whether the insulation in these spaces meets the U.S. Department of Energy's recommended R-values listed above. Measure the average depth of the insulation in the attic and below the floor, write down the measurements and the type of insulation used, and call a building-supply store for an estimate of the R-values. Alternately, check charts in books like those produced by the Massachusetts Audubon Society (see listing at the end of this section) to determine the R-value.

♦ If you're building a new home, research your windows carefully. Until recently, the most energy-efficient windows had R-4 ratings (most double-pane windows have an R-2 rating). Some new windows, employing argon-filled airspaces and two low-emissivity coated films suspended between glass panes, now have R-8 ratings. These windows cost 10% to 20% more than conventional low-e windows but the energy savings in colder parts of the country make them money savers. These "Superglass" windows are made by Southwall Technologies, 1029 Corporation Way, Palo Alto, CA 94303, 415-962-9111.

♦ Low-emissivity films made by Gila Energy Products (6615 West Boston Street, Chandler, AZ 85226, 800-528-4481) can be applied to your existing windows to increase their R-value. Low-e films reflect heat back toward the source: toward the sun in summer, toward your heater in winter. Consequently the films insulate and upgrade your existing windows.

♦ Loose-fitting windows can leak heated or cooled air five times faster than properly installed ones. Test your windows on a windy day: Take a candle and move it around the perimeter of each window (from inside the house). If gusts of wind disturb the flame, the wind is leaking through the window and you need caulking or rope caulking to plug the gaps.

Caulk from inside the house for best results. Caulking the outside creates a moisture barrier but is less effective for retaining heat.

♦ Use weatherstripping to seal gaps around the perimeter of your outside doors. Also install a door sweep

along the door's bottom edge. The materials more than pay
for themselves in a year.

♦ In winter, keep the drapes closed after the sun sets.
Drapes that fit snugly around the window reduce the
amount of cold air leaking into the house and will cut your
winter heating bill by at least $5 per window. On sunny
winter days, open the drapes and let sunlight flood the
house: wintertime sunlight carries a lot of heat.

♦ Pare your heating bills by wrapping fiberglass insulation around heating and air conditioning ducts in the basement, attic, and crawl spaces. If there is less than 2 1/2 inches of insulation around these ducts (measure the loft in several places), wrap them with more insulation. It is not difficult to do and the investment in added insulation will pay for itself in a season.

If you strip the old insulation off the ducts and add totally new insulation (not usually necessary), make sure you tape all the duct joints. Otherwise, heat will leak out of the ducts and into the insulation.

♦ Storm windows can cut in half the heat leakage through windows. The cheapest do-it-yourself windows are made from polyethylene plastic and are installed from inside the house with double-stick tape. You can buy kits from home centers and hardware stores. Cutting your own heavy-duty polyethylene plastic sheets and taping these over your windows is a cheaper, though less elegant, solution.

♦ Lay insulation over the back of your attic door (or hatch) and weatherstrip the edges.

♦ Aluminum foil reflectors behind radiators bounce the heat out into the room. They'll cost you under a dollar per radiator and lower wintertime heating costs by $4 per radiator.

If you want to make your own reflector, tape aluminum foil to cardboard. Or buy strips of thin foam insulation with a bright foil coating. Place these reflectors behind the radiator, foil coating facing the room.

♦ Apartments on the upper floors of a building will benefit from heat rising from below. Apartments on a building's middle floor will be heated from above and below.

♦ Reduce heat loss in the garage by tacking foam pipe insulation (3/4-inch diameter) to the bottom of the garage door. Set the pipe insulation about 1/2 inch from the outside edge of the door.

♦ If you're building a new house, make sure your outside doors are insulated.

♦ A variety of excellent, short books published by the Massachusetts Audubon Society (South Great Road, Lincoln, MA 01773-9988) list detailed yet practical advice for do-it-yourselfers wanting to cut the cost of insulating and weatherizing their homes. The titles include: *How to Weatherize Your Home or Apartment, All About Insulation,* and *Superinsulation.* Cost is $3.50 each.

♦ For quick answers to home-insulation questions, call the Conservation and Renewable Energy Inquiry and Referral Service: 800-462-4983 in Pennsylvania, 800-233-3071 in Alaska and Hawaii, 800-523-2929 everywhere else.)
For specialized questions about home insulation, write to the National Appropriate Technology Assistance Service (Box 2525, Butte, MT 59702).

PRODUCING HEAT

♦ Keeping your heat (or air conditioning) in the house is one major way to cut utility bills; the other approach is to produce that heat (or air-conditioning) more economically. Just like cars, some heaters are energy guzzlers, others energy sippers.
Super-efficient gas and oil furnaces are those that lose no more than 5% to 10% of the fuel's heat. High-efficiency models, meanwhile, lose about 15% of the heat. By contrast, most gas and oil furnaces lose 40% to 50% of the heat produced to vent the byproducts of combustion—water, carbon dioxide, nitrogen.
If you have a relatively new furnace, spending big bucks on a super-efficient heater won't be economical. But if you're getting ready to replace an old furnace or live in a cold climate where your fuel bills hit $1000 each year, the big savings of efficient heaters make them smart buys.
Use a heater's Annual Fuel Utilization Efficiency (AFUE) rating to compare the efficiency of the furnace you are considering. Also, contact the American Council for an Energy-Efficient Economy (1001 Connecticut Ave. NW, Suite 535, Washington, DC 20036) for their yearly guide, *The Most Energy Efficient Appliances.* Cost is $3.

♦ A properly sized furnace for your home or building will be able to keep the house at 70°F on the coldest days, but it will need to run nearly full time to do so. Furnaces are more efficient when they run longer and less heat is lost in the ducts, so it is better to have a smaller unit running nearly continuously than it is to have a big heater that turns off and on often.

If you're having your heater replaced, your contractor should do a thorough heat-loss analysis of your house and size the heater so it is just able to replace the heat that will leak away on the coldest days.

♦ As with any other work done to your house, make sure you get several bids when you need a contractor to install a new furnace. You'll find huge differences in the price quotes. See the *Household Tips* chapter for details about hiring contractors.

♦ Despite the age or type of heater you own, make sure it operates efficiently. Oil furnaces should be tuned up every year, gas furnaces every two years. A tune up costing $50 to $60 will typically save you $50 to $100 (assuming an annual heating bill of $1000).

Find a heating technician through your utility company or by consulting The *Yellow Pages* under Energy and Heat. To do some of this work yourself or to learn what a technician should be checking, get a copy of *Oil and Gas Heating Systems: Maintenance and Improvement* from the Massachusetts Audubon Society (address listed earlier). Cost is $3.50.

♦ Electric heaters work best when the filters, vents, and coils are clean. Vacuum or dust baseboard heaters often and change the air filter in forced-air furnaces every month or two.

♦ Whether your forced-air system is electric or gas, change the air filters every few months. A dirty filter increases the load on the blower, meaning your electric bills rise and the life of the blower falls. Because these filters typically cost about $1, most people trash their old ones. You can, however, lay a large piece of window screening over the filter, vacuum the filter clean (using a canister-style vacuum), and reuse it.

If your heater uses a permanent filter, clean it often (your owner's manual should tell you how to do so).

♦ After baking, open the oven door and let that heat warm the kitchen.

♦ Given the choice, use natural gas over electricity to heat your home and your water. Even in the Northwest, where electric rates are half the national average (around 4¢ per kilowatt-hour versus 8¢ per kilowatt-hour), gas cuts your heating bill nearly in half.

♦ Natural gas was once much cheaper than oil, but in most places this is no longer true. Consequently, converting the burner in your heater from oil to gas, a practice that was once quite economical, is no longer so clear cut. Determining the most frugal option now requires some calculating.

Assuming the gas burner replacing the oil burner has the same efficiency, it will take 140 cubic feet (1.4 ccf) of gas to generate the same heat as a gallon of oil. If your gas utility charges by 'therms,' 1.4 ccf of gas is nearly the same as 1.4 therms.

If 1.4 therms of gas is substantially cheaper than 1 gallon of fuel oil and you want to know how much converting to gas would save you over the winter, take last year's total fuel bill and divide it by the price of oil. This gives you the number of gallons bought. Multiply the number of gallons by 1.4 to determine the number of therms you would need. Multiply the number of therms by the per-therm cost. This is the amount you would have spent on gas last year.

♦ It may pay to give your furnace a facelift with the following modifications:

Oil furnace owners can replace the fuel nozzles with smaller versions, causing the furnace to run longer and reducing the heat loss that occurs when the furnace is off; do this when the furnace gets its annual tuneup and the few extra dollars spent will cut fuel bills 5% to 10%. Installing a valve that automatically dampers the flue when an oil furnace shuts off can save another 10% in fuel costs. Finally, flame-retention burners installed on old oil furnaces produce a smaller flame of higher efficiency: They cost $500 to $600 (installed) but reduce fuel bills 15% to 20%.

The pilot light on a gas furnace accounts for 5% of your annual fuel bill. Replacing it with an electronic ignition system typically pays for itself in three to five years. Electronic ignitions added to old systems are difficult to install properly so hire a technician who specializes in these installations.

♦ Forced-air heaters use a thermostat to start the fan that blows warm air through the ducts. If that thermostat is set too high, the fan comes on late and shuts off early, meaning some warm air gets trapped in the ducts where it does you no good.

The fan can be reset to turn on and off at lower temperatures so that all the warm air gets blown into the house. If you can't find your fan thermostat, get a heating expert to point it out. The fan should shut off at or just before 90°F and come on when the burner bumps the temperature up to 110°F. Furnaces with only one setting typically designate when the burner should go on, so set the temperature at 110°F.

♦ Hot water radiators should be bled of any trapped air twice each winter. Buy a radiator key at a hardware store. Then, while you hold a pot under the valve, keep the valve open until all the air has exited and only water streams out.

♦ The temperature in a room heated by either steam or hot water radiators can be regulated with a variety of valves that screw into the radiator's vents. These valves open and close the radiator when the heat falls below or rises above a comfortable temperature. They offer a cheap solution to controlling room temperature in old buildings regulated by one thermostat. Research and buy these valves at hardware stores.

♦ For more information about heaters, order: *Oil and Gas Heating Systems: Maintenance and Improvement* from the Massachusetts Audubon Society (address above). Cost is $3.50.

SUMMERTIME TIPS

♦ During hot spells, open the doors, windows, and drapes at night to let in the cooler air. Shut down the house (doors, windows, and drapes) come morning to seal in the cooler air.

♦ Close the vents to a forced-air heating system so the cool air from an air conditioner does not drain out of the house through the ducts.

♦ Use your barbecue more often in summer to eliminate cooking heat in the house and to reduce the strain on the air conditioner.

♦ If your summers are not extremely warm, consider an attic fan as an alternative to air conditioning. In temperate climates, this does a good job of cooling houses and costs much less than air conditioning.

♦ Awnings and canopies over the windows will cool a house in summer.

♦ It's a long-term trick: Plant trees around your house, especially along the southern and western exposures. By the time you retire and are living on a reduced income, the trees will be reducing your cooling bills. They'll also reduce the heat radiating out of the house in winter.

My life is a bubble; but how much solid cash it costs to keep that bubble floating.
                                      Logan Pearsall Smith

Hotels and Motels

Ridiculous—that's my one-word synopsis of hotels. People willingly pay $100 (even $200) per night to sleep through what they paid for. Of course, going too far in the opposite direction can be equally ludicrous. Shortly out of college, I flew to Zurich, Switzerland and arrived downtown after dark with a bad attitude about paying the exorbitant rates the hotels were quoting. I stashed my luggage at the train station and toted my sleeping bag to a park where I took refuge under a huge camellia.

The bush wreaked of excrement, but that was the least of my troubles. I knew nothing of Zurich and, once snuggled inside the coffin of my sleeping bag, worried about my safety. Through the hours of blackness I believed the footsteps I often heard around the perimeter of my bush were made by thugs who would gladly cut my throat for the chewing gum in my pocket.

Fortunately, in the vast midland between the Ritz and the pits there are many opportunities to secure a safe roof overhead without taking out a second mortgage. Next time you travel, consider these tips.

♦ The mother lode of budget lodging in the heart of major North American cities is the YMCA. The Y runs about 40 lodging centers in the U.S. and Canada (as well as an additional 50 lodging centers around the globe). They offer about the cheapest accommodations in the heart of major cities like San Francisco, Los Angeles, Vancouver, Houston, New Orleans, Chicago, Detroit, Miami, New York City, Boston, and Montreal. How cheap? For a double room you pay $36 in San Francisco, $30 in San Diego, $26 in

Denver, $30 in Miami, $42 in Boston, and $39 in New York City.

Accommodations are typically spartan but they are clean; you also have access to superb sporting facilities. You don't need to be a member and while some Y's still cater to men only, most accommodate women and couples. These accommodations are particularly popular among students and foreign travelers, but anyone needing safe, clean, convenient, and inexpensive rooms should use them.

For *The Y's Way International Directory*, listing the organization's properties and booking procedures, send a self-addressed, stamped envelope to: The Y's Way, 356 West 34th Street, New York, NY 10001.

♦ We think of hotel rates as immutable, fixed in stone, handed down from God along with the commandments. They aren't. They are commodities priced, in part, by the laws of supply and demand. And just as management can boost rates when a convention is in town, they can slash rates when business dies.

Every city has its slow periods and slack seasons, and business centers like New York, Boston, and Chicago have slack seasons every weekend. People with the courage to ask about discounts can often seize big savings.

To talk your way into a discount, it's best to call late in the afternoon or early evening; by then empty rooms are looking like lost opportunities. Working from a telephone, ask if the hotel has vacant rooms and at what rates. Casually query whether the hotel has any special rates being offered or whether they grant discounts to AAA members, students, senior citizens, AARP members, frequent fliers, clergy members, corporation employees, nearsighted penny-pinchers, or any other legitimate-sounding group. Even if you're self-employed don't hesitate to ask for a corporate rate.

If the hotel doesn't nibble, you'll need to let your fingers walk along to the next hotel listed in the *Yellow Pages*. If you do get a lower offer, don't take the first quotation as final, be willing to make a counter offer. Don't hesitate to be honest with a comment like, "Unfortunately, with my budget I need a room costing about $X. Can you offer a smaller room or can I qualify for a larger discount by paying cash?"

If you don't get the rate you want, cordially say you'll have to think over the offer; try a few more hotels in the *Yellow Pages*. Later, call back the hotel with the best offer.

♦ These same rules of negotiation apply to bed and breakfast accommodations (listed as such in the *Yellow Pages*). In fact, bed and breakfasts can be easier to deal with because you are likely to talk to the owner on the phone, and the owner possesses the power to make (and break) the rules.

♦ If you visit a city regularly, talk to the general manager of different hotels about establishing a special rate—you are, after all, assuring repeated stays and most hotels are willing to make an offer that is considerably better than their "rack" rate.

♦ Most hotels pull a dirty trick when quoting room rates—they don't add the city's occupancy tax (also called a "room tax" or "bed tax"), which is as high as 21.25% in New York City, 14.2% in Seattle, 13% in Baltimore, and 12.5% in Los Angeles. There is nothing you can do to alter these taxes, but when calling for room rates, ask if the quote includes the occupancy tax. Usually the answer is "no," so ask what the tax will be. Now you know the true cost of the room.

♦ Don't overlook friends (current and past) for a bed. College and university alumni associations are the best resource to find out where classmates have settled.

Friends are usually happy to see and house you. But if you want to be welcome again, think of yourself as rabble rather than royalty; do whatever you can to help.

♦ House exchanges are an excellent way for families to control lodging costs while visiting one city for weeks or months. Your homeowner's insurance should protect your home during a swap. Your car insurance should cover your car (if the swapper uses it) and you (if you use the swapper's car). Ask your insurance agent about these matters to be sure of your coverage.

People living in or near popular travel destinations (Disneyland, ski resorts, Hawaii, New York City, etc.) are particularly likely to arrange a swap—such homes are in high demand. As a denizen of Okmulgee, Oklahoma, however, you shouldn't give up hope—miracles can happen.

Of the thousands of exchanges taking place each year, the majority are organized through home exchange clubs publishing directories of people looking to swap. Joining such a club costs $20 to $40, but is a worthwhile expense because it gets your house listed in catalogs that are distributed to others hoping to trade places.

Exchange clubs to contact include: Global Home Exchange Services (P.O. Box 2015, South Burlington, VT 05401, 802-985-3825); Home Exchange International (22458 Ventura Boulevard, Suite E, Woodland Hills, CA 91364, 818-992-8990); InterService Home Exchange (P.O. Box 87, Glen Echo, MD 20812, 301-229-7567); International Home Exchange Service (P.O. Box 3975, San Francisco, CA 94119, 415-382-0300); Vacation Exchange Club (12006 11th Ave., Unit 12, Youngtown, AZ 85363, 602-972-2186).

♦ When traveling abroad, pay with your credit card whenever possible. Due to wholesale exchange rates, card companies get better deals than individuals. Those improved rates are passed on to the card holders.

♦ The *Guest Room Directory* lists about 250 Christian homes around the country (coast-to-coast and border-to-border) where travelers are welcome to spend the night free of charge. Many of these homes are in, or near, major cities. Others are in the heart of rural America, offering travelers a drastically different perspective of American life.

The *Guest Room Directory,* listing the families who offer guest rooms and the rules of visitation, is available for $8.95 (plus $1 for shipping) from the Christian Life Workshops (P.O. Box 2250, Gresham, OR 97030).

You'll actually receive three copies of the directory (there is no single-copy price). Use the spare copies as inexpensive but valuable gifts.

♦ Snobs snub them as bed-and-bath pit stops, but smart travelers recognize economy chains as one of the best values in lodging. That's why these chains are by far the fastest growing segment of the hotel industry.

Following is a listing of the 10 largest budget chains in the country and their central reservation numbers. Through the central number you can find out which properties are on course with your travels, inquire about any available specials, get the addresses and phone numbers of actual properties, and make reservations. Sometimes the central reservation numbers offer specials the individual properties don't (e.g., Comfort Inn's 30% senior-citizen discount is offered only through the central reservation number). More often, however, a specific property may offer a special that is not listed in the computers of mission control. The moral: Call both the central reservation number and the specific property to see who's got the deal of the day.

- Comfort Inns, 800-221-2222 (located in 48 states, Canada, Mexico, Europe).
- Days Inns of America, 800-325-2525 (located in 50 states, Canada, Mexico, France, Netherlands).
- Econo Lodges of America, 800-446-6900 (located in 47 states and Canada).
- Hampton Inns, 800-HAMPTON (located in 39 states).
- Hospitality International, 800-251-1962 (includes Red Carpet, Master Hosts, and Scottish Inns, and locations in 33 states).
- La Quinta Motor Inns, 800-531-5900 (located in 29 states).
- Motel 6, 505-891-6161 (located in 42 states).
- Red Roof Inns, 800-THE-ROOF (located in 30 states).
- Super 8 Motels, 800-848-8888 (located in 47 states and Canada).
- Travelodge International, 800-255-3050 (located in 47 states, Mexico, Canada, and Great Britain).

◆ All-suite hotels are more expensive than the economy chains just mentioned, but if you consider the total package price of room *and* board, they can save families money. How so? By using the kitchens that are part of the suites, a family can take its meals in-house rather than out on the town. The money saved on bread more than offsets the higher cost of beds.

Rooms can range from one-room studios with full kitchens for $70-$95 on weekdays (about $50 on weekends) at Residence Inns to multi-room suites for four at the

Embassy Suites Hotels for $70-$140 on weekdays ($70 to $90 on weekends).

- Embassy Suite Hotels, 800-EMBASSY (located in 28 states, some kitchen appliances, full breakfast included in price).
- Guest Quarters Suite Hotels, 800-424-2900 (located in 15 states, outfitted with some kitchen appliances).
- Quality Suites, 800-221-2222 (located in 18 states, some kitchen appliances supplied, breakfast included).
- Radisson Hotels International, 800-333-3333 (located in 17 states, cooking appliances vary with the properties, breakfast usually supplied).
- Residence Inn by Marriott, 800-331-3131 (located in 41 states, full kitchens available, continental breakfast included).

♦ Entertainment Publications (2025 Butterfield Road, Troy, MI 48084, 800-477-3234 or 800-521-9640) compiles discount coupon books for travelers. These books offer hotel rooms at half price (50% off the rack rates) and two-for-one coupons that can be used at restaurants, tourist attractions, and entertainment clubs.

Discount coupon books are assembled for 115 major cities around North America, including San Francisco, Los Angeles, San Diego, Seattle, Las Vegas, Houston, Chicago, Detroit, New York, Philadelphia, Orlando, Miami, Toronto, Montreal, and Vancouver. The books range in price from $25 to $40 and often pay for themselves the first time you use a coupon. Call the toll-free numbers listed previously for information or orders.

Entertainment Publications also assembles more general books for vacationers and business people who travel in wider circles. *Travel America Half Price* ($33 with shipping and handling), *Half Price Europe* ($42 with shipping and handling), and *Travel North America at Half Price*, ($28 with shipping and handling) all offer coupons for half-price hotel rates, and two-for-one coupons at attractions and restaurants in many cities.

While coupon books are available throughout the year for most locations, some cities with a brisk tourist trade sell out early each year. If you're sure you'll be using a particular book for business or pleasure, order it in October when the new edition hits the market.

♦ The Entertainment books just mentioned have a coupon in the back allowing you to purchase up to three other books in the Entertainment series at half price. If you will be ordering several books during the year, order just one book first to get that coupon, then order the rest. And if you really want to get the books on the cheap, buy your first book using the coupon given to you by a friend who already owns an Entertainment book.

♦ AAA members who are exploring their state or region will benefit from the free *Tour Books* of the states they intend to visit (get them from the local AAA office). These books rate different hotels and restaurants you'll find along your driving route. Use them in conjunction with the Entertainment books just mentioned—the *Tour Book* will help you find hotels and restaurants to meet your tastes, and the half-price tickets from the Entertainment books will make them affordable.

There are but two ways of paying debt: increase of industry in raising income, increase of thrift in laying out.

Thomas Carlyle

Household Tips

We had owned the house for only two months when the plumber socked me with a $750 bill to fix the broken sewage pump. Three weeks later when the pump failed again and raw sewage seeped under the house, I worried that we owned the set for the filming of *Money Pit 2*.

I called the plumber. He refused to guarantee his work in one breath and in the next told me he could pay a visit if I could pay his bill. I told old Toby that if he drowned in sewage tomorrow it wouldn't be soon enough—or words to that effect. Fortunately, I had followed advice I now pass on to you: When professionals work on your home, watch what they do and ask questions—you'll be better prepared for a repeat performance of the problem. Now I knew how to drain the sewage tank, disconnect the wiring and piping, and where to service the pump.

Into the tank I went, muttering filthy words. Distracted by my foul humor, I loosened the check valve that kept the neighbor's effluent from trespassing. Pandemonium exploded around me when the valve burst off the pipe and a firehose of raw sewage shot into the tank. Sewage in the face, sewage in the hair, sewage flowing over the top of my hip waders. Through it all, a newspaper headline preoccupied me, "Man drowns in home sewage tank." It would have pleased Toby.

Well, sometimes that's how the fight against entropy goes. I did manage to fish the valve out of the bottom of the tank and jam it back on the pipe. I managed to fix my pump and it cost me only sludge in the face and a tiny bout of hepatitis (joke). Since then I've managed to tame the money pit in a more gentlemanly fashion. Following are my tips for muzzling the monster.

♦ **Swinging doors.** Interior doors that swing open or closed by themselves don't need an expert or an exorcist to fix them. Remove the hinge pin from one hinge (place a nail in the bottom of the hinge and force the pin up by tapping up on the nail with a hammer), lay the pin on a concrete floor, and bend it *slightly* by striking it once or twice with a hammer. Reinsert the pin and the swinging will be gone or greatly reduced. If the door still swings slowly, repeat the procedure with the other hinge pin.

♦ **Rattling doors.** The racket of a rattling door gets aggravating after a while, especially when it awakens you. To fix the problem, use a screwdriver or pliers to bend out the tongue of the strike plate so that it exerts pressure against the edge of the door. Open and close the door a few times to fine tune how much to uncurl the tongue.

♦ **Non-latching doors.** It gets embarrassing when you're on the throne and, surprise, the door pops open. Inspect the hinges first and tighten any loose screws. If the problem persists, the door latch is not sliding properly into the hole on the strike plate. By closely examining the latch as you close the door, you can usually see which edge of the strike plate's hole is binding the latch. Use a file to enlarge the hole so that the latch slides in.

♦ **Clogged gutters.** Cleaning the gutters is one of those menial chores needing attention several times a year. If you're unable to prance about on the roof or yoyo up and down a ladder, you'll hire someone for the job. Minimize the problem (and expense) by laying long strips of plastic mesh like *Gutter Guard* over the top of your gutters. The product is inexpensive (about $2.50 for a 25-foot by 6-inch roll) and dramatically reduces the number of gutter cleanings needed.

♦ **Mossy roofs.** To reshingle an average three-bedroom house costs about $2000 for asphalt shingles and twice that for cedar. Given that the maximum life of an asphalt roof is about 20 years and cedar about 40 years, your roof depreciates about $100 a year. But let moss flourish up on high and it can easily suck five years of life away from your roof, meaning you've wasted $500. Lining the crown of your house with zinc stripping will keep moss from growing, and at a cost of $30 to $50 to line the average house, it's a good investment.

Note: if you've already got a pasture of moss growing on the roof, nuke it with a moss-kill product, then use the stripping to keep the moss from returning.

◆ **Squeaky floors.** Squelch creaks in wooden floors by sprinkling the offending joints with talcum powder. Let the powder sit a few days so it works into the joint.

◆ **Floor protection.** Prevent rocking chairs from scratching or denting hardwood floors by lining the bottom of the rockers with masking tape.

◆ **Exterior painting.** Most houses can be spray-painted in a fraction of the time needed to do the job by hand. With a good sprayer, even a novice can spread two coats of paint on an average-sized house (1400 to 1600 square feet) in a long day, provided the house is masked and all the necessary supplies are on hand.

Unless you frequently need a sprayer, rent it. This costs considerably less than buying an inexpensive sprayer, and rather than using amateur equipment worth $200, you'll have professional equipment worth $2000 that does faster, better work.

Rent sprayers from paint stores (see "Paint-Retail" in the *Yellow Pages*)—they rent equipment cheaply, because they hope to make money selling you paint and supplies. Call four or five stores. In 1991 my local paint stores rented similar-quality equipment from $45 to $65 a day. Rental shops were notably more expensive than paint shops. The same applies to the power washers used to prepare a house for painting: paint shops are cheaper than rental outfits.

◆ **Reusing solvents.** Dirty solvents like paint thinner and turpentine can be stored in a closed jar. After several days the contaminants (like paint) will settle out and the clear fluid on top can be poured off and used again.

◆ **Interior painting.** Amateurs who mask the molding, fixtures, and the floor below a wall will save time over those trying to free-hand it. They'll do a better job and save money, too, by not damaging fixtures, woodwork, molding, carpets...

On nonporous fixtures, an inexpensive mask is to rub petroleum jelly along the boundary line of the fixture. The jelly keeps the paint from hardening on the fixture.

The petroleum jelly trick works on window panes also, although people with a steady hand may find it faster to paint with a 1-inch or 1-1/2 inch sash brush (one with slanted bristles) and to use a razor blade to scrape off any mistakes. Scrape after the paint has hardened but before it cures.

◆ **Touch up jobs.** Use a *Q-tip* dipped in paint as a disposable brush for touch up jobs (inside or outside). You won't waste paint on the job or solvent cleaning up.

◆ **Extending paint life.** With an opened can, transfer the paint into the smallest can (or glass jar) available to reduce air contact. Make sure the seal is completely air tight by turning the can up-side down for several minutes and checking for leakage.

Adding 3 to 4 tablespoons of mineral spirits to the top of oil-based paint can also helps seal out the air. Don't mix in the spirits until you're ready to use the paint again.

◆ **Cutting holes in plywood and sheet metal.** If you own a power drill but not a saber saw, get a *Saw Drill*, a special bit with teeth on the shank. It does not cut with the precision of a saber saw but works fine for such chores as shaping holes in the backs of cabinets where electrical wires will run. And its low cost beats buying a saber saw.

Made by Vermont American (Box 340, Lincolnton, NC 28093, 704-735-7464), get it at a hardware store.

◆ **Damaged countertops.** Repair burns and chips in your counters with *Seamfil* (Kampel Enterprises, 8930 Carlisle Rd., Wellsville, PA 17365, 717-432-9688). The kit comes with filler, a wide assortment of colors, mixing charts to match colors, and additives for a glossy finish (it cures naturally to a matte finish).

A cheaper alternative is to fill small nicks and cracks with a wood-patching compound like *Zar Wood Patch* (United Gibsonite Laboratories, Scranton, PA 18501, 717-344-1202). Color the compound to the desired shade with watercolors or acrylic paints from an art-supply store.

Large, deep burns and chips may be difficult to patch adequately. Consider cutting out the damaged area and laying in a stainless-steel insert that will serve as a trivet for hot pots. Just Manufacturing Company (9233 King St., Franklin Park, IL 60131) supplies a variety of self-rimming inserts that will nestle into holes cut into the countertop.

♦ **Painted windows.** Even the Incredible Hulk won't be able to budge a window that's painted closed. Cut the paint between the window frame and the sash with a sharp razor knife or by running a putty knife along the seal and tapping it as necessary with a hammer. Bump the corners of the window frame and the window should open.

♦ **Jammed windows.** Another reason double-hung wood windows stick is from paint build-up in the sash channels. Run a chisel (bevel-side down) through the channel to remove excess paint (move the windows as necessary to scrape the entire channel). Then, with a block of wood that is narrower than the channel, sand with 100-grit sandpaper. Finally, spray the channel with silicone spray or rub on wax.

♦ **Worried about termites?** Their bite is definitely worse than their bark—in fact, you often don't know you have a termite problem until they have chomped holes in your house. Termites cause about $1 billion in damage in the U.S. alone. To ensure these are not your dollars: Relocate all wood piles that are beneath or alongside your house, cover attic vents with small mesh screens, ventilate all crawl spaces, check that the plastic vapor barrier under the house adequately covers the ground, and treat wooden sills on basement windows.

♦ **Old plugs.** Appliances that turn off and on when you jiggle the cord at the outlet need a new plug. Flat cords, with a groove running down the center, are used on most modern appliances. These are easy to fix. Cut off the old plug, push the end of the cord into a snap-on plug from a hardware store, snap the plug closed. Finito.

♦ **Fading furniture and art work.** Furniture or art exposed to high dosages of sunlight will fade quickly. The same ultraviolet (UV) rays that paint our skin red with sunburn, leach colors from pictures and fabrics. Relocate any valuable art so that it receives no direct sunlight. Furniture and less valuable art that is exposed to the sun's eraser can be protected by covering your windows with Gila or Sunshine films made by Courtaulds Performance Films (6615 West Boston Street, Chandler, AZ 85226, 602-961-3220 or 800-528-4481).

These films are not cheap but they'll cost you less than reupholstering the furniture or replacing your art prematurely. And they're not nearly so messy as slathering your possessions with sunscreen.

♦ **Insulating your windows.** The Gila/Sunshine films mentioned previously also increase the R-value of your old windows. These low-emissivity films reflect heat back toward the source: toward the sun in summer and toward your heater in winter. Consequently, they serve to "insulate" your windows.

♦ **Chimney sweeping.** Do this job at least once a winter, twice if you burn regularly. Scrape out the creosote buildup and eliminate the possibility that a hot or sparking fire could cause a chimney fire. Chimney brushes can be purchased at hardware stores and attached to a 10-foot length of aluminum conduit (3/4 in diameter). Tie and tape the brush securely to the pole so you don't accidentally lose it in the chimney—one of my favorite tricks.

♦ **Smoke alarms.** Some insurance companies offer lower premiums for houses protected by smoke detectors. Call your agent. Even if you can't get lower rates, you're foolish to live in a house without smoke alarms. The majority of fire-related deaths, not to mention a vast amount of property damage, happen at night in houses lacking alarms to awaken occupants.

Vacuum your alarm once or twice a year to remove dust that can desensitize the units. Change the batteries yearly and test the units every month or two.

♦ **Sticky locks.** Lubricate household and car locks by rubbing pencil lead (graphite) on a key and inserting the key several times into the lock.

♦ **Clogged sinks.** Try freeing them with a toilet plunger. If that fails and you own a wet/dry shop vacuum, suck the clot out. Alternate pouring hot and cold water down the drain, putting the nozzle down (or over) the drain, wrapping a wet towel around the opening of the drain (to improve suction), and turning on the vacuum. People without a vacuum can try *Drain King*, a ballooning device that attaches to the end of a garden hose. The balloon seals off the drain while the nozzle generates pressure to blow out the clot.

For additional tips about freeing clogged plumbing see the *Formula* chapter.

♦ **More storage.** If you have an uninsulated garage with exposed studs (no wallboards), nail horizontal boards between the studs to make shelves. Tilt the shelves toward the wall 10 to 15 degrees to keep items from falling off.

♦ **Filling large holes in wallboard.** Place a number of drywall screws around the perimeter of the hole. These screws resemble spokes of a wheel, with part of the screw penetrating the rim of the hole and the remainder of the shaft (and head of the screw) radiating into the void of the hole. Next, fill the hole with wood patch, plaster, or spackling compound. The screws serve to anchor the patch firmly in place.

♦ **Scratched furniture.** Scrapes in wood can be hidden with beeswax or with crayons, shoe polish, or felt-tip markers matching the wood color.

For valuable furniture, hide scratches with better quality touch-up pens available through large furniture dealers. Or order these supplies by mail through the Wood Finishing Supply Company (100 Throop Street, Palmyra, NY 14522, 315-597-3743) or The Woodworkers' Store (21801 Industrial Blvd., Rogers, MN 55343, 612-428-2199).

♦ **Loose furniture joints.** One loose joint leads to another so fix furniture whenever you notice a problem. Glue joints with yellow or white wood glue, don't nail or screw it. Be sure to remove old glue—glue adheres by absorbing into the wood and attaching itself to the wood fibers. Always put joints being glued under pressure with clamps or some substitute for clamps: elastic tie down straps (bungee cords) wrapped tightly around furniture, hose clamps around split dowels, and rubber bands around joints can all provide pressure.

♦ **White rings on furniture.** These water marks have discolored the finish but not the underlying wood. Use mineral oil (or baby oil) and a soft rag to remove furniture wax. Then, using a new rag, rub the ring with isopropyl alcohol. Rub fast and gently if the finish becomes tacky. A stubborn ring that won't lift may need light sanding with 600-grit sandpaper and baby oil. Wax the area when finished.

Note: Before working on a very visible surface, test this procedure on a hidden part of the furniture.

♦ **Dented wood.** Lift minor dents from wood by covering them with a wet rag and briefly laying an iron (set on high) over the rag.

♦ **Furniture nicks.** Furniture patch stick (from the hardware store) will fill in minor nicks. Rub wax over the patch and buff.

♦ **Deteriorating dishwasher racks.** The plastic-coated racks in dishwashers can cost upwards of $150 to replace, which means you better hang onto them as long as possible. Use a liquid-rubber compound (see *Repair* chapter) to coat any part of the rack that is peeling or rusting.

♦ **Stud finder.** In another book it might be a job for Christie Brinkley, here it's a job for an electric razor. Turn on the razor and put it against the wall. Move the razor and when the tone increases in pitch, you've found the stud. Or so you hope. On some walls the tone remains constant, so employ one of these other tricks:
  - Electrical outlets and switches are usually attached to a stud. Turn off the power, remove the cover plate, use a nail and hammer to determine which side of the electrical box is attached to the stud. Other studs should be located at 16-inch intervals from this one.
  - As a last resort, drill into the wall in an inconspicuous spot (behind a couch or along the baseboard) with

a thin bit. Once the bit penetrates the wallboard, probe left and right, feeling for the stud. From one hole you can explore a three-inch-wide area.

♦ **Tape measure life extender.** Fully extend your tape measurer and give it a shot of silicone spray. Good lubrication will more than double the product's life.

♦ **Nail holes.** In college days I kept the landlord from charging me for nail holes left in the wall by filling them with cream-type toothpaste. *Crest* works great for light blue walls, *Colgate* for white walls. Of course, you can use spackling paste, too. Color the paste with food color to match the wall.

♦ **Enlarged screw holes.** If the screw no longer grips the hole, place a glue-covered wooden sliver (tooth pick or matchstick) in the hole along with the screw. This works regardless of whether the hole is in wood, foam, plaster, or drywall.

♦ **Carpet dents.** After rearranging the furniture you can eliminate flattened areas of carpet by brushing up the matted carpet with a coin. Then place an ice cube on the flattened carpet. The cube will help swell the flattened fibers without wetting the remainder of the carpet.

Another approach is to steam the dent after rubbing it with a coin. Hold an iron a few inches from the carpet and steam the dent for a minute. Repeat as needed.

♦ **Axes.** When putting on a new handle, keep it from loosening by coating the blade-end of the handle and the hole in the axe head with epoxy glue. Protect the throat of the shaft below the axe head from missed blows by wrapping the area with cord. After making a length of coils about four inches long, wrap them with tape.

♦ **Appliance noise.** Silence noisy refrigerators, washers, and dishwashers by sliding one or two thicknesses of rubber-backed carpet under them. This dampens vibration and noise. Carpet stores sell scraps for almost nothing.

♦ **Heater filters.** Experts recommend changing the air filter in central heating systems on a monthly basis. Usually the filter doesn't actually need replacement, it just needs cleaning. Take out the filter, lay an old window screen over it, and vacuum the filter clean (both sides). This trick will double or triple the life of each filter.

♦ **Hiring a pro.** Use the *Yellow Pages*, suggestions from friends, recommendations from hardware store managers, building-supply stores, or the classified ads to find expert help. Ask several people to bid on the job. When I needed a ditch in my driveway repaved, the quotes ranged from $125 to $450. When I wanted tree stumps ground, the spread was $80 to $200. Such discrepancies are the rule, not the exception.

Don't automatically choose the lowest bidder. Do your homework to verify the contractor's credentials. Call several references. Check that he/she is bonded and insured and ask to see a copy of his or her license or bond. Call the Better Business Bureau to check whether complaints have been filed against the contractor. Heed your intuition if the low-ball pitcher strikes you as a lowlife.

Regardless of who you hire, sign an agreement stipulating the work to be done, the materials to be used, the time frame for starting and completion, the terms of the warranty, an explanation of how debris will be removed, a description of work you will perform, the cost, and terms of payment. Also, make sure a clause is included stating that the contract may not be changed unless a written amendment, signed by both parties, is added to the contract.

This may smack of paranoia but, because these professions attract a fair share of ungentlemanly people, most homeowners will get stung at least once by a gentleman's agreement (witness my experience with the plumber). Don't be afraid to negotiate and modify the contractor's agreement or to draft your own if the contractor seems content to work on a verbal agreement.

Regarding payment, *never* pay the full amount up front. Always keep a sizeable balance (at least 50%) that will be paid only when the work is complete. Before you pay in full, you also want all the lien waivers in hand. If for any reason you believe the contractor may not be paying his subcontractors and suppliers, withhold final payment or pay the suppliers and subcontractors yourself. Otherwise liens on your property could force you into something really ugly—paying for goods and services twice.

♦ **Solicitors.** It is risky business to use operations peddling their services door-to-door—say an asphalter, roofer, or radon tester who "is in your area" and who can offer you an amazing special today. You lack time to comparison shop to determine how good their "special" is. You lose the advantage of having several professionals look at the job and give you their opinions of what you do and don't need. You're not even sure if a door-to-door operation has a permanent address where you can lodge a complaint.

Should you succumb to such pitches, at least draw up a contract (as described previously) and don't pay until you are satisfied with all aspects of the job.

♦ **Quality work at lower prices.** Many contractors figure their time at $40 an hour, so finding one who agrees to let you help out can save you lots of cash. The bulk of the work a contractor does he'll do faster without you. Stay out of his hair. But most jobs have affiliated chores that any flunky can handle; these are the ones you want to negotiate over. Find out how much the contractor will shave off if you do the:

- Preparation. Perhaps there is siding, a porch or a driveway to be demolished before the contractor's work begins. Or maybe holes must be excavated for foundation footings or fence posts.

- Insulating and drywalling. In a new addition, installing the wall and ceiling insulation is easy (but itchy) work a contractor may be happy to escape. Nailing up the drywall may be another good job for you (but let a pro tape the joints).

- Painting. Any exterior or interior work you paint can amount to big savings.

- Clean-up. This is one job you can finish as quickly as the contractor and, as no one likes to pick up after himself, this is a job many contractors will delegate. If there are materials to be hauled away, negotiate to load the appropriate bins and let the contractor dispose of them.

- Landscaping. Backfilling dirt around the foundation or into ditches, replanting shrubs and grass are simple but time-intensive jobs you should consider doing.

♦ **More information.** Most home projects are not difficult to do yourself *if* you obtain good information. Such knowledge can come from the library or hardware stores—handyman magazines and books abound. Talk to knowledgeable friends and neighbors. Or cultivate a hardware-store guru whose opinion you trust and who can tell you what tools and supplies will be needed for home projects.

Magazines worth their subscription price in the money-saving tips you'll glean include: *The Family Handyman* (Subscriber Service Dept., Box 1956, Marion, OH 43302) and *Home Mechanix* (P.O. Box 54320, Boulder, CO 80322-4320). Both give you information on almost every imaginable home project: installing a TV antenna, turning broom closets into pantries, converting attics into livable space, installing skylights, controlling noise in your house, adding showers, making your own kitchen cabinets, adding a garage to the house... The November/December issue of *The Family Handyman* includes an index of all the subjects the magazine has covered in the last five years. Preview these magazines at the library.

♦ **Cross reference.** Other chapters in this book include additional tips to tame the money pit. See *Heating* for lowering home energy expenses, *Lawns* for yard care, *Stains* for maintaining your carpets.

Our houses are such unwieldy property that we are often imprisoned rather than housed in them.

Henry David Thoreau

Houses (Selling)

Houses. For many of us, they are the biggest investment of our lives. So come selling time, we should do what
we can to reap the rewards of our investment. This is a
domain where attention to details can add up to thousands
of dollars. Use the following tips: They will help you get
what your house is worth—or maybe even more.

♦ Put your house on the market early and give
yourself many months to find a buyer. Without time on
your side, you may be forced to drop the price below
market price to unload it.

Spring is a good time to place your home on the
market, as summer is the high-volume season. If you have
any choice in the matter, avoid selling in late autumn and
winter when the market freezes.

♦ First impressions count—with dates, bosses, and
yes, houses. Money spent on little projects that smarten up
the house's exterior will reap a big payback. Examples:
paint the trim and shutters, wash the siding, replace loose
or bent shingles on the roof, clean the gutters, repair holes
in screen doors, prune the shrubbery, mow and rake the
lawn, paint a rusty mailbox, replace broken window panes,
plant flowers by the front door.

♦ First impressions formed inside the house are
equally important. Get rid of the clutter that makes any
room feel small (put possessions in storage if necessary).
Keep the rooms tidy and clean. Make the house feel
brighter by painting the trim, washing the walls, replacing
dead light bulbs, or even using light bulbs of higher

wattage. Clean the carpets. Boil coffee or spices to give the home an inviting aroma.

Because you are too familiar with your house, get friends to inspect it and ask them to share their impressions, point out the defects noticed, and mention bad smells.

♦ Buyers give bathrooms and kitchens special scrutiny. Scrub the porcelain fixtures so they are shiny and work on removing any mineral stains. Repair the leaks in all faucets and toilets. Replace stained shower curtains. Eliminate clutters. Keep all appliances clean. Do what you must to make both rooms appear clean, large, and bright.

♦ Experts say that buyers view needed repairs very harshly and will subtract much more from their offer than it costs to fix problems. Consequently every $100 a seller invests in minor repairs of lost cabinet pulls, cracked glass, jammed doors, broken switches, holes in the wall, missing molding, scratched woodwork, etc., will keep the offers jacked up by $200.

That's good incentive to get the house in top shape before it hits the market.

♦ Give everyone who views the house a fact sheet. This points out the special qualities of the house. The sheet also helps potential buyers remember the house later, especially if the sheet includes a sketch or picture.

♦ As a seller, it pays to have your house inspected by a professional before placing it on the market. An inspection may uncover problems that, if left unfixed, could scare away a potential buyer or could undermine the asking price. A good inspection report also eases buyers' fears about the house—and a lower threshold of fear translates into a higher selling price.

♦ Increasing numbers of firms are selling houses for a fixed fee instead of a commission. That fee varies depending on the house and the firm, but usually the cost is about *half* what you pay an agency working on commission.

A good set-fee firm should handle the advertising, signs, and fact sheets; place the house in the multiple listings; perform a competitive market analysis (CMA);

qualify the buyer and help him or her with financing; negotiate the best price for you; and control the closing proceedings. And it should charge you only if the house sells. But don't take anything for granted. Ask about all services rendered and about the fees involved.

One main operational difference with many set-fee firms is that you may be required to show the house. This may require more time, but can work to your advantage, too, since no one knows your house better.

Help-U-Sell is among the oldest and largest set-fee firms and has offices around the country. Call 800-669-4357 for information and the number of their local office.

♦ Selling your own house can save you a bundle (6% to 7% of the selling price) but it's no breeze. It's time consuming and, because there is much to know, you can make expensive mistakes. However, if the big savings tempt you—savings that could amount to $10,000 on a $150,000 house—do your homework. Go to the library (or bookstore) and check out books like *How to Sell Your Home in the '90s With Less Stress and More Profit*. Also check the *Yellow Pages* (under Real Estate) and make some calls to determine how firms like *For Sale By Owner* can help you through the process (and at what cost).

The penny is well spent that gets a pound.
English proverb

Insurance

They've got 1001 different plans, 1002 ways to confuse you, 1003 ways to scare you, and then, when you actually file a claim, 1004 reasons not to pay you.

All of which make insurance a difficult product to buy. All of which make you wonder whether you've ever got enough of the stuff. And all of which contribute to the fact that you're probably paying more than you should.

HOMEOWNER'S INSURANCE

♦ In your insurance dealings, remember the Prime Rule: Insure yourself against large or disastrous losses, but not against small risks you can afford to pay out of pocket. Insurance is, after all, a losing proposition—over the years most everyone pays much more than they collect. The money you never see again finances the expenses and profits of the insurance company.

Applying this rule to homeowner's insurance, you should increase the deductible on your policy to $500 or even $1000. Compared to a policy with a $250 deductible, your premiums will be 10% and 25% (respectively) lower. Over time, statistics strongly indicate that these discounted rates will save you money.

♦ Refuse many specialized coverages available through your homeowner's policy—they often insure you against small risks you should cover yourself. Options to refuse include: stolen credit cards (card companies insure you against this already), fire department surcharges, debris removal, removal of damaged property, damage to vegetation (trees, shrubs, plants).

♦ Get the best value from your policy by forgoing market-value coverage of your home's content in preference to replacement-value coverage. It may cost $1500 to replace a stolen computer, but if you received market-value for a 4-year-old machine you'd collect only about $350. Replacement-value coverage of your possessions costs 10% to 15% more, but most budget-minded experts believe it provides better value for your insurance dollars.

♦ Know the true replacement value of your home and insure it for this amount against fire, wind loss, and acts of God. Underinsuring your home against its true replacement cost sets up a disaster scenario. Overinsuring it wastes money because, upon loss, you will be paid only the replacement value.

Remember, too, that you need to insure only the structures and possessions on your property. The land itself, which makes a huge contribution to your home's appraised value, doesn't need to be insured.

♦ Renters should (but often don't) know that landlords are not responsible for possessions stolen from or damaged in your apartment. Protect yourself with renter's insurance. As explained previously, opt for replacement-value coverage of your possessions.

CAR INSURANCE

♦ The type of car you own can *greatly* affect the cost of your auto insurance. Expensive cars are expensive to insure because they are expensive to fix. Meanwhile, some cars—notably sports cars—are in more accidents and are the proud recipients of a performance-car surcharge.

Don't put much stock in what car salesmen tell you about the cost of insurance—they're trying to make a sale, not enlighten you. Insurance agents routinely deal with customers who were misinformed by salesmen.

Call your insurance agent or look through *The Complete Car Cost Guide* (IntelliChoice, Inc., 800-227-2665) to learn what it will cost to insure the different vehicles you might purchase.

♦ Car insurance is no different from any other commodity; different companies charge different rates for the same basic coverage. Most policies are quite competitive, but in any given metropolitan area, the best shopper may pay half what the worst shopper pays for the same coverage. This equals a difference of hundreds of dollars.

Also, because many underwriters are always reworking their numbers in the attempt to become more competitive, the company offering the best deal can change from year to year. Every few years let several companies know the particulars of your policy and ask for their bid. Better yet, if you work with an independent insurance agent (one who handles the policies of many different companies), have him or her do it for you.

A few companies that consistently offer competitive rates include: Aetna Life & Casualty Group (203-273-0123), Allstate Insurance Group (708-402-5000), American International Group (302-761-3000), Geico Corporation Group (301-986-3000), Hartford Insurance Group (203-547-5000), Nationwide Insurance Group (614-249-7111), Travelers Insurance Group (203-277-0111), USAA Insurance Group (512-498-2211), USF&G (301-547-3000).

♦ What coverage should you get for your car? Most important is liability insurance covering bodily injury to others and damage to the property of others. Most people will also want comprehensive insurance to safeguard against non-collision loss (fire, theft) and collision insurance to fix cars damaged in an accident.

♦ How much bodily-injury liability insurance should you carry? Charles Givens, author of *More Wealth Without Risk*, conducted a study on the size of liability settlements in Florida (one of the lawsuit capitals of the country) and discovered the average settlement for *non-alcohol* related auto accidents was under $25,000. Non-drinking risk-takers willing to play the odds, will usually get away with carrying much less bodily-injury liability insurance than you are advised to carry.

Nonetheless, it is a standard recommendation (and probably a wise one for people who have accumulated ample assets) to insure themselves to the tune of their net worth.

Beyond that amount, the value of bodily-liability insurance drops sharply as it is extremely rare for juries to award settlements for non-alcohol-related accidents that exceed the defendant's net worth.

♦ Charles Givens recommends, however, that people who sometimes drive under the influence buy as much liability insurance as they can afford: Juries have no mercy when alcohol contributes to fatal or injury accidents. Settlements in these suits can be in the multi-millions and average around $250,000.

♦ If you have the good fortune of amassing a fortune, you'll want to protect yourself with more liability insurance; otherwise a jury perceiving you as a deep pocket could make you a victim of your own pocketbook. The smart way to fortify the liability shield isn't to add coverage independently to your auto and homeowner's policy but to purchase an umbrella policy that protects you on both fronts.

These policies are inexpensive (around $150 for $1 million) but are not always well advertised (insurance agents don't make much on them). Ask for them. To qualify for a personal umbrella policy, you may need to carry both your homeowner's and auto insurance with the same underwriter (not mandatory with all companies). You will also probably need certain liability limits on both your auto and homeowner's insurance (e.g., $300,000 and $200,000 respectively).

♦ Keep the Prime Rule of insurance in mind when deciding the deductibles on your collision and comprehensive insurance. The premium paid for a deductible of $200 averages 20% to 25% more than a deductible of $500 and up to 40% more than a deductible of $1000. Low deductibles cost so much more that over the years you would have to be in multiple accidents to make them a better buy than a high deductible.

♦ Once the blue-book value of your vehicle sinks to $1600 or $1700, scrap the collision and comprehensive insurance. Now, the return from a stolen or totalled car is not enough to justify the cost of the coverage. Play the odds. A few people will get burned (though not on a disastrous level), but the multitudes will come out smiling.

♦ Keep a low profile with your insurance company. If you place a claim on your collision or comprehensive—no matter how small—expect your *entire* car insurance premium to take a hike (up to 25% in some states) the following year. You'll pay the higher premium for three to five years, at which point a perfect driving record will eliminate the surcharge. If, however, misfortune forces you to place another claim before the slate is wiped clean, an additional surcharge will be added on top of the preexisting surcharge. These piggybacking surcharges can give your insurance premium more zeros than the national debt.

Avoid making claims until the damage done exceeds $500. Otherwise, the insurance company may well take back more in surcharges than they paid out in damages.

♦ Every driving violation on your record increases the likelihood of an increased premium. If given the opportunity to cancel a ticket by visiting traffic school, do it.

♦ Cars titled to young adults (ages 16 to 25) are an ugly sight when it comes time to ante up for insurance. When children want to be independent and insist on placing cars in their names, so be it—let them see if they can pay the inflated insurance premium. If you're footing the bill, however, bandage unnecessary hemorrhaging by putting your child's car in your name and insuring him or her under your policy as a driving-age child.

♦ A variety of car-insurance options violate the Prime Rule of insurance because they insure you against small risks. Avoid such coverages as emergency road service (emergency towing and roadside service) and specialty coverage of your audio equipment.

♦ A variety of other options should be bypassed because they violate the Second Rule of Insurance: Avoid policies that duplicate your coverage. Duplication can boost insurance bills big-time without significantly improving the quality of your protection.

Medical coverage bought through your auto insurance is one such example. It insures you and your passengers against doctor and hospitalization fees that were incurred because of a car accident. Your health insurance, however, should already provide this protection. And your passengers should be protected by both their own health insurance and your liability coverage.

Payment of funeral expenses found in uninsured motorist coverage is duplicated by the life insurance you should be carrying, as is death and dismemberment auto coverage. Coverage of lost wages is best handled through a disability plan, not through auto insurance.

◆ Some companies offer low mileage discounts if you drive less than a predetermined number of miles each year. If yours is a stay-at-home car, ask your agent about this.

◆ Also ask your agent about other discounts for which you may qualify. Insurance companies offer discounts for some or all of the following: vehicles with automatic seat belts, air bags, anti-theft security systems, or anti-lock brakes; drivers over 50 and those with perfect driving records over the last three years; students with good grades. If you don't ask, you may not receive.

◆ See the *Car Rental* chapter for rental-insurance tips.

LIFE INSURANCE

Life insurance is a wonderful misnomer. It should really be called "death insurance" because the intent is to protect family members who are financially dependent on you in the event of the Big Bummer.

The long-range goal of a family's wage earner is not simply to pay the bills but to build an estate with assets and investments capable of supporting the family once the wage earner is unable (or unwilling) to work. Each year the amount of death insurance required decreases because, theoretically, the growing estate should be drawing closer to the point of self-sufficiency. Until that time, however, death insurance is a stop-gap measure that leaves the family financially secure in the event that the wage earner fills a coffin before adequately filling the coffers.

◆ Through all this you may be asking, "What family?" If you're unmarried and are supporting no one other than yourself, you don't need life insurance. End of discussion.

Well, it should be the end of the discussion. Unfortunately, a quarter of all life insurance is sold to single people with no dependents. If that's you, cancel (or don't renew) your policy.

Pick up a policy later if you pick up some dependents.

◆ Another 10% to 15% of all life insurance covers children. Ridiculous. Life insurance should be bought for the wage earners upon whom the rest of the family depend. Okay, if your progeny is Macaulay Culkin or Brook Shields, you insure him or her. For 99.9% of the child population, however, the expense is a misappropriation of family funds.

♦ If you are a member of the venerable group known as DINKs (dual income, no kids) death insurance may again be unnecessary. Presumably both partners have careers and are able to support themselves. In fact, if your significant other suggests you take out life insurance, watch your back. Perhaps your beloved wishes to "arrange a little accident."

♦ Most whole life insurance, universal life insurance, and single-premium whole life insurance are a poor use of your insurance dollars. They provide death insurance but at inflated prices. The secondary benefits these policies tout (like savings and investment plans, college funds, tax shelters, or sets of Ginzu knives) are usually smoke screens to obscure the fact that you're getting taken.

True, some whole life and universal policies do give a reasonable return on your money, but if you buy inexpensive term insurance and put the money saved in a *good* investment (e.g., a mutual fund), you'll outearn the best of these policies. Meanwhile you'll avoid some truly horrible policies that literally rob you of the interest your money should be making for you.

♦ The least expensive insurance you can purchase is term insurance. This is death insurance pure and simple: You pay $170 a year, for example, and your beneficiary receives $100,000 if you check into the Pearly Gates Motel. This can cost 75% less than the mumbo-jumbo policies noted above and buys you the same death insurance. And if you take the money saved and sink it into a real investment (not a topic this book discusses), you might actually pay for your kid's college tuition when that financially tragic day arrives.

Several types of term insurance are available to you. Decreasing term insurance, in which payments are the same each year but the face value of the insurance drops, tends to be overpriced. That leaves annually renewable term (ART) policies and level premium term (LPT) policies as the choice buys for bargain hunters.

Annually renewable term insurance is often the cheapest option. Once you qualify for the insurance, renewal is guaranteed the following year if you pay the premium—a premium that increases every year.

Level premium term insurance lasts a given period (e.g., five, seven, 10, or 20 years)—and your payment and payoff remain the same during each year of the policy.

♦ Initially, annually renewable term (ART) insurance is likely to be cheaper than level premium term (LPT) insurance. But because the premium of your ART policy increases every year, it will typically overtake the fixed premium of your LPT plan.

There is a way around this. If you remain healthy and are physically able to qualify for a new ART policy, switch underwriters every three to five years. By sticking with the same underwriter year after year, you get stuck with higher and higher premiums.

It's the old loss-leader scenario. The insurance company entices you on board with a low come-on. Then, they up the rates each year, hoping that the increase between any two years won't justify jumping ship.

Which is exactly what you should do after about four years. By then, someone else's loss-leader will look much greener than where you're sitting.

♦ Purchasing an adequate amount of term insurance and disability insurance gives you the coverage supplied by credit life insurance and credit disability insurance at lower prices. Therefore, credit life insurance (where upon death, the borrower's loans are paid off), and credit disability insurance (where upon permanent disability, the borrower's loans are paid off) should both be considered unnecessary duplicate coverage.

MEDICAL INSURANCE

♦ If the daily commute doesn't kill you, paying your medical insurance might. Most people opt for a major-medical policy with a $100 or $500 deductible. Then, as medical expenses above the deductible roll in, they pay 10% to 20% of the expenses incurred. For all this "coverage" people pay thousands of dollars per year.

Health maintenance organizations (HMOs) work a little differently. Typically, an HMO charges a flat fee, no deductible, and an average payment of $5 per visit. In return, most medical conditions, emergencies, and visits are fully covered.

Whether an HMO saves you money depends on your location, the size of your family, and whether you want blanket coverage for every medical expense and emergency. For my family, the cost of the local HMO is just slightly higher than the traditional major-medical plans from companies like Blue Shield but provides more comprehensive coverage. In other parts of the country, reports show that families wanting 100% coverage of their family can save hundreds of dollars by using an HMO.

♦ There is a legitimate argument that many families——particularly young, healthy ones—may not be using their insurance dollars to best effect buying 100% coverage. A young family of four with discounts for healthy habits will pay roughly $4000 per year to an HMO. That's a lot to spend if you end up not needing the medical services.

By shopping the major-medical plans offered through companies like Blue Cross and Blue Shield, you may find a high-deductible traditional policy that, while not as comprehensive, does provide good coverage for major-medical problems at a lower price.

The price of these plans can vary significantly, so research the plans of as many companies as possible. Besides your local Blue Cross and Blue Shield, check the policy possibilities through Benefit Trust Life (708-615-1500), American Republic (800-247-2190), Central States Health and Life (402-397-1111), Time (800-333-1203), Banker's Life and Casualty (312-777-7000), Union Bankers (214-939-0821), Aid Association for Lutherans (414-734-5721), Metropolitan Life (212-578-2211), First National Life (205-832-1850), Pyramid Life (913-722-1110), Golden Rule (817-297-4123), Washington National (708-570-5500), Prudential (201-802-2642).

A good way to learn more about these companies and the quality of their service is to read the August 1990 issue of *Consumer Reports*.

♦ After deciding on a company's major-medical plan, you must decide how large a deductible to carry. It pays to study the numbers and to calculate your yearly medical expenses with each deductible, given a range of hypothetical medical bills (e.g., hypothetical bills of $500, $1000, $2000, $4000, and $6000 per year).

With no medical bills (e.g., no doctor, lab, or hospital fees), your total yearly "medical expenses" equal the annual cost of your health plan. If your medical bills are less than your deductible, your yearly medical expenses equal the annual cost of your health plan, plus the cost of those bills. And if your medical bills are more than the deductible, your yearly medical expenses equal the annual cost of your health insurance, plus the amount of your deductible, plus any percentage of the bills over the deductible that you are required to pay (some companies only pay 80% to 90% of the bills in excess of the deductible).

Sound complicated? It really isn't. Tedious is the word, but I guarantee this exercise is worthwhile. Reread the previous paragraph until the information sinks in, then calculate your total yearly medical expenses using the different deductibles and substituting a range of hypothetical annual medical bills.

When I graphed what I would pay for a standard Blue Shield plan for my family (Figure 1), some money-saving strategies became apparent. Compared to the $250 deductible, the $1000 deductible would save us $1130 at best (if we had no medical bills) and would still save us $440 if one family member incurred medical expenses over $1000 while the other family members remained relatively healthy (having several family members incur large medical bills the same year is unusual). Compared to the $500 deductible, the $1000 deductible would save us $650 at best and $200 if only one family member incurred substantial medical expenses.

What if our luck went sour and all three members of my family used up their personal deductible? The graph I plotted depicting this scenario (not shown) illustrated that the $1000-deductible policy would cost me $900 more that year. However, paying a guaranteed $1130 more *each* year for the $250-deductible to insure my family against the possible (but unlikely) loss of $900, made little sense. We got the $1000-deductible.

What should you do? Examine your medical expenses during the past three to five years. If your family is relatively healthy, you'll save big money by raising your deductible to $1000 (or possibly even $2500). Of course if your family is dealing with chronic health problems and more than one member will be using up his or her deductible, opt for a low deductible.

Figure 1: Medical Costs with Insurance

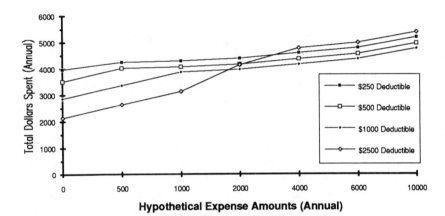

MORE INFORMATION

♦ More detailed information about some of the tactics prescribed in this chapter can be found in such financial books as *More Wealth Without Risk* by Charles Givens and *Money Dynamics for the 1990s* by Venita Van Caspel.

Fortune and misfortune are like the twisted strands of a rope.

Japanese proverb

Lawn Tricks

Ever stop to consider the logic of lawns? We spend money fertilizing and watering them for the privilege of mowing them more often. Then we pay the garbage man top dollar to haul away the clippings we so eagerly nurtured. Ridiculous when you stop to think about it, but such is the mania of Americans proving their superiority to the Goldschmidts next door.

If you're competing with the neighbors to produce the yard most resembling the 18th green at Pebble Beach, you're committed to an eternity of this insanity. But if you can be satisfied with a lawn that is less than PGA quality, yet perfectly healthy, these tips will save money and time.

♦ The easy way to establish a healthy but inexpensive lawn is to cut the grass long. Grass survives by drawing water and nutrients from the soil (a function of the roots) and by photosynthesizing these raw materials into sugars for the plant (a function of the blades). Long roots have access to more water and nutrients (meaning less watering and fertilizing for you) while long blades can produce more energy for the plant (meaning healthier grass).

To get long roots, however, you cannot cut the grass short. The roots will grow deeper only if the blades are allowed to grow higher. Without finding this balance between root and blade growth, all your watering, spraying, and fertilizing still won't make grass truly healthy.

Exactly how high your grass should be cut depends on many variables: climate, soil type, grass variety. As a general rule, grasses that thrive well in the northern climates should be kept around 3 to 3 1/2 inches high during most of the mowing season. Cut your lawn short (about 2 inches) for about a month in spring so sunlight reaches and warms the soil, then readjust your wheels for about a 3-inch cut. In October, as the cold temperatures return and the trees lose their leaves, *gradually* cut the lawn back down to the 2-inch range for the winter.

Southern grasses are different. Bermuda grasses, the most common grasses of the area, are long when kept at 1 1/2 to 2 inches. They can be kept at this height all year long. Thicker grasses like St. Augustine's and many coastal grasses can be cut at 2 to 3 inches throughout the year.

To learn more about your lawn, take a clump to a nursery and have them identify your grass. Then consult a book at the library, like *Building a Healthy Lawn* by Stuart Franklin, to determine the proper mowing height.

♦ Long grass has a multitude of benefits. It shades the soil better than short grass, reducing your watering. This same shade makes it difficult for sun-loving weeds and crabgrass to get a toehold in your yard. Deep, mature roots (which you now know are dependent on long blades) store larger food supplies so grass bounces back more readily from the dormancy of summer droughts and winter. These same food supplies make the plant more vigorous and resistant to weeds and disease. Finally, you won't need to cut long grass as often; short grass grows faster because the plant must use its stored foods to grow back the leaf it needs to photosynthesize.

What about the appearance of a long lawn—won't it look shaggy? No. It's the evenness of the grass more than its length that makes your patch a pasture or a lawn.

♦ An excellent fertilizer for your grass is your grass clippings. They provide a 4-1-3 fertilizer (4% nitrogen, 1% phosphorous, and 3% potash), an ideal formula for your lawn and a lot cheaper than store-bought fertilizers. Mow often and you can let the clippings lie in place. These clippings also create a mulch that keeps the ground wetter (minimizing water bills). Finally, you can save on your trash bill and on the time it takes to mow (lots faster when you don't bother with a catch bag).

♦ Letting the clippings lie can greatly reduce your fertilizing bills but won't eliminate them. Rain and waterings leach nutrients down into the soil, out of the lawn's reach. Occasionally you need to replenish these nutrients, and spring and fall are the best times.

If using synthetic chemical fertilizer, *don't* apply it according to the manufacturer's recommendations. These amounts are more than a yard can use in one shot. The excess nutrients cause the plant to grow too quickly without a corresponding root growth, meaning your grass isn't healthier—it just needs more mowing. Also, when you over-fertilize, many of the nutrients simply wash away with rain or waterings before the grass uses them.

Save money. Adjust your spreader so that the lawn gets only a half or a third of the recommended dosage. Several weeks later, apply another diluted dose.

♦ What's in the fast-acting liquid fertilizer the professional services use? The equivalent to what you find in a box of K-Gro Plant Food (available at K-Mart). Dissolve it in a bucket and apply it from a hose-end sprayer. Costs you about $2 versus the $30 to $40 a pro charges.

♦ If you do collect clippings, don't increase your garbage bill by disposing of the grass in an extra trash can. Compost the debris in a hidden corner of the yard. Mix in leaves, weeds, and vegetable food scraps and you'll produce compost for your flower beds or vegetable garden.

Or simply let the clippings sit and shrink. By autumn their volume will have shrunk dramatically and you'll be able to pack a summer's accumulation of clippings into one or two cans.

♦ With a healthy lawn, you should be able to stick your finger down through the grass and touch soil. With unhealthy lawns, your finger may get stuck in a layer of thatch, a mat lying over the soil which is composed of grass stems, roots, clippings, and runners. If the thatch layer gets 1/2 inch thick, you've got a problem.

Why? First, thick thatch keeps water, fertilizer, and air from reaching the soil. Second, grass roots start growing in the thatch rather than the soil, making the plant very intolerant to heat, frost, and insects.

If you have a thatch problem, collect your clippings until you deal with it. Using a thatching rake is one way to remove the problem. If you don't own a thatch rake, a cheaper—and in many ways superior—solution is to spray your yard with soap and beer.

Beer? It's no misprint. The yeast in beer helps break down thatch into fertilizer your grass can use. Add 1/2 cup of liquid dishwashing detergent per 16 ounces of beer in a hose-end sprayer and spray the lawn on a hot day. Don't worry about the brand of beer—your yard has not cultivated a palate yet so don't spoil it with *Lowenbrau* when *Buckhorn* will do. A six-pack will cover a third of an acre, and leave a can or two for you. Who said yard work is no fun?

♦ Many people think if you don't collect clippings you're guaranteed a thatch problem. Not so. Thatch depends on many variables—type of grass, climate, and how you maintain your lawn. Overfertilizing is one prime cause because it promotes too much growth. Fast-release fertilizers also kill many of the soil bacteria that break thatch down. Frequent, light watering is another cause of thatch; the grass roots are not forced deep in the search for water but are given reason to spread along the surface where they help weave the thatch mat. Pesticides and fungicides also aggravate thatch because they kill and weaken soil bacteria.

To prevent thatch, go light on the fertilizer and use heavy once-a-week waterings. Aerate the lawn to help water saturate the soil, and nurture the soil life that breaks down clippings. Finally, use the beer treatment at the beginning and middle of each summer.

♦ If you agree with the economics and ecologics of letting the clippings lie, a mulching mower reduces the likelihood of thatch. Mulching mowers slice clippings into tiny fragments and distribute the fragments evenly over the yard where they will break down rather than thatch up.

Mulching mowers are expensive, but not inordinately so if you need a new mower anyway. If you pay to have your clippings hauled, the economics look better still. Each quarter-acre of lawn produces 1.5 tons (225 bushels) of clippings per year; with a mulching mower, those clippings go back into the yard, not into the trash.

♦ Aerating can work wonders on a yard by getting water and fertilizer down to the roots. Wear golf spikes whenever you mow or work in the yard and you aerate with no extra time investment. If you don't own golf spikes, pick up a pair at a garage sale or order a pair of strap-on aeration sandals from a gardening catalog.

♦ Whether the moisture comes from the sky or a sprinkler, established lawns require about an inch of water per week to stay green. When the soil gets dry to a depth of 4 to 6 inches (use a trowel or a short length of pipe to get a core sample), it's time to irrigate.

Water slowly so the moisture sinks in rather than runs off. If you do the job properly, the soil will be very moist down to a depth of 6 inches.

You'll use less water (and time) giving the yard one good weekly soaking instead of several sprinkles. A thorough soaking is also better for the grass because, as the soil dries, the plant must maintain deep roots to find water. Sandy soils may require two waterings a week.

♦ Water your yard in the early morning or evening. Sprinkling at mid-day (or on windy days) can use three or four *times* more water. Yikes.

Experts greatly favor morning waterings so the grass can dry out during the day (better for avoiding fungus).

♦ On the average, Americans over-water their yards by nearly 30%. How long should sprinklers stay on to deliver an inch of water? A simple test (performed once) answers that question.

Set up four cans at different distances from the sprinkler and let the water run. Check the cans every few minutes and note the time it takes *each* can to accumulate an inch of water. Add these four times together, divide by four, and you're left with the average time to run the sprinkler.

For more thorough—and free—information about watering, order the booklet *Efficient Use of Water in the Garden and Landscape* from the Texas Water Development Board (P.O. Box 13231, Capital Station, Austin, TX 78711, 512-445-1467).

♦ If you really want to shave the water bill, you can stop watering a healthy, well-established lawn once the drought days of summer arrive. The grass will go into a brown dormancy. Worry not, grasses survived for millenniums before we came along with hoses. The grass will green up again when the rains of autumn arrive. In the meantime, enjoy your break from mowing.

If the rains of autumn never come, start watering again in mid- September so the grass revives and manufactures food for the winter.

◆ The best times to seed are very early spring or fall (mid-September). This is when the temperatures and moisture conditions are best. When you do seed, don't skimp—you need 15 to 20 seeds per square inch to produce a thick lawn or patch. Avoid using old seed, and get the right kind of seed. Seeds that aren't right for your climate, soil, or amount of sunlight won't grow well. Work with your local nursery to get a grass that's right for you, or send a stamped, self-addressed business envelope to The Lawn Institute (P.O. Box 108, Pleasant Hill, TN 38578). Request their *Grass Seed Recognition List* and the recommended varieties for your area.

◆ Overseeding your entire lawn every year or two is an inexpensive way to keep it thick and healthy. Grass plants in the lawn are continually dying and overseeding allows new grass, rather than weeds, to fill the vacancies.

Homeowners with new sod yards are particularly good candidates for overseeding. Sods are composed of a mixture of grass species and not all of them may like your soil. Overseeding allows grasses that can grow in your soil to fill in the ranks for grasses in the sod that can't.

Early to mid-September is the best time to overseed; early spring also works.

◆ Seeds that won't germinate (or that germinate slowly) run up water bills, waste time, provide the birds with food, and frustrate you. Here's a trick that gets seeds to germinate and grow fast. To each pound of seed, add 1 cup of cool weak tea (use 1 tea bag to make 4 cups of tea). Soak the seeds in the tea and refrigerate the works for 24 hours. Spread the seeds on your driveway to let them dry. Once dry, sow normally.

♦ Mowing properly plays a major role in keeping your lawn healthy and reducing the money and time spent on it. Most people wait too long between mowings and then, by cutting too much, shock the grass.

The blade is the plant's food factory so don't lop off more than a third of it at once. If trying to maintain grass at three inches, cut it before it reaches a height of 4 1/2 inches. When grass growth slows down during the dog days of summer, cut off even less.

Neglected yards that are beginning to resemble wild lands should not be shorn in one swoop. Cut the grass down slowly over the course of several mowings so it has several days to recover between each swing of the blade.

♦ Sharp mower blades reduce the need for pesticides and weed control. Dull blades rip rather than cut the grass, weakening the individual plants and making them susceptible to disease or encroaching weeds. Sharpen your blades several times each season. Owning two blades makes good sense: Replace the dull one when necessary and sharpen it at your leisure.

Other mowing tips include: cleaning the underside of the mower often (improves the airflow and helps the machine suck the grass upright); inspecting the yard for sticks, rocks, and toys (prevents dull blades and injuries); cutting in a different pattern each week (keeps the grass from leaning in one direction); refraining from mowing when the grass is wet (prevents grass loss caused by the blade tearing plants from the soil).

♦ If you sharpen your own blade, make sure to balance it before replacing it. The vibration caused by a lopsided blade can damage the engine. Balance the blade by hanging it horizontally from the midpoint. If one end dips consistently, file more metal off that end.

♦ A diseased lawn was likely weakened by improper fertilizing, poor mowing, or improper watering techniques. Keep lawns healthy as described above and you will have less cause to use insecticides and pesticides.

As for weeds, many of us blame our problems on the neighbor. "If they'd have picked those damned dandelions, we wouldn't have them in our yard." In truth, if you have weeds your lawn was not thick enough to crowd them out.

♦ Mower maintenance. Mowers are expensive tools. Neglected they may spend a lot of time with mechanics who charge $40/hour. Cared for, they can deliver season after season of faithful service.

- Change the oil often: Much of the dirt entering the mower gets deposited in the oil and sandpapers away at the piston and cylinder. Check your owner's manual for exact recommendations but, as a rule, change the oil every 25 hours (SAE 30 oil). For most home owners, that means changing the oil halfway through the mowing season.

- Check the oil often; run out of this inexpensive fluid and you'll be selling an expensive mower for scrap metal.

- Clean the air filter every 25 hours, too. If the filter gets dirty and clogged, the dirty air sucked into the carburetor will scour the moving parts. Check your mower's instruction pamphlet if you need help.

- The owner of one of the largest mower shops in Seattle says he sees more mowers ruined by corrosion than by any other cause. Wet grass matted to the bottom of the housing, combined with corrosive fertilizers, destroys the body long before the engine dies. Solution: Spend a minute after each use washing the mower. Tip the mower on its side and spray the bottom with a hose. Then wipe down the top of the housing with a wet rag.

- How well it works on your car I can't say, but *Armor All* does protect the bottom of your lawn mower. Clean the under side thoroughly of old grass, then spray on a heavy coat—it keeps grass from sticking and inhibits rust.

♦ Buying a mower. Personally, I'm a strong advocate of push mowers. Simple push mowers with a big-name 3.5 horsepower engine, a metal housing, and adjustable wheels are relatively cheap. Shop the sales and $150 will buy you a mower that can last a decade. These mowers are light and, unless your yard is huge, require little added effort to use. Consider that added effort good fitness training.

Self-propelled mowers add hundreds of dollars to a mower's price and, more than likely, hundreds of dollars to the long-term maintenance. Unlike simple push mowers in which brand-names are not that critical, self-propelled mowers vary greatly in the service they will require. Cheap mowers may cost you more in the long run. Read product evaluations in magazines like *Consumer Reports* and buy a model that scores high marks for reliability.

♦ Few people think about the gas they use in the mower, but they should. Gas has a short shelf life and not only loses much of its octane but starts turning gummy after only a month. That gum can do a professional job of clogging the carburetor. Don't risk using old gas from last season —start with fresh fuel. Store your fresh gas in a cool place and in an airtight container.

♦ A common reason that mowers visit mechanics during the active months of spring is because they were stored improperly during the inactive months of winter. After your last mowing in autumn, here's what you do:

- With the engine warm, change the oil. Run the new oil through the engine for a minute.

- Drain the gas, then run the mower until it is dry. Gas left in the mower over the winter can gum up the carburetor with varnish.

- Take out the spark plug, pour 15 or 20 drops of lubricating oil down the cylinder, and crank the engine a few times to disperse the oil. Clean and regap the plug before reinserting it.

- Scrape matted grass off the bottom of the housing. Use a rag and the motor oil you just removed to wipe the bottom of the housing and the blade (prevents rusting).

- Store the mower in a dry (and not overly cold) place. With the mower safely stored, sit back and enjoy your furlough from this neighborly game of suburban one-upmanship.

In our rich consumer's civilization we spin cocoons around ourselves and get possessed by our possessions.

Max Lerner

Libraries

Your tax dollars pay for it. It provides you with a means of saving hundreds of dollars each year. It can supply free music, movies, tax consultation, entertainment, forms, maps, and magazines, not to mention books. Yet only 20% of the populous regularly use the library.

The typical library user is moderately affluent. No doubt, in part, because the money saved ends up in the bank. Meanwhile, people who can least afford *not* to use the library, don't. Well, like they say, "Life is hard—especially if you're stupid." Of course, most nonlibrary users are simply unenlightened. So here is your enlightenment.

♦ Obviously, you can get books from the library. Not just some books but, if you are patient, most any book. If your branch of the county library doesn't own it, they'll get it from a branch that does. And if the book isn't in the county system, the library can place an inter-library loan (ILL) to get it. Doesn't matter if the book is an illustrated children's story, a trashy romance novel, Robert Fulghum's new best seller, a repair manual for Camaros, *The Etiquette of Tennis* by John MacEnroe, or *Why Cops Love Me So* by Zsa Zsa Gabor. If the book exists, your library can probably get it. And it costs you nothing.

♦ Many people don't use the library, figuring the book they want (say a particular cookbook) won't be in the system or (like a new best seller) won't be in. They figure a library visit will simply waste time and money.

The solution? Bring home a pile of the library's Book Request Forms. When you want a particular title, fill out a form and mail it back to the library. Write on the card that you are willing to wait for an inter-library loan (ILL) if the book is not in the system. Then wait. You'll be notified when your request arrives.

Alternately, call in your request to the library. If the desired book is available, ask to have it held (most libraries give you several days to swing by). If the book is checked out, ask to be placed on a waiting list. And if the book is not in the system, ask for an ILL.

♦ When you visit a bookstore, take several of the library's Book Request Forms with you. When you find a title that interests you, jot down its name and author on a form. Once you get home, mail the completed forms to the library and then wait to be notified when your books become available.

♦ Infants, toddlers, and preschool children all love books. Illustrated children's books, however, are expensive—especially considering how quickly young children outgrow their reading material.

My wife and I solve the problem at the library. Every few weeks we check out 10 books for our 3-year-old daughter. When those books go back, 10 new ones come home with us. Allison gets a hundred dollars' worth of new books every month.

Incidentally, children's books are like any other—you can request titles, so use the mail or phone to order the books your children enjoy.

♦ Libraries devote considerable funds and staff to their reference functions. When you have a question—almost any question—call. Need to know what the Burpy Company does, where to find the nearest chapter of the Twins Club, how Arnold Schwarzenegger spells his last name, the height of the Eiffel Tower, Ty Cobb's lifetime batting average, the cost of a 1988 Honda Civic, where to recycle toxic wastes, what community services can help a spouse with a drinking problem, the cheapest hotel in Los Angeles? Call the library.

A question like, "What's Miss January's phone number?" might stump them, but 90% of the time they'll find an answer or refer you to a reliable source. This service can save you an incredible amount of time, and, because *you* don't have to place calls all over the state answering a thorny question, it saves you money.

♦ My wife and I easily save over $150 each year checking out special interest magazines from the library. Except for the weekly news magazines, it doesn't matter whether most periodicals get read this month or next. Consequently, once or twice a month I'll check out back issues of interesting titles: *Backpacker, PC Magazine, Esquire, Consumer Reports, Omni.* For my wife, I'll pick up anything that has Princess Diana on the cover as well as a few magazines to redeem her mind after her royalty fix.

If you want a specific magazine, say the Demi Moore Issue of *Vanity Fair*, and your library doesn't have it, they can order it from another branch. If you just need a particular article, they'll have the article photocopied and sent to you at no charge.

♦ Books on tape are a popular resource found at most libraries. I get in twice as much "reading" now that I listen to books because I can "read" while I do menial work—commute, exercise, cook, wash dishes, rake leaves. Listening to a book makes all this drudgery infinitely more pleasurable; sometimes I even look for idiot's work so I can get along with the story.

You can buy books on tape or join clubs that send you a title every month. Both these options are expensive and you'll save a handsome sum getting these recorded books from the library.

Unfortunately, most of the good titles are often checked out when you visit. Here's how to work the system. Use the catalog listing the recorded books to fill out book request forms for three or four titles. When one book arrives and you go to fetch it, fill out book requests for another title or two. Maintain the routine and you'll always have good listening material available. All it costs you is a little gas money.

♦ Several friends who know I'm a serious audio "reader" now tape library books for me as birthday or Christmas presents. These gifts are actually illegal (making unauthorized copies of tapes violates copyright laws), but I was always taught not to look a gift horse in the mouth.

♦ Need forms to incorporate, make a will, file a divorce, establish a small business? Get them free from the library.

♦ What do most people get out of a cookbook? Usually just a few recipes that they're really anxious to try—which puts the per-recipe price of buying cookbooks up there with king crab.

Instead, reserve the books from the library, thumb through them, and copy the recipes you ache to bake.

♦ Most libraries now stock a good selection of popular films, documentaries, and instructional programs on video. Check out a few whenever you're in the library and you'll find yourself saving healthy sums on video rentals. Many libraries have enough good material that you could let the cable subscription lapse and still spend more time than you should in front of the TV.

♦ Need maps for your travels? Visit the reference area of the library. Among the topographic maps, road maps, and atlases, you can usually find and photocopy what you need.

♦ The records and compact discs available through the library can expand your musical taste. Experiment: The albums cost you nothing so sample new artists and styles of music.

♦ Parents can also hit pay dirt by checking out audio and video tapes for their children.

♦ Many stores will rent you computer time. But why pay when you can reserve free computer time at most libraries? Okay, you may not find state-of-the-art equipment, but if your needs are not overly complex, the library lets you compute and print free.

You can also expose yourself to vast amounts of software through the library. My library, a small branch of the county system, has 60 software programs ranging from computer games to educational software to big name packages like *WordPerfect*, *Lotus 1-2-3*, *Word*, and *Multi-Plan*. It's a wonderful place to test the merits of a software package before purchasing.

If you are not yet part of the computer world and are contemplating joining, logging hours with the library's hardware and software will help you determine what you should and should not buy.

♦ Monitor the library's evening programs for free seminars (preparing taxes or wills) and entertainment (travel-related films and slideshows).

Similarly, libraries sponsor educational and recreational programs for children of all ages. When you're checking out books, ask where the monthly calendar of events is displayed.

♦ Need tax help before the April 15 deadline? Call the library and ask if they can help. At this most maddening time of the year, it is quite common for IRS employees to volunteer time at the library to help fools like me who can't differentiate a Section C from a C-Section.

♦ Besides knowing the resources available through the county library, it pays to know the library resources of your local colleges and universities.

The nearby community college catalogs all the state topographic maps and navigation charts. I am an avid climber, hiker, and sea kayaker, so I have saved a fortune photocopying these maps and charts.

The maps I covet may do you little good, but dig around and you'll unearth your own treasures.

All complain of their lack of money, none of their want of brains.

Rumanian proverb

Lights

"Why is the house lit up like a Christmas tree?" It was the standard greeting from my father as he returned from work to find his family wasting money faster than he earned it. As a kid, I never understood how much utilities cost so I considered my dad an alarmist.

Once I left home and started paying the power piper myself, however, I quickly saw burning bulbs in a new light. Assuming average utility rates of 8¢ per kilowatt hour, a 100-watt bulb consumes 8¢ of electricity in 10 hours of use. Not much—unless you've got dozens of bulbs burning simultaneously. Suddenly all my father's begging and bullying made tremendous sense.

Had my father had his way we would have bumped around the house using Braille skills and greeted each dawn with mole eyes. But turning off the lights (or at least those lights not in use) is only one of many tricks to reduce your lighting bills.

♦ Light bulbs are rated in watts, a measure of the power they consume, but wattage does not tell how much light is produced—"lumens" tell that story. Lumens per watt, meanwhile, measure efficiency (like miles per gallon) and different types of light bulbs can be as different in efficiency as the Geo Metro and a Winnebago.

Incandescent light bulbs (the most common bulb found in homes) have changed little in the 110 years since Edison invented them, and 90% of the electricity that feeds them is still wasted in heat. They produce about 17 to 23 lumens per watt. Fluorescent bulbs, on the other hand, are three to four times more efficient, yielding 67 to 83 lumens per watt. Going fluorescent in areas that need light for long hours each day (e.g., the kitchen) is a big money saver.

Fluorescents still suffer from the misconception that their light is always cold, harsh, clinical. Nowadays many fluorescent tubes produce warmer hues that won't make your home feel like a hospital ward.

♦ Using more fluorescent lights is easy if you're building a house, but how do you capitalize on their efficiency in older homes? With compact fluorescents.

Compact fluorescents screw into the same fixtures as normal incandescent bulbs, and an 18-watt fluorescent can produce the same lumen output as a 75-watt incandescent. Assuming average power rates of 8¢ per kilowatt hour, one compact fluorescent burned for four hours a day saves you $6.66 a year, $13.32 a year if burned for eight hours a day.

♦ In the right situations, compact fluorescents save you a small fortune, but because the bulbs are about three times bulkier than incandescents, they don't fit all fixtures. And at a cost of $14 to $18 per 18-watt bulb, they may not pay off in locations where the light is "on" only a few minutes per day. However, in locations where the bulb burns daily for long hours, these bulbs squeeze pennies from electricity each time you flick the switch and will pay for themselves in a year or two.

Compact fluorescents also have incredible longevity. Their average life is 9000 to 10,000 hours, 10 times longer than the 750- to 1000-hour life of incandescents.

♦ Many utility companies around the country are participating in rebate programs to entice their customers to replace normal incandescent bulbs with compact fluorescents. For the utility companies, it's a conservation program; for you it's a chance to make these bulbs affordable. So if the front-end cost of compact fluorescents has kept you from capitalizing on their back-end savings, call the utility company. Currently, my utility offers a $7 per bulb rebate, making them about half price.

♦ When purchasing compact fluorescents, buy those encased in glass. Bulbs with a clear, plastic exterior can yellow over time. This yellowing ruins the quality of the white light.

♦ Circular fluorescents, like the GE *Circlite*, convert lamps with large shades (table lamps or hanging lights) over to fluorescent bulbs that can produce the lumen output of a 75- or 100-watt incandescent bulb with one-third of the power. Replace the old bulb with a screw-in fluorescent adapter (ballast), snap the circular bulb onto this adapter, and use the lamp shade to cover the underlying apparatus.

Like compact fluorescents, circular fluorescents have an average life of 10,000 hours. Purchased at large hardware and electric-supply stores, the ballast and bulb cost $9 to $15. For technical data and information on where to purchase them locally, contact General Electric (800-626-2000) and Lights of America (800-654-7976).

♦ The 13-watt Lumatech fluorescent flood lamp, made to replace the incandescent 75-watt reflector bulb used in recessed ("can") ceiling fixtures, is among the few fluorescent floods available. With a price of about $40, however, this is not a cheap option *unless* that particular light stays on much of the day. Call Lumatech (510-654-4300) to locate a local outlet for the bulb.

A cheaper way to employ fluorescent bulbs in a recessed fixture is to use 15- or 18-watt compact fluorescent (globe or capsule style) together with a reflector that bounces the light lost in the "can" back into the room. Such a reflector can be purchased for $11 with a satisfaction guaranteed warranty from the Seventh Generation catalog (Colchester, VT 05446, 800-456-1177).

♦ Incandescent bulbs filled with halogen can replace both standard "reflector" and "parabolic aluminum reflector" (PAR) bulbs with good results. A halogen 90-watt PAR bulb delivers as many lumens as a standard 150-watt PAR bulb, a power saving of 40%. These halogen lamps cost about twice as much ($8 to $9 versus $4 to $5) but they often last longer. And because you'll save an average of $9.50 in electricity over a halogen bulb's life, it's like getting the bulb free. Well, almost—they'll seem anything but free when you buy them.

♦ General Electric is now marketing a commercial PAR bulb called the *60-watt Halogen IR* that produces as many lumens as a normal 150-watt PAR bulb. Over its life this halogen bulb, which is 2 1/2 times more efficient than a standard bulb, will save $14 in energy (assuming average energy rates).

Purchase the bulb (about $11) through commercial lighting outlets. Call GE (800-626-2000) for more technical information and for a local supplier.

♦ Currently no halogen "reflector" bulbs are made for the recessed "can" fixtures found in the ceilings of many homes. The thin glass in reflectors cannot withstand the pressures used to make halogen bulbs. Nonetheless, the halogen PAR bulbs mentioned earlier can replace reflector bulbs in many fixtures. A 90-watt halogen (PAR-38) produces the same light output as a standard 150-watt R-40 reflector while a 45-watt halogen substitutes for a standard 75-watt reflector.

The same applies for smaller reflectors; a 50-watt Halogen (PAR-30) produces as much light as a 75-watt R-30 reflector.

Halogen PAR bulbs are a little shorter than reflectors so a socket extender (available from electric-supply stores for $2 to $3) can be used to lengthen the bulb.

♦ Many fixtures for outdoor flood lights hold two bulbs, but not everyone needs their driveway or backyard lit up like Candlestick Park. Cut costs by screwing a dead bulb into one of the sockets or unscrewing one bulb just enough to disconnect its power.

♦ Outdoor fixtures that turn on and off by means of built-in heat/motion detectors and timers are far more economical than keeping the outdoor lights burning long hours each night. These fixtures can be bought at hardware and electric-supply stores for $12 to $25 and even idiots who are smart enough to follow instructions can install them.

At night the lights turn on whenever the fixture detects a warm body moving in the surveyance zone. They turn off a few minutes later when that body has either died on the spot or has moved along.

♦ Extricating the base of a broken bulb from a socket is child's play, so don't panic and call the electrician. Turn off the electricity at the circuit box, then stuff a kid's rubber ball (like the ones used to play jacks) or a golf-ball sized wad of *Silly Putty* into the *inside* threads of the bulb. Once the ball or putty is packed into the threads, twist it (counterclockwise). The broken stem will screw right out.

If Conan originally screwed in the bulb and the ball keeps slipping, glue the ball to the inner threads with epoxy cement. Return later to unscrew the mess. Don't let your kids see what became of the ball you borrowed or they may not cooperate next time you come begging.

♦ General Electric sells a line of "A" bulbs (the common bulb used around the house) called the "Energy Choice" and their marketing hoopla says their 52, 67, and 90 watt bulbs replace normal 60, 75, and 100 watt bulbs, respectively.

What you need Paul Harvey to tell you is that these bulbs, which cost about two-thirds more than normal bulbs, may replace 60, 75, and 100 watt bulbs but they aren't as bright as the bulbs they replace. Consumers trying to be environmentally conscientious are hoodwinked into paying more for dimmer bulbs. That's the rest of the story.

♦ With standard incandescent light bulbs, you get more lumens from a single 100-watt bulb than from two 60-watters. Also, it takes six 25-watt bulbs to match the lumens of a 100-watter.

♦ Incandescent bulbs turned on and off with a dimmer will last far longer than those operated with a normal switch. The dimmer reduces the huge power surge that destroys the filament of many bulbs. A variety of inexpensive, easily installed dimmer switches are available to replace wall switches. For lamps, several types of dimmers clamp quickly to the power cord.

♦ Incandescent bulbs advertised as "long-life" bulbs possess thicker tungsten filaments. This makes the filament last longer but the bulbs are dimmer than standard bulbs of the same wattage. These bulbs may be useful in hard-to-reach places, but considering they cost more to buy and operate they are not the miser's choice for general use.

♦ Don't buy the long-life buttons that fit between an incandescent light bulb and the socket. Advertisers say the buttons prolong bulb life (true) but they fail to mention that the buttons siphon energy away from the bulb and reduce the amount of light produced. You would save both energy and the cost of the buttons simply by buying a lower-watt bulb, but it's so much more fun getting scammed.

Note: Because some buttons significantly increase the temperature of the socket base, the safety of some of these products has also been questioned.

♦ If your night light burns out, a Christmas tree bulb is a cheaper substitute than an official night-light bulb.

♦ Turning lights on and off frequently shortens bulb life. Turn off an incandescent light when you leave the room for more than a few minutes. Standard 75- and 100-watt bulbs cost only between 50¢ and $1, yet they are so inefficient they consume about $8 in power during their 1000 hours of bulb life.

Fluorescents are a different story. An 18-watt fluorescent retailing at an average price of $16 will cost only $13 to operate over its 9000-hour life. Because the bulb is more expensive than the power it consumes, many experts recommend leaving the light on in rooms you will be revisiting within half an hour.

♦ Come Christmas time, consider the economy of laziness; don't hang lights around the perimeter of the house. If friends shovel flack about how your house is the neighborhood black hole, tell them at least one person cares enough about the world we are leaving our children to make personal sacrifices. If you're not into the holier-than-thou shtick, just tell them the truth, "Bah Humbug."

♦ To buy or get more information about the bulbs discussed in this chapter, call The Lightbulb Place (White Electric Co., 1821 University Avenue, Berkeley, CA 94703, 510-845-8535, 1-800-468-2852); Seventh Generation (Colchester, VT 05446, 800-456-1177); Sylvania Lighting Center (100 Endicott St., Danvers, MA 01923, 800-LIGHTBULB); GE Answer Center (800-626-2000).

When you have money think of the time when you had none.

Japanese proverb

Mail Order

Mail order: Is it a rip off or a steal?

Depends on where you do your shopping. In a former career, I was a merchandiser for a mail-order company producing a slick, full-color catalog. Each page featured copy and beautiful studio photographs of just a few products. You would read 32 reasons why each widget could make you happier, healthier, hipper, smarter, sexier. Good copywriters possess the power of persuasion to make coal sound like a diamond. And they know how to make the price of that diamond sound trivial.

But when you buy from slick, colorful, wordy catalogs, you're usually paying top dollar. These publications are an expensive way to generate business—the thick catalogs my company produced several times a year cost 80¢ each to produce and mail. They went out to half a million people and the company expected only 5% or 6% of those folks to send in their cash. The other 94% of the catalogs went from the mailbox to land fill. That meant the unlucky few who placed orders had to be gouged to keep the boat afloat.

The merchandise I bought for the company sold for at least twice what we paid for it. Often it sold for four times the wholesale cost. These margins were higher than at most retail stores.

On the other end of the mail-order spectrum are the discount houses—the ones with advertisements in the back of stereo, camera, computer, and electronics magazines. The ads have no copy—they list a million products at prices way below retail. Are these prices for real? Can you trust the firms? Do the firms deliver?

Yes. On all counts. I've bought computer printers, cameras, camera lenses, a camcorder, stereo components, and hundreds of rolls of brand-name film from these discount houses. I've paid 25% to 50% below local retail. By buying from out-of-state firms, I've avoided paying sales tax (8.2% in my locality)—on a big-ticket purchase like a computer, that alone can save you a few hundred dollars. Finally, mail-order shopping saves me a few dollars of gas money. And through it all I've yet to encounter any problems (knock on wood) with service or fraud.

I am not alone. In polls conducted by consumer magazines, the vast majority of people who shop by mail say they'll continue to do so. Of course, you've probably heard the hard-luck cases. Unfortunately, some people refuse to do their homework. Here's how to do it.

♦ Know exactly what you want—manufacturer, model number, desired options, accessories... That means doing your homework before calling the companies. Talk to friends. Find out, in detail, what they recommend. Read *Consumer Reports* and magazine reviews to zero in on what you want. Visit several retail stores to see what you like and to learn the local prices.

This is research you should do before any major purchase, whether you buy locally or by mail—don't consider it extra work.

♦ At the library get current copies of magazines listing the mail-order companies selling the product you want (e.g., *PC Magazine* for computers, *Popular Photography* for cameras, *Stereo Review* for audio equipment). Make a list of firms that might sell the product you want. There are usually plenty of choices so I tend to favor ones with toll-free phone numbers.

Now ask the librarian for a back issue of the same magazine that is several years old. Star the firms that were advertising back then—few firms stay in business that long if they don't keep customers happy.

♦ Call the most promising firms on your list for price quotes. Find out exactly what comes with the product (cases, warranties, etc.), whether the product is in stock, if you can get the desired options, the shipping costs, how long delivery will take. A few mail-order firms may be impatient with you or tell you the toll-free number is for orders only. Don't take it personally—just cross them off the list. You deserve good treatment and there are plenty of places that will treat you civilly while giving you price quotes over their toll-free number.

The telephone salesperson will pressure you to order on the spot. You're not ready until you've compared the quotes of four or five mail-order houses *and* compared those prices to local retail shops. Be firm: Tell anyone who puts on the squeeze that you'll call back.

♦ Before ordering from a completely unfamiliar company, consider checking with the Better Business Bureau nearest the company's headquarters to see if any complaints have been filed against the company.

For a directory of BBB offices, contact the Council of Better Business Bureaus Inc., 4200 Wilson Blvd., Arlington VA 22203, 703-276-0100. Send a self-addressed, stamped envelope with your request.

♦ If you place a telephone order, say exactly what you want. List all the options and accessories you expect to receive. Spell your name and address. State your phone and credit card numbers slowly and clearly.

Salesmen will typically try to hang up fast. Don't let them, until they've repeated *everything* to you (product model number, accessories, options, your name, address, phone number, and credit card number). Have the bill tallied (with shipping included). Write down the salesperson's name and your purchase-order number. Verify that the product is in stock, when it will be shipped, and when you can expect it. Write it all down and file the info.

♦ When placing an order by mail, print neatly and fill out the order form completely. Make a photocopy of the order form, or at least keep a record of what you ordered, the catalog number, the catalog or advertisement you ordered from, the firm's address, the date you ordered.

♦ When dealing with reputable firms (and you shouldn't be ordering until you've established that a firm is reputable) pay with a credit card. You receive faster service because the company need not wait until your check clears.

With a credit card, you're also protected if the product never arrives, is damaged in shipping, or if the product does not live up to the advertised claims and you become entangled in a warranty dispute. How? Through the power of the Federal Trade Commission's Fair Credit Billing Act, you can withhold payment of disputed charges. See the *Credit Card* chapter for details.

♦ Don't send cash—maybe the post office will send your order to Tanzania, maybe someone who processes your order will suffer from sticky fingers. Why test fate?

In addition, once the company has your money, your negotiating power in the event of a dispute diminishes. Might as well stack the deck in your favor and pay with a credit card (first preference), or a check or money order (second preference).

♦ Some companies try to charge you shipping insurance. Cross out any line on an order form (or resist any telephone pitch) charging for optional shipping insurance. Legally, it's the shipper's responsibility to insure the safety of the merchandise. And if you've paid by credit card, you can call on the Fair Credit Billing Act in a sour situation.

♦ File the phone numbers and addresses of the mail-order houses with whom you've been happy. Next time you need a similar product, you'll know one possible outlet. Naturally, you'll still want to check with several competitors before placing a new order.

♦ Keep the original box and padding in which the product arrived until you decide to keep the purchase. If you decide to return the product, you will have all the necessary packaging.

Note: Some manufacturers' warranties are void unless the product is returned in the original box. Read the warranties carefully before deciding the long-term fate of the goods and their packaging.

♦ In the *Mail-order Appendix* of this book, you'll find a list (not comprehensive) of reputable companies. No matter what you need—photo equipment, computers, stereo components, furniture, office supplies, clothing, sports equipment, medicine, toys—you can buy it through the mail.

♦ Serious mail-order shoppers and people living in small communities with little retail competition should purchase a copy of *The Wholesale By Mail Catalog 1992* (HarperCollins Publishers, P.O. Box 588, Dunmore, PA 18512, 800-331-3761). It lists mail-order sources for just about any product, be it automobiles or audiotapes, books or boats, clothing or clocks...

The book also explains the ABCs of ordering, paying, complaining, and returning merchandise.

♦ The Sears Catalog is another excellent resource to keep at home because you can order virtually anything through it: toilets, house fixtures, tools, clothes, toys, furniture, appliances—at one time you could even mail order prefab houses.

The prices at Sears aren't necessarily the best, but they are mid-range and will give you the basis for deciding whether offers through other catalogs are a steal or highway robbery.

You can buy catalogs at any Sears store or order them over the phone (800-366-3000). Cost is $5 but if you order anything, the $6 coupon in the catalog lets you recoup your investment.

♦ In mail order, the term gray goods is not synonymous with shady deals or black markets. Gray goods come into the country via legitimate importers but not through the recognized U.S. dealers or distributors. So while the goods are legal, they may or may not have a U.S. warranty.

This is no biggy for something like printer ribbons, but is a definite concern if you're ordering an expensive camera. Consequently, be sure to ask whether the goods are "gray" and to get a guarantee that you will be receiving a valid U.S. warranty before you ante up.

♦ If you have trouble resolving a problem with a firm, contact the Direct Marketing Association Action Line (6 E. 43rd St., New York, NY 10017). If the firm is a member of the DMA, the DMA will intercede to resolve the problem.

Medical Expenses

It has been said that for a thousand years medicine was an art, for a hundred years it was a science, and now in the last 10 years it has become big business. You needn't look far to see the truth of the claim—everything about medicine (doctors' fees, cost of drugs, hospital charges, health insurance premiums) comes with prices that terrify even the wealthy.

I don't pretend to have the solution to our health-care system—controlling medical costs and providing every American with affordable medical care are immense problems. I can, however, bandage some health-related wounds that bleed you of more money than they should. By helping you reduce the money spent on doctors, self-limiting illnesses, drugs, hospitals and more, this chapter will reduce your charitable contributions to big business.

COLDS AND FLUS

♦ Colds and flus are both "self limiting." In other words, they run their cycle and go away on their own. Nothing a doctor prescribes will actually shorten the amount of time you are sick. Save yourself a doctor's visit and let the illness run its course. The bite of a flu will last three or four days while the worst of a cold can last five or six days. It's not unusual, however, to have lesser symptoms for weeks.

♦ What's the cheapest way to weather a cold? Ignore cold medicines that claim to do everything. Instead, identify which active ingredients fight the symptoms you are suffering at the time. Buy single-ingredient medications (preferably generics) to ease those symptoms.

People with colds normally suffer from congestion, sore throats, fever/headache/muscle ache, *or* coughs. But they don't suffer from all these symptoms simultaneously. If you're congested and take a drug with both a decongestant and a cough suppressant, you'll pay much more for that medication than for a simple decongestant. Likewise, some decongestants add aspirin or acetaminophen to their formulas and charge you a fortune for the pain relief that a penny's worth of aspirin delivers.

When you have a cold, fight muscle aches, fevers, and headaches with pain relievers containing aspirin, acetaminophen, or ibuprofen. Stymie sore throats with medicated lozenges and sprays containing phenol compounds, benzocaine, hexylresorcinol, or menthol. Stop coughs with suppressants containing dextromethorphan, codeine, diphenhydramine; medicated lozenges containing menthol; or with expectorants containing guaifenesin. And relieve congestion with topical decongestants containing phenylephrine, oxymetazoline or xylometazoline, or with oral decongestants containing pseudoephedrine.

◆ The advice for fighting a cold also applies to the flu. According to the *University of California at Berkeley Wellness Letter*, one of the most-respected health newsletters, flu medicines are made from basically the same ingredients as cold medications. Also, flu medications are often expensive combination medicines containing a fever-lowering pain reliever, an antihistamine, and a cough suppressant.

Avoid the high cost of these combination medicines by sticking to single-ingredient medications that relieve the symptoms you're suffering at the time (see the last entry for the active ingredients you need).

◆ Hard candies and warm-saltwater gargles deliver about the same sore-throat relief as lozenges and sprays packed with phenol compounds, benzocaine, or menthol.

For a saltwater gargle, use 1/4 teaspoon salt mixed with 1 cup water. Using a stronger concentration of salt may do more harm than good.

♦ Steam-borne eucalyptus oil is also helpful for soothing sore throats, reducing coughs, and relieving congestion.

♦ Because flus can cause complications with people over 65 years of age or those with respiratory problems, high-risk people should get an annual flu shot. It's cheap insurance against the major problems a flu can precipitate. These shots are unlikely to give you a low-grade case of the flu. Recently, a double-blind study showed that people receiving flu shots suffered no more side effects than those receiving a placebo shot.

♦ Popping penicillin or other antibiotics will not speed up your recovery from a flu or cold. Both illnesses are caused by viruses, and antibiotics work only on bacterial infections. Unfortunately, surveys show that nearly two out of three Americans believe antibiotics kill viruses and bacteria alike.

♦ Do devices that shoot steam up the nose, like *Viralizer*, shorten colds and flu? A double-blind study published in the *Journal of the American Medical Association* found these sprays ineffective in killing the germs causing the illness and in shortening the course of illness. Sounds like P.T. Barnum developed this product.

DOCTOR TRICKS

♦ Despite your age or sex, using a family-practice doctor as your personal doctor is a safe and economic approach to obtaining excellent health care. Visits with a family-practice doctor can cost half what a specialist charges. What's more, family-practice doctors are trained to deal with the widest array of problems and are well-qualified to deal with the gamut of health problems you'll encounter over time. They can handle a good 85% to 90% of your ailments and will refer you to a specialist for the situations beyond their expertise. Only then do you pay the premium price charged by a specialist.

When picking a family-practice doctor, make sure he or she is board-certified, has completed three years of residency, and has been recertified at seven-year intervals.

♦ My brother Alan, a doctor, recommends talking to your doctor about reccurring problems suffered by yourself or a family member, be it your frequent urinary tract infections or your child's ear infections.

These problems are expensive if you follow the standard course of action (arrange an appointment for a prescription and a follow-up visit to verify your recovery). If, however, you are assertive and demonstrate an understanding of the affliction and its symptoms, you can often cut a deal.

Ideally when a reccurring problem strikes, you want to be able to call the doctor, discuss the problem, and obtain a written prescription without the formality of two expensive visits.

A doctor who won't work with you on these problems you recognize and understand is not meeting your needs: Ask him or her for a referral to another doctor. If you look for another doctor, discuss your problems and come to an understanding before signing on.

♦ Doctors often prescribe what the patient wants. If the patient wants medicine for a flu or cold (two illnesses that have no cure other than time itself), a doctor is likely to prescribe medications that will, at least, do no harm.

The reasons are two-fold. A patient who expects to leave with a remedy will be disappointed if sent away empty-handed: And if he leaves unhappy, he may not come back. Then, there is the placebo effect: It is well-known from studies of medications that a third of the test population receiving a placebo (e.g., sugar pills) will experience the desired benefits of the actual drug. All of which means that a doctor may be prescribing drugs or tests for you not because he or she believes you need them, but because you believe you need them.

Unfortunately, the drugs or tests may be expensive. As a pragmatic penny-pincher you may not want a doctor to play voodoo games. So get in the habit of asking doctors, "If you had this condition, what would you prescribe for yourself?"

What a doctor would do may cost hundreds of dollars less than what he or she prescribes to patients who seem desperate for a remedy.

♦ If you decide to employ the last trick and are not completely happy when the doctor says, "I wouldn't do anything—the problem will go away in several days," ask what he or she recommends if you are no better after several days. If that recommendation involves taking a prescription medication, ask the doctor to write the prescription now so that you needn't schedule another appointment if you don't improve.

Many doctors will do this if they judge you to be reasonable and responsible.

♦ A sick toddler who is well enough to play several hours during the day is probably not sick enough to warrant a doctor's visit. However, if the child has been very listless all day and uninterested in playing, call the doctor.

♦ Getting shots for either your children or yourself is usually substantially cheaper through the county's public health department than through a medical clinic. For example, a measles-mumps-rubella shot for my daughter costs $8 at public health, and $36 from my doctor (plus the cost of seeing the doctor if the shot is not given during a normal check-up).

I can also get the shots I need for travelling (cholera, hepatitis-B, typhoid, gamma globulin, polio...) from public health at a reduced cost. A typhoid shot costs me $9 through public health; my medical clinic would charge me $10 for the shot plus $19 to administer it.

Look up your local public health number under "Health" in the county government listings of the phone book.

DRUGS AND MEDICATIONS

♦ Shop around for any medications taken regularly. Prices vary considerably among pharmacies and no single outlet has the best price on every drug. Recently, when my wife needed an expensive allergy medication, I found a $32 difference between the cheapest and costliest quote. Then, I checked prices with several reputable mail-order pharmacies (see *Mail-order Appendix*) and found two that undersold the cheapest local store.

You can order over-the-counter and prescription medications through the mail from sources like Pharmail, Medi-Mail, and America's Pharmacy. For prescription medications, enclose the doctor's prescription with the order.

Members of the American Association of Retired Persons (people over 50 can join for $5 a year), should call the organization's pharmacy-by-mail (800-456-2277 or 703-684-0244) for price quotes on the medications they require regularly.

♦ Avoid filling prescriptions at hospital pharmacies where prices are usually much higher than at discount drugstores.

♦ Generic drugs give you big results without the big gouge; typically they are half the cost of brand-name drugs and sometimes even less. A 1989 survey revealed that the prescription blood-pressure medication Inderal sold for as much as $40 per hundred tablets while its generic equivalent, propranolol, could be found for less than $5 per hundred.

Do generics work? Yes. Nearly half those on the market are made by the very companies that developed the brand-name product. The other half are sold by firms specializing in generics. These firms must prove to the U.S. Food and Drug Administration (FDA) that their products are bioequivalent (work in and on the body in the same way) to their brand-name brethren.

A scandal in 1989, in which several FDA employees accepted bribes from generic-drug companies, rocked the public's confidence in generics. But the FDA has purged itself and the evidence shows that the vast majority of generics will deliver the same therapeutic value as brand-name drugs. A few generics are controversial in their efficacy. This, combined with the fact that the brand-name companies work hard at spreading misinformation about generics, has many people reluctant to try them. If you have any doubts, most pharmacists will give you an informed (and honest) opinion about whether the generic drug you need will deliver the same results as a name brand. Ask.

♦ Tell your doctor when he or she is writing your prescription that you would like to take a generic medication if one is available.

Your comment serves two purposes. First, if your doctor has no objections it will eliminate any doubts you might have. Second, some doctors habitually check a box on their prescription form stating that the prescription be dispensed as written. If the doctor checks this box and lists a brand-name drug, a pharmacist cannot substitute a generic for you. By asking about generics, you'll tip the doctor not to check that box.

♦ A rose by any other name is still a rose. Keep that thought in mind when evaluating over-the-counter medications. You'll get the same headache relief from 325 milligrams of aspirin regardless of whether it's labelled Bayer or Brand X. Meanwhile, 200 mg of ibuprofen will give you the same relief whether the bottle reads Advil or Acme, and 325 mg of acetaminophen will do about the same whether the pills are Tylenol or TyTabs.

Buy your generics from a reputable pharmacy or chain and you can rest assured the medication will duplicate the efficacy of the name brand. That applies to the gamut of medications: pain relievers, decongestants, cough suppressants, antihistamines. If you're unsure whether a $7 bottle of Robitussin will give you the same cough relief as a $4 bottle of Robicop, ask the pharmacist which one, on a cost-benefit basis, is the smart buy.

♦ Generally, over-the-counter generics cost about half as much as the name brands. Following are a few examples from the pharmacy I frequent: Afrin nose spray is $7.43 versus $3.39 for the same quantity of generic, Bayer Aspirin is $8.49 for 200 tablets versus $3.99 for 300 tablets of generic. Advil is $10.99 for 250 tablets versus $7.57 for 500 tablets of generic ibuprofen.

♦ The three common over-the-counter analgesics are aspirin, acetaminophen, and ibuprofen. All work well for minor pains. Ibuprofen is often preferred for sprains, sore muscles, and menstrual pain. Generic aspirin, however, is the cheapest of the three and, if it has given you faithful relief without upsetting your stomach, stay with it.

The "extra strength" rage is a marketing maneuver to lure bigger bills out of your wallet. Example: 100 tablets of Anacin delivering 400 mg of aspirin per tablet cost $5.89 while 40 maximum-strength Anacin delivering 500 mg of aspirin per tablet cost $5.39. Milligram for milligram, maximum-strength Anacin is 91% more expensive, making that pill hard to swallow.

If you have an "extra-strength" headache, three tablets of aspirin or acetaminophen (usually 325 mg each) give you nearly the same dosage as two extra-strength tablets (usually 500 mg each).

Note: Maximum adult dosages for aspirin and acetaminophen are 1000 mg every four hours. Maximum adult dosages for ibuprofen are 800 mg every eight hours. For equivalent pain relief, 200mg of ibuprofen equals about 600 mg of acetaminophen or aspirin.

♦ Pills usually come to the pharmacist in bottles of 100 and your prescription will cost more if the pharmacist must break open a bottle and count pills. Ask your doctor to prescribe any pill you or your children take regularly in multiples of 100.

♦ Talk to the pharmacist about where to store the drugs you purchase. Most drugs store better if refrigerated, but there are exceptions.
Bathroom cabinets are among the worst storage places due to the room's vacillating temperature and humidity.

♦ Chewable medicines are usually the most expensive—often twice the cost of their liquid equivalents.

♦ A medicine a child won't take is not cheap no matter how cheap it is. Ask your pharmacist about the children's medications you need and see if any of the options (generics, pills, chewables, liquids) have putrid reputations. Occasionally the cheap trick here is to buy a costlier alternative.

EMERGENCIES

♦ Using the services of a hospital emergency room make for an expensive patch job. Services rendered there cost twice what a doctor's office would bill. Moreover, many insurance companies won't pay the hospital bill if, in the end, the visit was not deemed a true emergency.
Rush to the emergency room if you slash through your arm with a chain saw, but if the injury is really not particularly threatening (e.g., a laceration requiring stitches) call your doctor's clinic. They'll juggle their schedule to see you.
If your clinic is closed for the evening or you don't have a doctor, visit a local "doc in the box" (urgent-care clinic). Most of these clinics have extended hours and don't

require appointments. Costs will be higher than a family-practice clinic, but much lower than an emergency-room visit.

♦ To help you stay out of the emergency room, consider what the doctors who work there call the most common, preventable injuries.

- Major trauma. Studies have proven that seat belts reduce automobile fatalities by over 40% and serious injury by larger percentages still. Buckle up—even for short trips. And use a lap/shoulder-belt combination when available. Without a shoulder belt, you increase the odds of injuring the back, spinal cord, head, spleen, and liver. That explains why all cars since 1990 come outfitted with lap/shoulder belts in the front *and* rear seats.

- Whiplash. Keep the seats' head restraints at a height that supports your entire head, not just the nape of your neck.

- Accidental gun shot wounds. Keep guns unloaded and locked away. Store ammunition away from the guns.

- Poisonings. Store all house- and garden-chemicals, medications, and vitamins (some are toxic in large quantities), out of children's reach. Lock them up if possible and mark them all with labels that a child understands mean "Danger!"

- Mowing accidents. Clear the lawn of sticks, rocks, and toys before mowing. Wear safety glasses. Always stop the mower when removing catch bags, adjusting wheels, etc.

- Bicycling Accidents. Over 1000 people die each year from bicycle accidents; 85% of these deaths are attributed to head injuries. Doctors know that many of these deaths and thousands of additional cases of brain damage would be prevented if riders donned proper helmets (ones that are ANSI or SNELL approved). Don't get on a bicycle without one. The advice also applies to kids riding tricycles and anyone riding a motorcycle. What about people who, despite the evidence, refuse to wear helmets? Maybe they have nothing worth protecting.

- Broken necks (and permanent paralysis). One of the most common causes is from diving into unfamiliar (and shallow) water. The diving rule: Go feet first until you know exactly what's down there.

- Dislocated shoulders and elbows. Even if children deserve it, don't yank them around by the arm—these joints are easy to dislocate.
- Choking. Keep nuts, cough drops, sucking candies, grapes, hot dogs, chunks of raw vegetables, seeds, marshmallows, etc. from children under 4- to 5-years-old. Alternately, cut these foods into smaller pieces that aren't a choking hazard.
- Slips and falls. Keep walkways and stairways free of toys, clothes, books...

HOME REMEDIES

♦ Acne. Chocolate rarely contributes to an acne attack, neither do scores of other foods with bad reputations. Primarily, genetics is to blame, which gives you yet another guilt trip to lay on your folks. Ironically, with women the makeup they apply for beautification is also responsible for the volcanic outbreaks.

Oils in the makeup are the culprits, so use oil-free products. Also, be sure to wash off that fake face every evening. Unsure how oily your makeup is? Test it by rubbing a dollop onto a sheet of typing paper with a 25% cotton-rag content. Over the course of a day, oil from the makeup will expand outward from the dollop. A very tight ring of oil is okay, but if the slick looks like an aerial photo of the Exxon Valdez disaster, switch brands.

♦ Allergies. If you happen to know that dust mites trigger your allergies, be aware that mattresses and pillows are mite havens. Protect yourself from the zoo by wrapping your mattress and pillow (under the sheets and pillow case, of course) in plastic.

Also, wash your mattress pad frequently in *hot* water and use synthetic pillows because they, too, can withstand hot-water washes.

♦ Allergies. Non-prescription allergy pills are far from ideal. Some dry you up but put you to sleep. Others keep you awake but don't work long. All of them are pricey.

Recently, a friend told me her solution for surviving hay fever season: Using her finger or a *Q-tip*, she coats the inside of each nostril with a thin layer of petroleum jelly (get the petroleum jelly at least an inch up each nostril). Apply as needed.

The remedy got me through my yearly bout of hay fever with nary a sniffle. Placebo effect? Perhaps, but because it's cheap and does no harm, it merits a try.

For more mainstream information about allergies, order *Hay Fever* from the Asthma and Allergy Foundation of America, 1717 Massachusetts Avenue, NW, Suite 305, Washington, D.C. 20036 (send 75¢).

♦ Antacid. Baking soda makes a good antacid (1/2 teaspoon soda per 1/2 cup water) and it's exceedingly cheap compared to tablets. People with high blood pressure should avoid it, however, because it is packed with sodium.

♦ Cuts, blisters, scrapes. Research backs up the claims that antibacterial salves with neomycin, polymyxin B, and bacitracin ointment (*Neosporin, Polysporin,* or generic triple antibiotic ointments) heal skin wounds faster than mercurochrome, *Bactine spray,* merthiolate, hydrogen peroxide, Campho-Phenique, and tincture of iodine. Some tests indicate that most of these other solutions actually delay healing—they *do* kill germs but are nondiscriminate and also assassinate the skin cells you're trying to save.

♦ Calcium supplements. When boiling bones to make soup broth, add a little vinegar to the water. The vinegar extracts calcium from the bones and fortifies your soup with more calcium than an equal quantity of milk.

If you get additional calcium through supplements, be aware that some brands don't break down in the stomach fast enough to be of value. At home, pop a pill into half a cup of vinegar and stir the vinegar every five minutes. If the pill dissolves or breaks apart into many pieces within 30 minutes, it's acceptable. If it maintains its original shape, it's a waste of money and should be exchanged for another brand.

♦ Canker sores. I get numerous canker sores each year—the penalty paid for the tons of candy I consume. Expensive medications like *Cankaid* don't work for me, but rubbing the sore with a cheap styptic pencil (the kind used to heal shaving nicks) usually heals the sore overnight. To use: Wet the pencil and rub it against the sore for about 10 seconds before bed (yes, it hurts).

♦ Snoring. Light and moderate snorers rarely shatter the airwaves unless they are lying on their backs. Spouses who want to sleep through the night without the annoyance of sonic booms can sew a small pouch onto the back of their partner's night shirt. A tennis ball tucked into the pouch will keep the spouse off his or her back.

If after you implement this trick your S.O. (make that S.O.B.) starts snoring on his or her stomach, smack the tennis ball with a racket. If you're too civil for barbarism, use the inexpensive foam earplugs from drugstores to dampen the roar.

♦ Sunburn. The best remedy for relieving the itch and pain of sunburn is to apply a lotion made from the aloe plant, right? While some evidence suggests this may be true, a larger body of evidence indicates that cold water and cold compresses affords the best relief. Save your nickels and let cold water, wetted shirts, or wet washcloths ease the discomfort.

HOSPITALS

♦ Currently, the average cost of a hospital stay is $900 per day and rising so, whenever possible, stay out of these centers of expense. Some studies indicate that 40% of all hospital stays among the nonelderly are unnecessary, and may be recommended more for the doctor's convenience and welfare than for your financial welfare. Discuss the financial ramifications with your doctor and explore options. If your procedure is done at an outpatient surgical center (these centers do over 1400 different procedures) you can often cut your surgical costs in half *and* eliminate the hotel component of your bill.

♦ Non-profit hospitals can be 20% cheaper than their capitalistic competitors. Teaching hospitals are also likely to charge higher rates to help finance their gee-whiz technology. If your ailment and cure don't require Star-Trek technology, stay out.

♦ To reduce the odds of having a costly complication, use the hospitals that specialize in the procedure you need (a specialty hospital should do a few hundred such procedures each year).

♦ Find out when the hospital's billing day begins and ends and plan your arrival and departure around those times.

♦ For elective surgery, find out what diagnostic tests are required and have these tests performed on an outpatient basis before the surgery. This can reduce the number of days you are in the hospital and slash the size of your bill.

♦ Specialists may be necessary for your surgery, but tell your doctor you want to be consulted for approval if one is to be used.

♦ You think eating and shopping at an airport are expensive? Compared to hospitals, airports are like bargain malls. Food, drugs, and toiletries are all outrageously expensive if the hospital sells them to you.

If you won't be on a special diet at the hospital, have your family and friends bring you meals (you'll need to receive pre-approval from the administration for a food discount). Ask your doctor what kind of medications, vitamins, pain relievers and supplies you'll need during your stay and bring your own pharmacy. When the hospital must supply drugs or medications, ask your doctor to prescribe generics. And before leaving the hospital ask what medications and supplies you've already paid for; take those items with you, leave everything else.

♦ Don't pay your hospital bill when you check out. You need time to study the charges first. Do get an itemized bill before leaving, however. You don't want to dispute charges at this instant, but you want to start reviewing the bill promptly and carefully with a fresh memory of what services and supplies were actually rendered. Why? Because studies show that hospital billing errors are the norm rather than the exception and that you are three times more likely to be overcharged than under-charged.

If your insurance does not cover or only partially covers your procedure, keep a detailed diary of your stay. Note when and how long the doctor visited, the tests performed, medications and supplies used... The secretarial work is worth the bother—one study figures the *average* size of a hospital overcharge is $1250. With that much at stake, you don't want to let figures slip through the cracks in your memory.

INFORMATION

♦ If you want solid recommendations based on the best evidence available, find out what the well-respected organizations advocate. The recommendations of the Surgeon General, American Diabetes Association, American Cancer Society, National Cancer Institute, and American Psychiatric Association are supported by many carefully performed studies.

Other highly rated (and highly readable) sources of medical and health information include: *University of California, Berkeley Wellness Letter* (P.O. Box 420148, Palm Coast, FL 32142), *Tufts University Diet and Nutrition Letter* (P.O. Box 57857, Boulder, CO 80322), the *Consumer Reports Health Letter* (P.O. Box 52148, Boulder, CO 80322), *Harvard Health Letter* (P.O. Box 420300, Palm Coast, FL 32142), and *The Johns Hopkins Medical Letter, Health After 50* (P.O. Box 420179, Palm Coast, FL 32142).

These newsletters summarize the crux of many complicated health, medical, and nutrition subjects in language you can understand. They are assembled and reviewed by medical experts and their recommendations are based on the results of careful studies.

♦ Books with information to further reduce your medical costs include *The Doctors Book of Home Remedies* by the editors of Prevention Magazine Health Books, *Take This Book to the Hospital with You* by Inlander and Weiner, *Getting the Most for Your Medical Dollar* by Inlander and Morales, and *The New Medicine Show* by the editors of Consumer Reports Books.

♦ Toll-free hotlines can help you find health-related information ranging from abortion and AIDS to spina bifida and SIDS. For a directory of different hotlines, order *A Guide to Health and Consumer Toll-Free Hotlines*. Order the guide for $1 by sending a stamped, self-addressed business envelope to Hotlines Guide, Essential Information, P.O. Box 19405, Washington, D.C. 20036.

MISCELLANEOUS

♦ Need an inexpensive calcium supplement? Try *Tums* antacid (calcium carbonate). *Tums* give you 200 mg of calcium per tablet and are cheaper than many supplements.

♦ Considering a bubbler or whirlpool, costing about $150, to convert your bathtub into a spa? If you're thinking these bathtub spas will improve your health, think again. Physical therapists report that a hot bath or shower will deliver the same health benefits.

If you think such a device will make your baths more enjoyable, make sure you're willing to spend the time assembling, disassembling, and cleaning it. Nearly half of *Consumer Report* readers who own these units and who responded to a survey said they would not buy one again.

♦ Puffing a pack of cigarettes a day costs over $730 a year—not to mention the extra $75 to $150 a year you pay in added health insurance over a non-smoker.

But that's just the tip of the fag. Smokers miss more work than non-smokers so figure in lost wages. They also miss a lot of life: A recent study showed that the average life-long smoker who is now 30 will die at the age of 64.8 while the average non-smoker who is now 30 will live to be 82.7 (an 18 year difference).

Dying from smoking may also be very expensive since smokers often die after battling heart disease, emphysema, or cancer—none of which are a cheap way to visit the pearly gates.

Inexpensive programs to quit smoking include: *Freedom from Smoking*, sponsored by the American Lung Association (get a local number from the phone book); *Fresh Start*, sponsored by the American Cancer Society (contact the local chapter or call national headquarters at 404-320-3333).

♦ The American Psychological Association (APA) does not endorse subliminal tapes and messages because double-blind studies have consistently shown that the likes of stop-smoking, lose-weight, and enhance self-esteem programs do not alter human behavior. Unfortunately, a recent survey indicated that two out of three people believe these programs, that now constitute a $50-million-a-year business, can work. Lots of people have had the subliminal wool pulled over their eyes.

♦ Dozens of unsubstantiated health schemes—chelation, laetrile, mega-vitamins—are modern-day versions of snake oil. They promise to kill your ills but actually feed on your savings. Neither a single study nor an individual's testimony is cause for jumping on a health-related band-wagon. Before you engage in an expensive program—be it for weight loss, cancer prevention, or addiction cure—look for legitimate studies to verify the claims made.

Remember, too, that great breakthroughs in medicine are rare so "miracle cures," and "astounding advances" should raise as much skepticism as curiosity.

♦ Every year 7000 women die unnecessarily from cervical cancer. Unnecessarily because cervical cancer is usually curable if caught early. An annual Pap smear from age 18 on (or once a woman is sexually active) is cheap insurance.

SKIN, SCREENS, AND SUN

♦ Visiting the tanning booths to make yourself a body beauty? Save your money and lower your chances of skin cancer to boot. Tanning salons promise a safe tan without a burn because their lights emit ultraviolet A (UVA) rays rather than the burning ultraviolet B (UVB) rays.

Traditionally, UVB rays have taken the rap as the thugs of the electromagnetic spectrum and modern sun-screens were designed to neutralize them. The sun protection factor (SPF) of a screen tells how much of the UVB light is filtered out (an SPF of 15 means that treated skin gets 15 times more protection than untreated skin).

Recent studies, however, indicate that UVA rays are far from innocuous. They accelerate the aging of skin, impair the tissue's immune reaction, and—even if you are tanned—make the skin more susceptible to skin cancer. Unfortunately, the SPF rating of sunscreens accounts for UVB rays only and there is still no standardized system telling you how much UVA protection you're receiving. Nonetheless, you will receive broader-based protection from sunscreens claiming some UVA protection.

♦ Since 1960 Americans have witnessed a 300% increase in the cases of malignant melanoma and squamous cell skin cancer, two of the more lethal forms of cancer. The good news: These are two of the most preventable forms of cancer if you protect your skin from strong sunlight. Keep your skin covered or, when you do bare it, use a sunscreen giving some UVA protection and an SPF of 15 or higher.

Use sunscreens even if you are tanned. Otherwise, the UV rays will continue to damage the skin's blood vessels and elastic fibers. The cumulative effect of years of "bagging rays" is an increased likelihood of skin cancer and hag-like wrinkles—not quite what sun worshippers have in mind.

♦ Buy waterproof sunscreens. They cost nothing extra, yet cut down dramatically on reapplication (they don't sweat off easily). Buy name-brands and major store-brands by price: Impartial product tests have found few differences in the quality of widely distributed sunscreens, yet screens like *K-Mart Solace* can be two to six times cheaper than national brands.

♦ Special screens for the face and nose carry a whopping sticker price and won't do anything that *K-Mart Solace* can't. Also, if you don't want to buy screen for your lips, rub on normal screen (keep your lips parted for a minute while the screen penetrates). Note: This trick is not recommended for children.

♦ Sunscreens for babies are formulated for sensitive skin and are unlikely to use paraaminobenzoic acid (PABA) as an active ingredient. If you find a good buy on children's sunscreen, there's no reason not to use that formula on adults too. The opposite is not necessarily true; some adult formulas may have ingredients like PABA that are not as kind to sensitive skin.

♦ Despite advertisers' claims, no moisturizing cream is known to "nourish" or slow the aging of skin—all of them simply reduce the skin's dryness. Two very inexpensive, yet effective, moisturizers are petroleum jelly and mineral oil.

As with most cosmetic products, expense has little to do with quality and a lot to do with marketing. Doctors often recommend the simplest (and cheapest) moisturizers because the expensive creams often contain perfumes, dyes, and emulsifiers that can irritate sensitive skin.

♦ Additional medical tips can be found in the *Babies and Children, Fitness, Insurance,* and *Nutrition* chapters.

With money in your pocket you are wise and you are handsome and you sing well too.
                                        Yiddish proverb

Miscellaneous Tricks

Most chapters in this book are pure breeds—well, at least they focus on a common theme. This one is the mutt: It brings you cheap tricks from many walks of life. To help you relocate particular suggestions later, they are listed below in alphabetic order.

CANDLES

♦ Candles burn longer and without much dripping if you refrigerate them for several hours before use.

♦ Large, decorative candles that have melted down in the center are difficult to light, but they don't need to be thrown out just yet. Insert a smaller candle (like a votive candle) into the hole and your decorative candle suddenly has a second life.

CARPET

♦ Dirt particles are like little knives that, when stepped upon, slice the life out of your carpet. Consequently, an easy way to double the life of your carpet is to vacuum twice as often (twice a week).

Sound like too much work? It's not if, for every two out of three cleanings, you concentrate on just the traffic lanes. These lanes can be cleaned in a matter of minutes.

♦ Other ways to extend your carpet's life: 1) Place good mats at the entrance to every outside door 2) Go Japanese: Wander the house in socks or slippers only.

CASSETTE TAPES

♦ Look for cassette tapes at rummages, garage sales, thrift stores. Don't worry about what's on the tapes, you can record over them. Often you can buy good tapes for 25¢ to 50¢.

CLEANING TRICKS

♦ Drapes. Give them a partial cleaning by tossing them in the dryer with several damp towels. Dry the lot for half an hour.

♦ Floors. Mop the floors with a piece of waxpaper and you'll give them a quick shine.

♦ Oil stains. Spots on garage floor can be sprinkled with kitty litter. Rub the litter in, let it sit for a day or two, then sweep it up. Alternately, soak several sheets of newspaper with water and press them firmly onto the stain. Let the newspaper dry thoroughly, then remove the paper. Most of the stain comes up with the paper.

♦ Screens. Rub metal screens from both sides with a rag dampened in kerosene. This cleans and preserves the screens.

♦ Socks and underwear. To get dingy white cottons white again, boil them (after washing) in water containing several slices of lemon.

♦ Thermos bottle. Add a few tablespoons of baking soda and fill with warm water. Let sit for several hours. Rinse.

COMPACT DISCS

♦ CDs that are lightly scratched and deliver poor sound quality can be improved by coating and buffing the CDs with *Data Mud* (available at record stores). You'll get the same dramatic improvement in sound quality at much lower prices, however, if you polish damaged CDs with *Rally* auto wax. *Carefully* coat the CD with a thin film of wax, then buff with a very soft, clean, lint-free cloth.

CORRESPONDENCE

♦ If you have a complaint or inquiry with a catalog company, use the business-reply envelopes from inside the catalog (meant for sending in your order) for your correspondence. The postage is usually prepaid.

FIRE EXTINGUISHERS

♦ A few fire extinguishers around the house are cheap insurance for an emergency. Of all residential fires, 80%

start in the kitchen; keep a bicarbonate extinguisher handy here. Keep an all-purpose extinguisher in the garage/shop and in the cars.

♦ A big box of baking soda (sodium bicarbonate) makes an inexpensive fire extinguisher for dousing kitchen pan fires. The baking soda is nonflammable *and*, when thrown on flames, produces carbon dioxide which helps suffocate the fire.

FLOWERS

♦ Refrigerate cut flowers at night and you'll nearly double their life.

GARBAGE BAGS (Plastic)

♦ In a review of plastic garbage bags, *Consumer Reports* found that many store-brand bags were as strong as the national-brand bags and significantly cheaper (about 50% less in large sizes, 30% less in medium). Try several different brands and it won't take long to hone in on a store giving you high quality for a low cost.

GARBAGE BILLS

♦ They go up every year and with the shrinking landfill space and tougher standards for burning rubbish, garbage bills will continue to rise. Beat the system: Cut the bills in half by doubling up with your neighbor.

For the past two years, my family has shared a garbage can with the neighbors and we have yet to have our garbage runneth over. Now that our neighborhood has curbside recycling, we could take on even a third neighbor.

Hint: Call your garbage company and ask about the maximum-size container allowed. Many companies accommodate huge cans that will swallow the trash of several families.

GIFTS

♦ Instead of spending money on presents, volunteer your time for house cleaning, lawn work, massages, baby-sitting, cooking, haircuts, manicures.

♦ When a wine you like is on sale, stock up on it. Use these bargain bottles as gifts when you have dinner with friends. Do the same with jams or chocolates if these are the gifts you tote when you go a-visiting.

GIFT-WRAP

♦ Call home-decorating stores and ask them to save their wallpaper scraps and old books of wallpaper samples for you. Use the paper to wrap gifts or to make craft projects with your children.

♦ Newspaper cartoons make colorful wrapping paper.

HAIRCUTS

♦ Call the local beauty schools and ask what they charge for haircuts. The cost of a full-service appointment complete with consulting, hair wash, and cut will be way below what beauty salons charge. Using these schools works much like a normal shop. Call ahead to arrange an appointment (you can reserve students you've used in the past); then come in and get chopped. With hair being the vanity pacifier it is, only you can decide whether you're pleased— you will, however, receive professional-quality service.

Try it. If you're displeased, the damage is temporary—like our family proverb says, "The difference between a good cut and a bad one is about five days." If you're pleased, however, you'll have found a long-term means of saving yourself $9 or $10 a cut.

INVITATION

♦ A cheap but interesting party invitation: Blow up a balloon, write the invitation on the balloon, deflate the balloon and mail it.

LABOR

♦ Seattle has a non-profit organization called the Millionair Club Charity that, among other things, helps people without jobs find part-time work. Residents and businesses alike can hire workers through the charity for roofing, lawn work, manual labor, construction clean-up, simple carpentry jobs, house cleaning, window washing, painting, janitorial work... These workers are screened by the charity and do quality work at the low rate of $6 to $7 an hour. Friends who have used these workers said they received real value: people who worked hard for reasonable rates.

Seattleites can call 206-728-5627 for more information about the Millionair Club. Residents of other cities should call their Chambers of Commerce or Better Business Bureaus to see if their area has a similar program.

LOCKS

♦ When car locks freeze, you don't need a de-icing liquid or a battery-warmed blank to thaw the locks. Put your hot air to work for a change. Using a straw (or a piece of paper rolled up like a straw) blow on the lock for a minute. It works.

LOTTERY

♦ If you play your state's Lotto, quit. You can't change the laws of chance and those laws are stacked against you—way against you. Most states with a Lotto-type game give you 1-in-14 million, 1-in-18 million, or 1-in-23 million odds of winning per ticket sold. Imagine your name is in the New York City telephone directory: The odds of someone opening the directory and pointing to your name are better than winning these games.

Washington State, where I live, gives "good" odds of winning: 1-in-7 million chances per ticket sold. But even these good odds are so bad they are beyond comprehension. If you bought a ticket once a week for 67,000 *years*, the odds of *not* winning those drawings would still be better than the odds of winning once.

The only way to win is not to play. Then you reap the benefits of state services paid for by Lotto players at no cost to yourself. Not a bad way of winning the game.

LUGGAGE

♦ Want a color of soft luggage that will give you the most mileage? Avoid light colors—they show dirt too quickly. Meanwhile, very dark colors show the whitish haze caused by abrasion. That leaves colors of medium intensity as your best bet. Tweeds are especially effective at camouflaging dirt.

NEGOTIATING

♦ When shopping thrift stores, garage sales, rummage sales, wear well-worn clothing. If you want to dicker over prices, you'll make better headway if you look needy.

♦ More stores than you would expect are willing to bargain. This may be less true for department stores, but even here there are cases where you'll get a bite if you fish for a better price. To test whether there is any room for negotiating, try a few innocent questions. What kind of discounts are given for cash? What kind of discounts are given for buying two of something? What price will an item be when it goes on sale? Can you get the sale price now? Will a store match the price of a competitor?

The questions can be asked in a non-abrasive manner and the answers will quickly tell you whether the store owner/manager will budge on price or whether you should mosey along to another store.

If you are hoping to negotiate, don't act too interested in an item and don't hesitate to walk away if you don't get some cooperation.

PARKING

♦ If your car barely fits in the garage, hang a length of rope (knotted at the low end) from the ceiling. The knot should touch the car's windshield when the car is correctly positioned. It's a simple way to keep from driving through the back of the garage some day.

PESTS

◆ Got birds roosting where you don't want them? Scare them away with rubber snakes purchased from novelty stores. Or hang strands of monofilament fishing line around the eves, light fixtures, and down spouts where birds like to roost—the sensation of the nearly invisible line scares the birds.

◆ Pouring pots of boiling water down the hills and holes of ants will destroy a colony cheaply.

♦ Remove aphids and spiders by washing plants with a mixture of water and mild detergent. For large jobs use a hose-end sprayer filled with detergent.

♦ Spraying flies with hair spray immobilizes them long enough to kill them.

♦ Make inexpensive fly paper by dabbing honey on a strip of yellow paper. The yellow paper draws the flies, the honey holds them.

♦ The belief that cedar chests repel or kill moths is a myth. Cedar chests simply keep moth larvae (the guys who do the munching) away from your clothes because the tight seal keeps egg-laying moths out. But dirty clothes that enter the chest with moth eggs or larvae on them will emerge later with holes—and the damage can easily spread to other clothing. Consequently, the first step in protecting stored clothing is to clean everything (machine wash, hand wash, or dry-clean).

Moth larvae dine on anything containing wool, fur, or feathers. Unfortunately, they also chew through cotton, silk, acrylic, and polyester if the fabric has stains or salts that can nourish them. So for added protection, wrap items for storage in plastic bags.

PETS

♦ After using the broiler pan, soak it in water overnight to loosen the meat drippings. In the morning, pour the resulting broth over the dog's dry food. Turns another boring meal of dry food into an Alpo day.

♦ Using large kitchen garbage bags (three-ply) as litter-box liners costs about a quarter as much as buying official cat-box liners. And they work. If your cat claws through single garbage bags, then double-up the bags—this still does the job for half price.

♦ Pine needles in the dog house or under Fido's pad reputedly repel fleas.

PHOTOGRAPHY

♦ The mail-order discount houses are famous for selling big name photography gear at low prices. Many pros order their gear through outlets like those mentioned in the *Mail-order Appendix.* I've ordered cameras, lenses, tripods, and camcorders without a hitch. If you know what you want, it's a great way to buy. Make sure you're not purchasing gray-market goods, so that you get a valid U.S. warranty (see the *Mail-order* chapter).

Question the other details, too. Does the camera come with the manufacturer's lens (instead of a cheap Brand-X one)? If the camera has auto-focus ability, is the accompanying lens an auto-focus one? Will you receive all the normal straps and cases?

♦ Film is also an excellent buy through the discount mail-order houses. Current mail-order prices for 36 exposures of Kodachrome run under $8 for film *and* processing. The same film and processing costs $15 at K-Mart and $13.50 through the cheapest retail outlet I've found in Seattle. Savings are comparable for Fujichrome, but buy processing only if the mail-order house is selling U.S. mailers for the film (foreign mailers cost extra to have processed).

♦ Mail order is also where you'll find great deals in film processing and print making. Prices are often half of what you'd pay at drugstores or department stores. And low price does not mean low quality. It usually means that you have eliminated a middleman who was enjoying a feast. See the *Mail-order* Appendix (Photography Services) for addresses of processing labs.

One disadvantage of mail-order processing labs is time—no next-day service. Expect to wait a week (two for some labs) before you see your priceless photos. On the plus side, there's no driving or special errands to run—just walk to the mailbox.

What do you do about work that you deem to be substandard? If an enlargement is too dark, washed out, or has poor color balance, and you decide the problem is in the processing (not the quality of your negative/slide), don't hesitate to send it back. Include a note describing the problem and request a remake. A good lab won't charge you for its errors. I've requested remakes on several occasions with different companies and have never had the lab balk.

POTS AND PANS

♦ The inexpensive non-stick pans I've owned have worked just as well as the expensive ones. Give you three guesses what I recommend.

SALES

♦ Whether you're buying skis, lawn mowers, clothes, or tires, there is a season when you can get your item on sale. August and January are among the two best months for sales because most stores are making the transition from one season to the next.

SAWDUST

♦ Sawdust from the shop can reduce the treachery of icy sidewalks and driveways. And it blows away on its own in spring.

SHARPENING

♦ Sharpen scissors by cutting up a piece of 220-grit sandpaper into thin slices.

♦ Sharpen a dull sewing-machine needle by stitching through a piece of fine-grit sandpaper.

SILVERWARE

♦ Laying pieces of aluminum foil in your silverware box reduces tarnishing. This is cheaper than buying commercial strips that reduce tarnishing and is easier than polishing.

SPOUSES

♦ A friend of my brother's was dating two women simultaneously and was smitten by each. He had the good sense to understand, however, that by keeping two in the bush he may never get one in the hand, so he decided to end one relationship. To determine which, he had a credit check run on each. One woman, with her large loans and extended credit cards, looked to be a bad risk. He eventually married the other girl.

A credit check of a potential spouse (if you have the connections to snoop for you) may be romantically and morally distasteful, but, pragmatically, it's a stroke of genius. After all, once you utter, "Til death do we part," your spouse (not a house or car) becomes the biggest expense in your life. It is he or she who will have a pivotal role in the type of house you buy, the kind of car you own, whether you need to keep up with the Joneses... Get stuck with a spendthrift and for better or for worse you can forget about the "for richer" part of the vows.

STORAGE

♦ An old dresser drawer is excellent for storing items under beds. Attach casters to the bottom of the drawer for easier retrieval.

♦ If storage in your home is a real problem, consider this table. Bolt together two or three kitchen cabinets. Have a formica table top made to your specifications that covers these cabinets. Attach the tabletop to the cabinets and you'll have your storage and a table too.

♦ Short on space for your linens? Store extra sheets and blankets between a bed's mattress and box spring.

♦ If you are tight on space in your clothes closet, save the plastic rings formed when you open a gallon milk bottle with a screw-on cap. Slip this plastic ring over the hook of a hanger and you've created a place where you can hang one hanger onto another. This trick lets you hang two or three hangers in a chain and effectively doubles or triples the amount of clothing you can pack in a closet.

To implement this trick without drinking 50 gallons of milk, make rings (about 1.5" in diameter) from sturdy cord.

THE Nth DEGREE

Some tricks go to outrageous measures to save a penny and even if you deem the following unworthy of your time, they're fun to know about.

♦ Tired of poking fingers through the end of rubber gloves? Push a cotton ball down each finger first.

♦ Your pencil getting too short to hold? Lengthen it by screwing a long drywall screw into the eraser.

♦ The fluid in your spray bottle getting lower than the uptake tube? Drop pebbles or marbles into the bottom of the bottle to raise the fluid level.

♦ Your sandpaper wearing out too fast? Reinforce the backside of the paper with several strips of masking tape and the paper lasts longer.

♦ Water poured down the drain could often be used on your plants. Water used to boil eggs, water surrounding frozen fish or from an aquarium, even water from the bath will benefit your plants.

TOOL STORAGE

♦ Keep your garden tools from rusting by sticking the metal portion in a bucket of sand treated with a cup or two of motor oil (used motor oil works fine).

VACUUM

♦ Don't mind rolling up your sleeves and getting dirty to pinch a penny? Then don't throw out the vacuum cleaner bag when it is full. Shake or pull out the dirt and lint; then reuse the bag.

Some bags are very fragile and tear if you pull dirt out the entrance it went in. To reuse these bags, pull apart the opposite end of the bag, then shake out the dirt. Once empty, roll up the newly opened end and staple it shut with eight or nine staples. Only empty these fragile bags once, but reuse heftier bags several times before tossing them.

WATER PURIFIERS

♦ According to the Environmental Protection Agency (EPA), less than 1% of the water from public systems presents any kind of health hazard. Still, water-treatment businesses have created nearly a billion-dollar industry selling people equipment and filters to treat water that is already safe.

Because some of these companies pull dirty (and dishonest) tricks to convince people that their water is dirty, don't sign any checks for equipment until you've done your own unbiased research. Call your local water district or health department for information about the area's water quality. If you voice legitimate concerns, agency employees may come out and test your water at no charge.

WEDDING

♦ Ask who else is saying "I do" at the same facility on the same day. Maybe you can split the cost of flowers?

Poverty has many roots, but the tap root is ignorance.
Lyndon B. Johnson

Nutrition

Deciphering fact from fiction in the nutrition arena is no easy job. Advertisers feed us so many half-truths (or even lies), we hear so many inflated claims about the merits of X and the dangers of Y, and we read so many inaccurate articles that we become bundles of misinformation. To make my point, I challenge you to a true/false quiz. Test your nutrition knowledge and learn some related cheap tricks in the process.

Most of these questions (and answers) are adapted from a research questionnaire prepared by my brother, a family-practice doctor who spent two years performing nutrition research. The correct answers to his questions were agreed upon by a panel of nutrition experts including five Ph.D. nutritionists and two directors of family-practice clinics who also teach medicine.

True or false: The only scientifically-proven ill effect of sugar is cavities?

A: You can't live on sugar alone any more than on bread alone (which the body breaks down into sugar) but sugar does have a healthy wreath of misconceptions surrounding it. A task force formed by the U.S. Food and Drug Administration has tried to correct these misconceptions.

For starters, sugar does not *cause* diabetes although diabetics must control sugar intake because they lack insulin to process it. Next, while sugar does contribute toward hypoglycemia in diabetics, exceedingly few non-diabetics get low blood sugar rebounding from eating too much sugar. Meanwhile, double-blind studies fail to support the claims made by many parents that sugar transforms angelic children into jittery monsters who bounce off the walls. Other studies fail to show a link between sugar and high blood pressure, heart disease, cancer, or gallstones. The answer: True.

Cheap trick application: If cavities and weight control are not a problem, don't spend extra on sugar-free products.

True or false: The American Diabetic Association recommends honey rather than sugar as a sweetener?

A: A sugar is a sugar. For all practical purposes, different types of sugars (refined and unrefined) are metabolized in nearly the same fashion. Honey, like refined sugar, converts into glucose. The same story applies to carbohydrates, which are complex sugars (simple sugars bonded together). Enzymes break down the bonds and the resulting simple sugars are converted to glucose. The answer: False.

Cheap trick applications: Don't fall for the health-food gimmicks peddling different forms of sugar (unrefined sugar, honey, brown sugar, fructose, molasses) at higher prices.

True or false: For good nutrition information, consult your doctor?

A: Although the public is encouraged to consult their physicians for dietary advice, carefully controlled studies have repeatedly documented that physicians, as a group, do not offer reliable nutrition counseling. Medical personnel and organizations have reliable nutrition information at their disposal, but doctors don't know the facts—partly because nutrition is rarely included as part of a doctor's medical training, partly because doctors are contaminated by the same misinformation that sullies the rest of us.

Other dubious sources of nutrition information are "nutritionists" (anyone can use this label). Also, don't be impressed by a Ph.D. in nutrition unless you know the degree is from a reputable university. The answer: False.

Cheap Trick Application: Don't spend money getting dietary consultation from physicians unless you know they have special nutrition training or have a registered dietitian working with them. Also, take what you read in most magazines (even popular "health" magazines) with a pound of salt—magazine articles are often riddled with errors or do not report new findings in proper context.

Get your nutrition counseling from a registered dietitian. They've received four years of nutition training to earn their degrees. Other highly rated (and highly readable) sources of nutrition information include: *University of California, Berkeley Wellness Letter* (P.O. Box 420148, Palm Coast, Florida 32142), *Tufts University Diet and Nutrition Letter* (P.O. Box 57857, Boulder, Colorado 80322), *Consumer Reports Health Letter* (P.O. Box 52148, Boulder, Colorado 80322), and the *The Johns Hopkins Medical Letter, Health After 50* (P.O. Box 420179, Palm Coast, FL 32142).

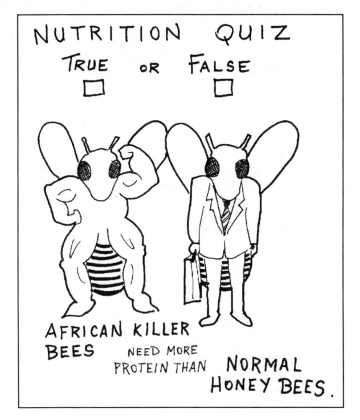

True or false: Athletes need a higher protein diet than non-athletes?

A: Sugars—not proteins—provide the energy to sustain heavy exercise. Continued exercise does build muscle mass but the registered daily allowance (RDA) for protein accommodates the protein needs for growing muscles. The RDA for protein is 56 grams for men, 44 grams for women.

Interestingly, the sporting community is a most susceptible group to nutrition myths and unsubstantiated fads. The desire to win makes athletes willing to embrace outrageous schemes in the hopes of gaining a competitive edge. The answer: False.

Cheap trick application: As an athlete, don't waste your food budget consuming excess protein—meats, cheeses, and other forms of protein are the most expensive part of a balanced diet. Approach expensive foods, drinks, and diets for athletes with skepticism, keeping in mind that capitalistic America wants your pecuniary contribution more than your personal best. Follow the advice of a registered dietitian—preferably one with a sports specialty—instead of the newest fad.

True or false: Milligram for milligram, synthetic vitamins are as useful to the body as natural vitamins.

A: The body doesn't care how a vitamin is made. It is the advertisers who make a big deal—and big profit—creating the illusion that "natural" vitamins are better. The answer: True.

Cheap trick application: Buy the vitamins giving you the most milligrams for the least money.

True or false: Legally, any nutrition claim about a product is permitted as long as those claims are not made on the label.

A: People can say or write anything they want about a product or vitamin as long as it isn't an advertisement. That is our right by the first amendment: It protects our right to tell the truth, and to lie. If I choose to write a book claiming that vitamin C cures colds (even though the bulk of evidence fails to support the premise), that is my right. If I want to write an article saying that vitamin E will turn wimps into studs, I can. My book will have hypochondriacs yanking vitamin C off the shelves while my article will have the sexually impotent chomping vitamin E like popcorn.

In advertising, false claims are outlawed, but misleading ones are not. For vitamin C, the ad might say, "Just the thing for a cold." The ad leads consumers to a false conclusion without lying. The answer: True.

Cheap trick application: Ignore claims made by the manufacturers and promoters of nutrition products—they have a vested interest. Be very skeptical of spiels touting "wonder vitamins" or "miracle elixirs": Snakeoil salesmanship is alive and well and it feasts off gullibility. Miraculous claims that survive the scrutiny of real tests will promptly make the mainstream. You'll read about them in *Time*, *Newsweek*, and the reputable magazines mentioned earlier.

True or false: Bottled water is healthier than tap water?

A: Bottled water doesn't need to meet any higher standard of safety than your municipality's standards for tap water. Some bottled waters are drawn from the local water system, and although they may receive additional filtration and treatment, they may not.

Tests performed by reputable consumer organizations show that bottled water is no safer than the tap water from most municipal water systems and that some bottled waters contain disturbing levels of arsenic and fluoride. The answer: False.

Cheap trick application: Get off the bottled water bandwagon (that goes for seltzer and Perrier, too). Just drink tap water. If your local water has a bad bite to it, freshen the taste by adding lemon slices and chilling it.

True or false: Enriched flour is a good source of vitamins and minerals?

A: After enrichment white flour is nutritionally very similar to whole-wheat flour. The vitamins and minerals added are just as useful to the body as those found there naturally. The one important component found in whole-wheat flour but nearly absent in white flour is roughage. Nevertheless, the answer is true.

Cheap trick application: Don't let health-food claims persuade you that white flour is a nutritional vacuum, but do use more whole-wheat flour to benefit from its roughage. Regardless of the flour used, don't buy it from expensive health stores. Shop the normal aisles of the supermarket and get whatever brand (national or store brand) is cheapest. Brand loyalty is a waste of bread.

True or false: It is well known that many obese people don't eat any more than average-weight people.

A: Skinny people don't buy it, but the answer is true. The basic fact about weight is this: If you eat more calories than you burn, you'll gain weight. Many obese people eat no more than their thinner brethren, but they burn off less—they are underactive more than overfed. Meanwhile, some obese people have very efficient basal metabolisms and simply use fewer calories sustaining life—too bad such efficiency translates into jelly bellies.

Cheap trick application: No amount of money spent on the newest diet or scientifically formulated foods will change the facts—to lose weight you must consume fewer calories than you burn. Like it or not, that leaves you with three courses of action: eat less, exercise more, or eat less and exercise more. None of these options is easy—they involve changing habits, changing lifestyle patterns. If you expect it to be easy, you're not ready to succeed.

If spending big dollars on a diet provides the impetus needed to stick to a difficult task, then it is money well spent. But if you can summon an iron will without this financial blackmail, dieting is a cheap proposition. Eat a balanced, low-fat diet, taking in fewer calories than in bygone days. On top of this, boost your metabolism with regular exercise. It doesn't need to be rigorous: Walking a mile burns about as many calories as jogging the mile, it just takes longer to fry them.

That is all the theory you need to know. The facts about weight loss are exceedingly simple—it's the execution that is tough.

How did you score?

9: Did you cheat?

8-7: Ever consider a career in nutrition?

6: Better than average.

5-4: Average score—which is the same as guessing.

3-2: You're misinformed, uninformed, or both.

1-0: I'll be kind and shut up.

Paper Products

My sister and I once laughed at my grandmother's tight-wad ways. Here was a woman who rinsed and reused paper towels until they dissolved into balls of pulp, doubled the life of paper napkins by tearing them in half, and whited-out the writing on the greeting cards she received so she could resend them.

I'm not sure whether cheapness is a contagious or congenital condition, but today I practice similar ploys. I keep a small straw basket next to the sink where I store used paper napkins and towels. When I need to mop up grease from the frying pan, wipe my oily hands after car work, or sop up spills, out come the contents of that basket. I'm not the only victim of the affliction: On a Thanksgiving visit to my sister's, I watched her tear the paper napkins in half before they went onto the table.

Following are some other tricks my sister and I employ to minimize what we spend on paper products. If my grandmother were still alive to read the list, she'd be the one laughing now.

♦ Keep a cloth towel in the kitchen and use it for drying your hands. Toss the towel in the laundry when it's soiled. Save paper towels for truly dirty work (blotting bacon grease, wiping oily hands, mopping spills).

♦ Paper towels come in many different qualities and it is worth buying two different grades. Use the cheapest grade for everyday use (wiping hands, minor spills) and the heavy-duty grades for hefty chores (washing windows, rubbing grease off auto parts).

♦ Toilet paper and paper towels are notorious for being sold in bulk packs where the per-roll price is *higher* than the per-roll price of singletons or small packs. Don't make any assumptions about bulk buying—do your math.

♦ Substitute cloth napkins for paper ones. Teach family members to refold and leave their napkins at their place for the next meal. You can use cloth napkins this way for at least a week before washing them.

At my house we use a variation on the theme: We each have a different napkin holder. After each meal, our napkins go into our personal napkin holder. At the next meal, there is no question whose napkin is whose—my wife grabs the lion napkin holder and I, symbolically, reach for the monkey.

♦ Use paper napkins for picnics and really messy meals (spare ribs, spaghetti) but make them go twice as far by tearing them in half before setting the table. Open them and tear (or cut) them along the crease. Fold the two resulting pieces in half and the finished napkins will *look* normal on the table.

♦ Save used paper napkins and towels. Keep them in a coffee can under the sink and employ them for messy chores later (working on the car, painting...)

♦ Out of coffee filters? Use a single-ply paper towel of reasonable quality or a facial tissue as a substitute and you may discover you can dispense with filters and save money. Both facial tissues and paper towels have the necessary wet strength needed for the job.

The #4 filters for my Braun coffee maker are four times more expensive than an equal number of paper towels. Because I cut paper towels in half and make two filters from every towel, the #4 filters are actually eight times more expensive.

The basket filters for machines like Mr. Coffee are considerably cheaper, but an inexpensive roll of single-ply paper towels is still likely to cost 30% less (60% less if you cut the towels in half).

Note: Not all paper towels drip water as quickly as coffee filters. Pay attention the first time you brew a really large pot of coffee to make sure the water exiting the grounds is keeping pace with the water entering.

♦ Squash your rolls of toilet paper so that the cores are flat and rotate awkwardly over the central dowel of the dispenser. This discourages kids and guests from rolling out miles of paper per use.
Note: This works only if the central dowel of your dispenser does not rotate.

♦ Keep facial tissue in the house for visiting guests, but when you blow your own nose or remove makeup from your eyes, use toilet paper instead of facial tissue. Two squares of medium-quality TP give you plenty of paper for a good nose blow or eye wipe, yet cost a third of what you pay for a sheet of medium-quality facial tissue. As for softness, the two papers are nearly identical.

♦ I once wrote a letter to my senator suggesting that the form letters mailed to his constituency be printed on both sides of the paper. I argued the practice would significantly reduce the cost of his mailings and save taxpayers' dollars. The senator never adopted my suggestions, but you should. Use both sides of your writing paper.
   And don't discard the reams of paper you receive in the mail that are printed on one side only. Use those sheets for scratch paper, writing letters to friends, coloring paper for kids... Why purchase note pads costing about a penny a sheet when the paper you throw away will do the job?

♦ The paper collected above can be bound into pads by means of a simple trick. Grab a 1/2-inch stack of like-sized paper (e.g., 8 1/2 inches by 11 inches) and tap the stack on a hard surface until the bottom edges of all the sheets are flush. Clamp the wad of paper using giant paper clips (make sure the edge of the pad remains flush). Stand the pad between two large books that are leaning against each other in an A-frame configuration. Spread a paper-thin layer of liquid plastic like *Goop* or *Shoe Goo* (see the *Repair* chapter) across the top of the pad. Let the liquid plastic harden and, *voilà*, you've created a pad of paper.

In 15 minutes (less time than a trip to the store) you can lay up a dozen pads, but the glue takes several hours to cure.

♦ A package of stick-on mailing labels (size: 3 1/2 inches by 1 inch) will net big savings over time. The large manilla envelopes you receive in the mail are often closed only by a metal clasp in the back and are marred on the front with only a label and postage mark. Use your stick-on labels to cover the old label and postage mark, then reuse the envelope.

Another way to remove an old address from an envelope is with the sticky side of cellophane tape. The tape will lift out certain types of inks if applied lightly. For indelible inks, apply the tape firmly and then pull it off; it will peel off the top layer of the paper and the ink with it.

♦ I receive many books by mail and am especially careful to salvage the padded envelopes they come in; these padded envelopes retail for about 70¢ each. By tearing off old labels (or covering them with several stick-on labels), I can reuse the envelopes for mailing my own fragile items.

♦ Much of your mail does not need to be sent in envelopes. Fold your letters in half (or thirds) and staple them shut. Write the address on the back of the page, stamp the letter, and mail it.

♦ Make postcards from the photographic prints you don't intend to keep as part of your permanent photo collection. Friends will get more enjoyment from these pictures than your drawers will.

The minimum size for a postcard is 3 1/2 inches by 5 inches. If the prints are larger than 4 1/4 inches by 6 inches, cut them down so that you qualify for postcard rates (larger cards can be sent without an envelope but require the same postage as a letter).

♦ For additional paper-related tricks see the *Greeting Card* and *Reuse* chapters.

Repairs

When you sit on your sunglasses and break the frames, lacerate your hip waders on barbed wire, or abrade a hole in the toe of your tennis shoes, what do you do? If you are Donald Trump, you trash the damaged goods. But if you're among the humble majority who do not earn thousands of dollars an hour, you grab the glue. Epoxy on the bridge of the glasses, contact cement to patch the waders, and liquid rubber on the toe of the tennis shoe, will fix for pennies those items costing dollars to replace.

With over 15,000 glues on the market, which glues do you need? Some glues are so specialized they could help Trump-types patch a failed marriage or a crumbling empire. We the humble, however, don't need specialty glues. We need a team of all-purpose glues that will repair the most breakdowns for the least money. Usually that means stocking four or five different glues.

♦ Epoxy cement, a two-tube glue that you mix, is a star player of that team. It creates a very strong, waterproof bond that sticks to most hard surfaces (metal, plastics, wood, porcelain). It also fills gaps on surfaces that won't be flexed. Slow-setting epoxies (24 hours to cure) are the strongest, but the 5-minute varieties still receive good grades for strength. The quick sets are better when bonding parts and pieces that cannot be clamped. Elmer's, Duro, and Devcon are all widely available, good-quality epoxies.

Be creative using these glues. Consider how you can increase the size of the gluing surface. To fix a broken ski pole, for example, insert a glue-smeared wooden plug inside the pole at the point of the break: this splints the pole and greatly enlarges the gluing surface on both sides of the break. When gluing items with a hidden side, glue splints (e.g., old popsicle sticks) over the break on the hidden side.

♦ My neighbor, Elmer, is a fix-it expert who handles the tough repair jobs around the block. The all-purpose glue he praises with fanatical fervor is *Marine Tex*, an epoxy putty. It bonds materials together like a glue and acts as a putty to repair leaks in fuel tanks, water tanks, piping, food containers, cracks in the crankcase of engines.... It bonds to metal, plastic, fiberglass, wood, glass and is impervious to water, oil, grease, fuel, brine, and detergents. The glue has both incredible tensile and compressive strength and won't shatter under heavy blows. Amazing stuff. Get it from marine-supply stores or contact the manufacturer (Travaco Laboratories, 345 Eastern Ave., Chelsea, MA 02150, 617-884-7740).

♦ Elmer also does many remodeling jobs around the neighborhood and he uses *Liquid Nails* (made by The Glidden Company and widely available from hardware stores) for a wide array of construction jobs. It firmly bonds large and small sections of wood, panelling, ceramic tile, corkboard, or foam panelling to wood, brick, or cement.

♦ I'm more of a lover of flexible glues. As an avid outdoorsman, I must often patch holes in rubber boots, tarps, rubber rafts, tents, running shoes, and hiking boots. Liquid-rubber glues like *Shoo Goo*, *Goop*, *Aquaseal*, and *Freesole* are priceless members of my repair team. They all emerge from a tube as a viscous liquid you can spread over rubber, nylon, neoprene, plastic, canvas, leather. Then they harden into a flexible, tough patch.

The different brands of these glues vary tremendously in their ability to bond to slick surfaces like rubber and plastic. Of the five or six brands I've tested over time, *Aquaseal* and *Freesole* are the runaway winners. They cost more and are slow to cure (at least 12 hours), but there is little comparison in how well they bond to the soles of running shoes, the leather of hiking boots, or the rubber of hip waders. Get them at scuba diving shops, backpacking shops, marine supply stores, or contact the manufacturer (McNett Corporation, 1405 Frazer, Bellingham, WA 98226, 206-671-2227).

When applying these glues, keep the patch neat by putting masking tape around the boundaries of the patch. If patching a gaping hole, rub tape to the underside so that the glue can pool and cure without draining away.

♦ The other important flexible glue in my arsenal is contact cement. Use it to glue rubber patches to tires or rafts, attach velcro to non-porous surfaces, anchor masonite to countertops, bond a square of linoleum that has worked free. It is waterproof, and lets you bond two surfaces together in a matter of minutes.

♦ Wood glue (Elmer's white glue) and carpenter's glue (Elmer's yellow glue) are inexpensive, strong adhesives for interior use on a wide variety of porous materials—wood, paper, particle board, cardboard. Carpenter's glue has a shorter clamping time, is more water resistant, and sands easier than white glue.

Resin glues, like *Weldwood Plastic Resin Glue*, are strong, waterproof wood glues excellent for outdoor use. Franklin's *Titebond II Wood Glue*, sold at most home centers, is a no-mix glue that it is well-suited for outdoor use.

♦ Watching late-night TV ads, you would think that Superman himself could not tear asunder something repaired with *Super Glue*. But many people I know, myself included, have had little success with instant adhesives like *Super Glue* and *Krazy Glue* and favor other solutions.

To be fair, some people find these adhesives, called cyanoacrylates, very useful for gluing items that can't be clamped (porcelain, pottery, fingers, eyelids). Apparently these glues just don't stick for people of my IQ.

♦ Duct tape: It's not technically a glue, but I think of it as one because it has 1001 uses for splinting broken items and temporarily patching holes. In the car, I've used it to repair leaking engine hoses, mend broken wires, or cover nicks in the windshield until they are fixed properly. Around home it can splint broken handles, repair wires, seal minor leaks in pipes, clamp odd-shaped items for gluing. In the field, it can fix punctures in air mattresses, seal water leaks in rubber boots, mend holes in tent floors, hold bandages to a wound, splint ski poles.

Buyer's tip: Many modern duct tapes contain a low thread count (horizontal threads 1/8 inch apart), making the tape quite weak. Good tape has a finer thread mesh (more like the mesh of a screen door).

♦ Mouse and rat traps make inexpensive and effective clamps for gluing a wide assortment of items. Tape, hose clamps, bungie cords (elastic straps), and heavy-duty rubber bands can also supply excellent pressure while gluing awkward items.

♦ When repairing machinery, gaskets must often be replaced. If you don't have a new gasket, make your own from silicone products like *GE Silicone High-Temp Instant Gasket*. Directions on the package tell you what to do.

One common need for a new gasket is in the LCD waterproof watches made by companies like Casio. Whenever the battery is changed, the casing gasket should be replaced or the watch may lose its waterproofness. But this may involve shipping the watch to the manufacturer and a $20 fee. Forget it—that's probably more than you paid for the watch.

Take the watch home, use needle-nose pliers to screw the watch's back from its face plate, coat the threads with a thin layer of gasket-making compound, and screw the halves back together. Your watch is waterproof again but can be disassembled later when you need another battery change.

If a man has money, it is usually a sign, too, that he knows how to take care of it; don't imagine his money is easy to get simply because he has plenty of it.

Edgar Watson Howe

Restaurants

Buck Peterson offers one approach to eating on the cheap while traveling. In *The Original Road Kill Cookbook*, he lists tongue-in-cheek recipes for preparing the fruits of the highway—skunk, opossum, dogs.

Me? I'm a blue-blood type who takes a vastly different approach to eating on the road. Yup, it takes something hoity-toity—like a can of chili cooked on the engine block for 45 miles—to satisfy my regal taste. Employing an automobile as a rolling stove is fast (stop at any rest area, open the heated can, and scarf), it's cheap, and there's plenty of variety (choose from canned goods or leftovers wrapped in foil).

Unfortunately, my wife can't stomach that approach. For her, the pleasure of travel entails sampling new restaurants. This gives her taste buds a break from the stock menus we prepare at home and, because she does most of the cooking, a break from the drudgery. Our different ideologies have resulted in some thunderous food fights.

Happily, we've negotiated a workable compromise: Jan gets the pleasure of dining out more often than I prefer and, in return, lets me minimize the damage through use of the following tricks.

♦ **Visit ethnic neighborhoods.** Chinatown in New York or San Francisco, the International District in Seattle, the Greek neighborhoods of Chicago, and scores of others all offer a diverse choice of good, cheap restaurants.

♦ University districts are also bursting with good eateries. They must offer good value since their clientele (students) have deep stomachs and shallow pockets.

♦ Hotel employees are sometimes compensated to suggest particular restaurants to guests. For advice on where to find good food at good prices, ask disinterested locals—store clerks, grocers, butchers, bakers, even candlestick makers.

When asking for recommendations, be specific: Ask locals where *they* go when they want a steak, pancakes, seafood, Mexican food,... Tell them that good prices are as important as good food or, out of regional pride, they may send you to the city's best (and most expensive) restaurant.

♦ Pass up restaurants frequented by business people. These are usually expensive, probably because an expense account is picking up most tabs.

♦ Avoid eateries in locations where food is not the primary business. This eliminates restaurants at hotels, bus stations, sports stadiums, movie theaters, airports, bus stations, and amusement parks.

When visiting sports stadiums, movie theaters, and amusement parks, bring your own food.

♦ Skip restaurants that don't post menus outside. Once inside you'll probably be too embarrassed to take a hike—even if the prices frighten you.

♦ Thousands of restaurants offer bargain rates during the slow times of day. Breakfast specials, the ubiquitous lunch special at Chinese restaurants and pizza houses, and early-bird dinner specials at fine restaurants are examples of the many daily specials offered.

Anyone willing to go against the grain a little (e.g., arrive for dinner before 6:00 p.m. or dine out for lunch rather than supper) can easily chop 30% to 50% off their restaurant bills.

♦ Happy hour is also a good way to scrounge a cheap meal. Many restaurants offer discounted afternoon drinks and free hors d'oeuvres, meaning that for the cost of a drink a dedicated cheapskate can pack away enough food to skip dinner altogether.

♦ Variable pricing is very much in effect at most restaurants. Usually the main courses, which come with a salad and a side dish, are the best value. Hors d'oeuvres and drinks are overpriced and pull in much higher margins (profits). The price of alcoholic beverages is particularly bloated, giving you a sobering reason to stay sober.

Come dessert time, coffee is usually a good value but the affiliated fineries (dessert) are accompanied by prices that match their calorie counts.

Keeping all this in mind, it is quite possible to eat a nice meal at a nice restaurant at a nice price if you're willing to avoid the known evils.

♦ If you order a soft drink (despite the above advice), order it without ice. Soft drinks are usually stored in pressurized cylinders and the drinks cool to refrigerator-like temperatures when they come out of the cylinders (it's a fact of science that by releasing pressure you reduce temperature). Skip the ice and you get twice as much to drink—and every drop of it is cold.

On rare occasions you'll be served warm pop from a bottle. Not to worry. Order a glass of ice water, drink the water, then pour the ice into the pop.

♦ Large soft drinks at restaurants invariably give you much more pop for the penny spent. Compared to medium sizes, a large drink often provides twice the pop for a 20% price increase.

Families can exploit the situation by ordering one or two large pops (with no ice) and a number of glasses of ice.

♦ At home, don't overlook the value of clipping newspaper and magazine coupons for local restaurants. When the urge to dine out strikes and it's too late to capitalize on a lunch or early-bird special, you can pull out the coupons to find a restaurant whose food and fare are both appetizing.

♦ Finally, when it's just you out on the highway and nobody is forcing you to eat at a restaurant against your better judgement of value, prop a baking potato, some fresh road kill (wrapped in foil), and a can of corn against the engine and bake them all for 100 miles. There's nothing like rolling into a motel with home-cooked vittles waiting your arrival.

Reusing and Recycling

My grandmother raised a family during the Depression and, for survival's sake, cultivated the skill of making everything work double or triple duty. Nothing got trashed until she wrung every ounce of usefulness from it.

When times changed, old habits did not. To her, good times could shatter tomorrow so she maintained frugal ways and squirreled away dollars for the next crash.

No doubt about it, the woman was eccentric. Later, her means were substantial, yet she spent hours crocheting plastic bags into door mats instead of wasting money on store-bought mats. The idea was wondrously clever, the finished product wondrously tacky.

Many of my grandmother's tricks, however, were both ingenious and elegant. The Christmas tree ornaments she fashioned from the lids of mason jars looked beautiful. Her foil wrapping paper looked store-bought—until you removed it and found a potato-chip bag turned inside out.

I thought of Grandma immediately when I read an article in *Popular Photography* listing 68 ways to use the film canisters housing 35mm film. Even she could have learned some tricks here. Consider the following:

♦ **Advent calendar.** Cut a sheet of cardboard into the shape of a Christmas tree. Glue the bottoms of 25 canisters onto the cardboard. Glue a picture to the outside of each lid and place a surprise in each canister.

♦ **Condiments.** Fill film cans with ketchup, mustard, or salad dressing for sack lunches and picnics (pill bottles work well for this, too).

♦ **Clamp protector.** Glue the cap from a film canister to the swivel end of a C-clamp to protect a wood project from clamp damage.

♦ **Drug and cosmetic receptacles.** Kodak film canisters with their tight-sealing lids carry shampoo, hand cream, toothpaste, aspirin, sun screen, and other personals on short trips.

♦ **Electric cord holder.** Remove the top and bottom of the canister. Use the hollow cylinder to corral the excess loops of electrical cords that normally roam wild behind your desk, dresser, couch.

♦ **Fishing bobber.** Lay the fishing line across the top of the canister and snap the lid on. To weight the bobber for improved casting, add water to the canister.

♦ **Hair rollers.** Use as is.

♦ **Salt and pepper shakers.** Poke holes in the lid with a fat needle (hot needles make the job easier).

♦ **Spaghetti measurer.** Stack uncooked spaghetti into a canister. A full canister makes spaghetti for two.

♦ **Stamp dispensers.** Cut a 1-1/2-inch slit in the side of the can, slide a roll of stamps inside, feed the stamps through the slit.

♦ **Swimmer's kit.** Tape a lanyard to the canister. Use this floatable, waterproof container to tote a car key and a few dollars.

♦ **Travel sewing kit.** Load a canister with threaded needles, buttons, safety pins, and straight pins.

♦ **Weights.** Fill them with sand to anchor fabric when cutting patterns.

If someone can assemble 68 ideas for reusing film canisters, think what a little meditation could devise for the other gems we trash. I have, and this chapter lists dozens of tricks for making discards work double duty. Put your brains to it and you'll add many excellent ideas to the list.

BLANKETS, SHEETS, TOWELS

♦ **Aprons.** Many old bath towels have enough good fabric left to fashion aprons.

♦ **Bath Mats.** Old, large towels can be converted into good bath mats. Fold the towel in half and stitch the three sides.

♦ **Born again.** The centers of towels and sheets wear faster than the edges. When the centers wear thin, cut the towel or sheet lengthwise down the middle and stitch what were formerly the outside edges together in the middle. Hem the new outer edges to prevent unraveling.

♦ **Dish towels.** Cut old or stained linens into dish towels. Stitch the edges to prevent unraveling.

♦ **Washcloths and hand towels.** Cut the good parts of old (or stained) bath towels into washcloths and hand towels. Stitch the cut edges.

CLOTHES

♦ **Bras, panties, and slips** that have grown dingy over the years can be given respectability (and, thus, new life) by dying them in strong, hot tea. After the hot soak, rinse the items in cold water. Note: Wet all items before soaking them in the tea.

♦ **Handkerchiefs.** Old linens, T-shirts, and pajamas all make good handkerchiefs. Stitch the cut edges to prevent unravelling.

♦ **Maternity pants.** Convert seldom-used pants into maternity pants by replacing the zipper with a triangular panel of like-colored stretch fabric.

♦ **Short skirts.** Lengthen skirts that are too short for fashion or your taste with a band of wide ribbon or lace.

♦ **Short slips.** Convert old or unused full-length slips to half slips by snipping off the bodice. Roll over the fabric at the waist and sew in a waistband of 3/8-inch elastic.

COFFEE CANS AND LIDS

♦ **Camping pots.** Put coffee cans, full of food or water, right on the fire and cook. When you get home recycle the can (no clean up).

♦ **Cutting boards.** The plastic lids of large coffee cans make cutting boards for onions and other odoriferous foods. They also make disposable cutting boards for picnics.

♦ **Dehumidifiers.** Fill a coffee can with charcoal briquettes. Cover the can with a plastic lid, punch holes in the lid, and place the can in a closet. The charcoal helps keep the closet dry.

♦ **Drain plug.** Cut the rim off a plastic lid. Place the lid over a drain (kitchen sink or shower) and the suction will seal off the drain.

♦ **Paintbrush cleaner.** Pour thinner or water (depending on the paint used) in a coffee can. Cut an X in the can's plastic lid. Slide the handle of your paintbrush through the X and you can suspend it in solvent overnight without bending or rumpling the bristles.

♦ **Winter emergencies.** Fill several coffee cans with sand and store them in the car. If you get stuck in snow, sprinkle sand around the tires for the necessary traction to get going again.

EGG CARTONS

♦ **Desk organizer.** Throw away the top of an egg carton and use the bottom to keep your paper clips, tacks, stamps, and other sundries sorted. If you don't need a dozen compartments, cut the box down to the desired size (or buy a half-dozen eggs).

♦ **Fire starter.** Fill the carton with lint from the drier and you've got good tinder to start a fire.

♦ **Jewelry storage.** Use egg cartons to store children's jewelry and costume jewelry for adults.

♦ **Crafts.** Cartons make good craft objects for kids. For example, cut the bottom of the carton in half (lengthwise) and let kids paint the long rows of humps into a caterpillar.

♦ **Packing material.** Use the foam cartons when sending (or moving) fragile items.

♦ **Seedling nursery.** Put half an egg shell in each compartment of the carton and fill them with rich soil. Plant seeds in each egg shell. When the sprouts are ready, plant them—eggshell and all. As the plants grow, the shells will break and provide nourishment.

♦ **Sock organizer.** Keep a carton in a child's dresser and place a pair of socks in each section.

♦ **Thread box.** Keep your threads organized by placing one or two spools in each compartment.

FABRIC SOFTENER SHEETS

Used fabric softener sheets can give you additional service performing any of the following chores: shining your shoes, dusting (dust sticks to them), cleaning eyeglasses (they prevent fogging), shining furniture, deodorizing your shoes, scenting closets or drawers, polishing silver.

MARGARINE TUBS

♦ **Food storage.** Save margarine tubs and lids to store leftovers (containers from the same brand of margarine will stack better in the cupboard). Most tubs can be slipped right into the microwave for reheating leftovers.

♦ **Sandbox molds.** Let kids use them in the sandbox to make towers and castle turrets.

♦ **Wintertime faucet protector.** Cut a circle (2 inches in diameter) in the lid of a large margarine tub. Slide the lid over the faucet and screw it to the house's siding. Wrap the faucet with fiberglass insulation or rags and then snap the margarine tub to the lid screwed on to the siding. The tub creates a coat for the faucet, keeping the insulation dry, and the faucet from freezing.

MAYONNAISE AND PICKLE JARS

♦ **Bulk-food storage.** Because of their air-tight, waterproof, rodent-proof seal, jars are good for storing bulk dry goods like excess salt, sugar, flour, pancake mix, cereal, etc. Wash all the odor out of pickle jars first.

♦ **Nuts and bolts.** Nail the lids of mayonnaise jars to the ceiling of the shop (be sure to tie into a joist). Fill the jars with nails, screws, or bolts. The jars screw onto the lids and won't clutter up your work bench.

♦ **Canning.** My dad uses mayonnaise jars and pickle jars (rather than mason jars) for canning. After canning, he keeps the jars upside down until the contents cool. If there is no leakage he trusts the seal.

MESH BAGS

♦ **Nets.** Run a hanger (or stiff wire) through the holes at the entrance of mesh bags and bend the wire into a hoop. Secure the two ends of the wire into a handle. Kids can use these as butterfly nets or fish nets.

♦ **Potato storage.** Transfer potatoes from plastic bags into mesh bags and hang them in a cool, dry place. The air circulation will keep the potatoes longer.

♦ **Scrub pad.** Cut a mesh bag into like-sized pieces. Bunch the pieces and tie them tightly around the center with a cord. Use this creation as a scrubber.

♦ **Washing bag.** Put delicate fabrics inside, close the top with a large diaper pin, and wash on a gentle cycle.

MILK CARTONS (CARDBOARD)

♦ **Building blocks.** Stuff one milk carton inside another so that the bottoms of the two are at opposite ends of the resulting block. You've just made a building block.

Make more blocks as empties become available and soon you'll have a set for forts, castles, and walls.

To spiff up the blocks, wrap the four long sides of the block with stick-on shelf paper (the ends are white and can be left alone).

♦ **Fire starters.** Wax-coated cardboard cartons burn a long time and will ignite your kindling.

♦ **Flares.** Stuff several cartons with a sheet of newspaper and keep them in the trunk of the car as emergency warning devices. If you need a flare, light the paper and hold the carton upside down while the wax catches fire. Once the carton has caught fire, turn the carton right side up and set it down as a marker. It will burn for seven or eight minutes. Drop a stone in the bottom so the wind doesn't turn your flare into a forest fire.

♦ **Freezer storage.** Fill a carton with soup, staple closed and freeze.

♦ **Planters.** Cut off the top half, punch holes in the bottom and use them as starter pots for seedlings.

MILK and BLEACH BOTTLES (PLASTIC)

♦ **Bailers.** Cut off the bottom of milk or bleach bottles, tape on the lid, and you've got a good bailer for a canoe or row boat.

♦ **Buoys.** Fill the bottles with styrofoam packaging peanuts and tape on the lid to make buoys marking crab pots, boat anchors, deadheads in the lake.

♦ **Bulk cleaners.** If you make the cleaners mentioned in the *Formula* chapter, you will need a supply of gallon containers.

♦ **Clothes pin holder.** Cut a fist-sized hole high in the jug, through which you can grab clothespins stored inside. Hang the jug on the clothesline by the handle and slide the bottle down the line with you as you hang clothes.

♦ **Emergency drinking water.** Clean bottles, fill with water, tape on the lid and store them in the basement for emergency drinking water. Some people purify the water first so it can sit without growing microbes. Buy 2% tincture of iodine at a drugstore and add 10 drops per gallon. Don't worry about trace amounts of bleach from bleach bottles—it too helps purify the water.

♦ **Ice blocks.** Fill a milk bottle 7/8 full with water and freeze it. Then put it in your cooler for picnics or car-camping trips. After the ice melts, you have cold drinking water.

♦ **Old oil.** After changing your car's oil, store the old oil in plastic bottles. When the garage gets cluttered, tote the bottles to a local service station or recycling center that will dispose of it properly. *Don't* pour the oil down the sewer or drop it in the trash.

♦ **Universal gym.** When filled with water, two bottles (one in each hand) serve as weights for myriad upper-body exercises (see *Fitness* chapter).

MISCELLANEOUS

♦ **Belt holder.** Tear the front and back plastic covers off an old three-ring binder. Screw the metal, three-ring assembly to the closet wall or door. Snap your belts in and out of the rings.

♦ **Bird feeders.** Slather pine cones with hardened bacon grease before rolling the cone in seeds or crumbs. Hang the cone in a tree for the birds.

♦ **Blankets.** Convert dead electric blankets into normal blankets. Along the foot of the blanket, slit open the channels containing the wires and pull out the wires. Where necessary, make other incisions to remove the wires. Sew up the incisions. After washing, the slits are nearly invisible.

♦ **Boxed wine and juice.** Save the empty foil bladders from boxed wine or boxed apple juice. Pull the rubber nozzle off the bag, rinse the bag out, then pour in bottled wine, or juices made from frozen concentrates. Replace the rubber nozzle. Now, holding the bag with the nozzle higher than the wine, open the nozzle with your thumb, and suck the spare air out of the bag. Presto, you've just vacuum-packed your wine (or juice) and increased its shelf life.

♦ **Bumper pads.** Cut slits in old tennis balls and slide them over sharp projectiles that you or your children are prone to hit, like the ends of the guide rails on a table saw. Or use them to protect wooden floors by covering the hidden legs of heavy furniture.

♦ **Button bottles.** Use plastic pill bottles with wide tops to store your button collection.

♦ **Caulk cap.** Seal a partially used tube of caulk by twisting a plastic electrical connector onto the end. These connectors twist on and off quite easily.

♦ **Chrome shine.** Crumple used aluminum foil into a ball, dip the ball in water, and use it to rub any rust spots on chrome furniture. The shine in the chrome will return quickly.

♦ **Crayon container.** Kids can use metal band-aid boxes to carry crayons.

♦ **Coffee table.** An old piano bench with the legs cut down becomes a functional coffee table. It's a good conversation piece, too.

♦ **Firestarter.** Cut old bicycle and automobile inner tubes into two-inch squares. Light the corner of the square and it will burn for about five minutes—long enough to get medium-sized kindling burning with less fuss than newspaper. These squares are excellent for camping, too—they burn even if they get wet.

♦ **Game pieces.** Save toothpaste caps for this use.

♦ **Garden hose hanger.** Screw a large, plastic plant-pot to your house's siding with three 2-inch screws and flat washers (the bottom of the pot lies flush against the house). The rest of the pot now functions as a hanger to support a coiled hose. Furthermore, hose accessories can be stored inside the pot.

♦ **Gift wrap.** Old wallpaper that is in good shape after being stripped off can be rolled up and recycled as wrapping paper. Also, many stores sell their wallpaper scraps for almost nothing and that makes for cheap wrapping paper.

♦ **Groundsheet.** Store an old roll-up window shade in the car trunk. If you have car trouble out on the road, keep yourself clean by rolling out the shade as a groundsheet. Or use it as a groundsheet on picnics.

♦ **Hot pad.** Ceramic tiles left over from home projects can be employed as hot pads, trivets, or coasters. To protect wooden furniture, glue several felt pads to the bottom of each tile.

♦ **Knee pads.** Stack several styrofoam meat trays together and use them as knee pads when weeding the garden or scrubbing the floor.

♦ **Kneeling pad.** Stuff styrofoam packing pellets into an old hot water bottle and you're left with a great kneeling pad for house and garden work.

♦ **Knife rack.** Screw empty thread spools to a wall (or inside a cabinet) with the flat surfaces of the spool ends against the wall. Place the spools in a horizontal row, each butted against the next. The gaps between the spools make a slot for the blades, the handles rest on the spools.

♦ **Knitting supplies storage.** Tubes from *Pringle* potato chips make excellent containers for storing a ball of yarn, knitting needles, and crochet hooks. Poke a hole in the plastic lid and feed the yarn through it. When working with multiple balls of yarn, tape together several tubes and put a ball of yarn in each.

♦ **Mobiles.** Cut out the pictures from colorful greeting cards and fashion them into a child's mobile.

♦ **Odds-and-ends storage.** Screw plastic berry-baskets inside closet and cabinet doors. Store spice packets, spice tins, and other small sundries here.

♦ **Oil dispenser.** Fill an old dishwashing-detergent bottle with motor oil. The lid of these bottles makes it easy to top off small engines (lawn mowers, chain saws, generators) without making a mess.

♦ **Paint pads.** Scraps of high-density-foam carpet padding make excellent disposable paint pads that are much cheaper than store-bought models. Cut the padding into tapered pieces of foam, resembling the pads from the store. Clip the foam with a clothes pin and use the pin as your handle. When finished painting, throw away the foam pad and keep the clothes pin.

♦ **Paint strainer.** From an old window screen, cut a circle that is just smaller in diameter than the paint can (use the bottom of the can as a template). Place the screen on top of the paint and push it down through the paint with a stirring stick. As the screen moves down through the paint, it will drag paint lumps along with it.

♦ **Place mats.** Leftover pieces of wall paper can make attractive place mats. Glue the wall paper to matting board, then coat the creation with plastic spray.

♦ **Puppets.** Make finger puppets from the fingers of old rubber gloves.

♦ **Puzzles.** Mount old Christmas or greeting cards onto thin cardboard (like a cereal box) with spray-on adhesive. Cut the cardboard into puzzle pieces (an Exacto knife cuts odd shapes better than scissors do).

♦ **Quilt.** Sew a quilt out of baby blankets that are no longer in use. Or cover an unsightly—but warm—blanket with two sheets. Sew the first sheet to the blanket (good side up, bad side against the blanket). Place the second sheet over the first (good sides kissing) and sew the perimeter of three edges. Invert the quilt (so the good sides are now out) and sew the fourth side. Finally, sew about five evenly spaced rows of stitching along the length of the quilt, making sure you stitch through all three layers.

♦ **Saw blade cover.** Slit a section of old garden hose, longitudinally, and slide the slit hose over straight saw blades.

♦ **Sewing toy.** Use a hole punch to make designs in styrofoam meat trays. Kids can use lengths of yarn to "sew" the designs. Make a safe "needle" by wrapping the first inch or two of yarn with tape.

♦ **Scouring powder.** Fill an old spice container or parmesan cheese canister with baking soda (or a mixture of two parts baking soda and one part soap powder).

♦ **Scrapers.** Old plastic credit cards make good ice scrapers for windshields or putty scrapers for filling holes in the wall.

♦ **Screwdriver holder.** Nail a plastic berry-basket to the wall of your shop. The blades of screwdrivers will slide through the holes in the baskets but the handles will not.

♦ **Scrubber.** A crumpled ball of aluminum foil works as a dish scrubber.

♦ **Shower-curtain liner.** Use old shower curtains as liners for new shower curtains. The old curtains take the beating, extending the life of the new ones.

♦ **Soap pads.** Cut old sponges into soap pads. Put these pads in soap dishes to keep bar soap high and dry. Your soap will last much longer.

♦ **Soap sock.** To eke the most out of your soap, put those thin slivers you normally discard into a sock. Use the sock like a washcloth in the shower.

♦ **Squeegees.** Use old windshield wipers for washing windows around the house. Keep one in the car for wiping dew off the windows in the morning.

♦ **Stuffing.** Save lint from the dryer; it's a clean stuffing for Christmas decorations and dolls.

♦ **Swing.** Hang an old tire on the tree outside.

♦ **Trivets.** Convert old puzzles into place mats or trivets. Sandwich the completed puzzle between two layers of clear, plastic contact paper.

♦ **TV dinners.** Don't throw out the partitioned trays from TV dinners. Save them for your own leftovers. Cover them with foil or plastic wrap (depending on whether you'll be reheating leftovers in an oven or a microwave) and put them in the refrigerator.

NEWSPAPER

♦ **Burning logs.** Roll newspapers into a log with a 3-inch diameter and wrap a length of bailing wire around the center of the log. They'll burn in a wood stove at a ratio of one newspaper log for every two or three wood logs.

♦ **Gift wrap.** The comics make colorful and cheap wrapping paper.

♦ **Grease sponge.** Put a crumpled piece of newspaper in a cooling frying pan to absorb the excess grease you plan to throw away.

♦ **Kitty litter.** Ripped into thin strips, newspaper substitutes for kitty litter. It controls odors well and goes into the trash after use.

♦ **Windows and windshield cleaner.** After washing and drying, rub windows and windshields with newspaper. It eliminates any film or streaks left on the glass. Paper towels work well too, but newspaper is free.

♦ **Odor absorber.** Newspaper absorbs odors well. When moving, pack the inside of the refrigerator and freezer with loosely crumpled sheets.

♦ **Shoe dryer.** Pack wads of newspaper into wet shoes to dry them faster. The practice also helps shoes dry without as much damage to the leather.

♦ **Package stuffing.** Mailing parcels? Wadded newspaper protects what you're mailing.

♦ **Oil stain remover.** Saturate newspaper with water and lay it over stains in the garage. Rub the paper firmly onto floor. Let it sit until the paper dries thoroughly, then pick it up. Stains come up with the paper.

♦ **Weed prevention.** Spread sheets of newspaper (several layers thick) around flower beds and walkways. Cover with bark dust and gravel. The paper prevents weed growth for a season or two before decomposing and becoming part of your soil.

NYLON SOCKS and PANTYHOSE

♦ **Clothes protector.** Wash fragile clothing and hosiery in old pantyhose sealed at the top with a safety pin. The pantyhose protects the valuable contents inside.

♦ **Deodorizer.** Fill the foot of an old nylon with cedar chips, tie off the foot, and cut the nylon above the knot. Hang this bag in the closet as a deodorizer. The same idea can be used with any mixture of spices and herbs.

♦ **Rubber bands.** The elastic bands from pantyhose (and men's briefs) make excellent bands for keeping large boxes closed.

♦ **Socks.** Cut down pantyhose with runs above the knee into socks to be worn with slacks. Snip the hose above the knee and, using the elastic from the waist band, make two leg bands. Turn over the top of the sock and sew on the leg bands.

♦ **Stuffing.** Stuff pillows, craft projects, dolls, etc. with old nylons.

♦ **Tie-up cords.** Cut lengthwise strips from old pantyhose. Use these strips to tie tomato plants to poles. The pantyhose stretches so it won't cut into the stalks as they grow.

♦ **Tub and sink scrubber.** Wrap an old nylon around an old tennis ball to make a scrubber.

♦ **Wall scrubbers.** When it is time to wash the walls, slip an old nylon sock or pantyhose over your hand. They clean well without shedding lint.

♦ **Mop cover.** Cover your mop with an old nylon. When finished mopping, throw the nylon away. Your mop stays cleaner and lasts longer.

♦ **Paint strainer.** Pour lumpy paint through old nylons to strain the lumps.

♦ **Potato and onion storage.** Fill old nylons with onions or potatoes and hang in the garage. The nylon allows air circulation and keeps vegetables from molding. If you isolate each onion or potato with a knot in the pantyhose, it is easy to slit the pantyhose and pull out one vegetable.

PLASTIC BAGS

♦ **Disposable gloves.** Working with irritating chemicals or mixing up meat loaf? Keep your hands clean by wearing plastic bags over your hands. Rubber band, or tape the bags to your wrists.

♦ **Food storage.** Save plastic produce and bread bags for storing leftovers, preparing lunches, freezing foods, etc. If you ever need to buy plastic bags again, you're not trying very hard.

♦ **Freezer bags.** The stiffer, crinkly bags used to line cereal and cracker boxes are better freezer bags than normal plastic bags—they reduce moisture loss and freezer burn.

♦ **Golf balls.** Use extra (or dirty) plastic bags to make practice golf balls. Wad several bags into a golf-ball-sized core then wrap the works with a skin of masking tape. Keep about 25 balls in a box for driving practice in your backyard. The balls don't travel too far but still hook or slice according to the demons of your swing. Considering a bucket of 60 balls costs about $4 at public courses, this is much cheaper (and less time-consuming) practice than visiting the local driving range.

♦ **Sandwich bags.** Trim off the tops of bread bags; they make perfect sandwich bags.

♦ **Yarn holder.** Put a ball of yarn in a plastic bag and feed the end through a hole in the bottom of the bag. Tie off the top of the bag. The yarn will feed out as you knit but will not unwind or tangle in the work basket.

PLASTIC PAILS
(5-gallon size used for paint or bulk foods)

You can get these pails free for the asking at fast food stores like the local Dairy Queen. Of course, if you've painted your house lately, you may have several around. Use them for:

♦ **Bailers.** Keep these pails on power boats as either a bailer or fish bucket.

♦ **Camping food storage.** When car or canoe camping, these containers are excellent for carrying food supplies—with the lids on, they are water and rodent proof. They also double as stools for sitting around the campfire.

♦ **Food storage.** Wash the pails well and use them to store bulk foods or emergency supplies. Place waterproof lid on tightly and store.

♦ **Planters.** Wrap the buckets with foil and they make attractive, large planters.

♦ **Stair Master substitute.** See *Fitness* chapter.

♦ **Washing Machine.** By cutting a one-inch hole in the bucket's lid and adding a toilet plunger to the bucket, you've made a washing machine for a summer cabin. Add clothes, water, and detergent to the bucket; place the plunger in the bucket; and snap on the lid, threading the plunger's handle through the hole. Rapidly pump the plunger up and down for several minutes and the clothes will wash nicely. Pour off the soapy water and do several rinse cycles the same way.

♦ **Water storage.** If your water supply is undependable, fill up several buckets with water, attach the lids tightly, and store for emergencies. Treat the water to ensure it remains pure. Purchase a bottle of 2% tincture of iodine from a drugstore and add 10 drops of iodine per gallon of water, stir water, cap the bucket.

PIE TINS

♦ **Bird repeller.** To keep birds out of your fruit trees, hang several pie tins on branches from which the tins can spin in the wind.

♦ **Dust pans.** Cut disposable pie tins in half and you're left with two dust pans.

♦ **Grease catcher.** Punch holes in an aluminum pie tin and place the tin over hot frying pans spattering grease.

♦ **Vegetable steamer.** An aluminum pie tin with holes poked in it (one or two holes per square inch) makes a good steamer. Pour one-quarter to one-half inch of water into a pot with a slightly larger diameter, put the pie tin in the pot (rim side down), pile the vegetables on top of the pie tin.

PILLOW CASES

♦ **Dust cover.** Worn or stained pillow cases can cover valuable—but seldom-worn—clothes in your closet. Slip the case over the clothing and poke the hanger out the sewn seam on the opposite end.

♦ **Patio-chair cover.** Cover patio chairs stored for the winter with old pillow cases.

PLASTIC PEANUT BUTTER JARS

♦ **Camping food storage.** Backpackers, canoeists, hunters, and fishermen can use plastic peanut butter jars for toting food on camping trips. They are water- and rodent-proof, light, and unbreakable. They can also double as cups or glasses.

♦ **Knickknack storage.** Plastic peanut butter containers withstand kid abuse well; use the larger sizes (they come in 18-ounce and 28-ounce sizes) to store sundries—puzzle pieces, plastic alphabet sets, toys.

♦ **Paint storage.** Small quantities of paint will store longer in a glass mayonnaise jar than in the original paint can. To ensure that the jar will open easily, coat the threads of the lid with a dab of petroleum jelly.

PLASTIC POP BOTTLES (2-liter size)

♦ **Canteens.** Fill plastic pop bottles with water and take them on camping trips.

♦ **Bailers and scoops.** Cut off the bottom, screw the lid on firmly, and they make good bailers for small boats and sand scoops for kids.

♦ **Funnels.** Cut off the bottom and throw away the lid and you've got a funnel. Cut the body down to make the funnel any size. Great for changing car oil.

♦ **Bowling pins.** Save 10 bottles, put a little sand in the bottom of each (for ballast), screw on the lids. Kids can bowl them down with a medium-sized rubber ball.

♦ **Ice cube.** Fill about 7/8 full with water and freeze the day before a camping trip or picnic. Use this "ice cube" in an ice chest to keep food cool. After the ice melts, drink the cold water.

SINGLE SOCKS

♦ **Bandages.** Cut off the toes of socks and use the ribbing to hold bandages or cold compresses on elbows, knees, shins. Use kids' socks for kid-size injuries.

♦ **Broomstick horse.** Stuff a sock, insert a broom stick and tie off the sock to the broomstick. Decorate the sock with buttons for the eyes and ribbon for the mane.

♦ **Cuffs.** The tubes of heavy socks can serve as cuffs to lengthen sweatshirts or children's coats. Measure, then sew around the circumference of the sock above where you will cut the sock (prevents unravelling). Cut and sew on the new cuff.

♦ **Dusters.** Put an old sock on each hand and dust away. Works very well on venetian blinds, too.

♦ **Floor protectors.** Wrap old socks around the legs of heavy furniture being moved. Protects the floor, walls, and the furniture itself.

♦ **Hand puppets.** Sew faces onto the toes and make them into a menagerie of hand puppets for your kids.

♦ **Mittens.** Use two similar single socks or a matched pair with worn toes for this job. Pull the sock inside out and pull it over a hand to measure the fit (the ribbing pulls up over the wrist and the thumb projects into the heel of the sock). Mark where you will cut the sock.

Alternately, pull the sock inside out and lay it flat on the table. Have the user lay his or her hand on the sock, thumb projecting into the heel and fingers pointing toward the toe, and mark the sock. Once marked, sew the lines with a zig-zag stitch. Cut away the extra fabric and invert the sock so the good side faces out again.

♦ **Rags.** Slit cotton socks open and sew a few together to make larger, flat rags for dusting and cleaning.

♦ **Soap holder.** Put slivers of soap in a sock and let kids use this to wash themselves. The practice uses less soap and kids can find the sock in the tub (they often have trouble finding a soap bar).

♦ **Sock ball.** Put one sock into the toe of a second sock. Twist the second sock and pull its sleeve over the lump formed in the toe. Repeat several times until the sleeve of the second sock is wrapped up in the ball. Put the ball in the toe of a third sock and repeat the process of enlarging the ball by wrapping the sleeve of the new sock around the lump in the toe. When the ball reaches the wanted size, hand stitch the seams along the outside to keep it from unravelling.

♦ **Washers.** With a sock on each hand, simultaneously wash both sides of screens, wicker chairs, or playpen netting. On the first pass, dip the socks in soapy water. For the second pass, dip the socks in fresh water and rinse off the soap.

Showers

I enjoy guests but, like most people, I have personality quirks that make me a believer in Benjamin Franklin's belief, "Fish and visitors stink in three days."

One of my foibles centers around showers. I have a mental meter that clicks on like a taxi meter whenever I hear the shower running. I can bully my own family into short showers, but lecturing guests on the subject doesn't qualify as gracious hospitality.

Nonetheless, my mental money meter measures the five gallons of hot water swirling down the drain every minute. Here in the Northwest, where electric rates are 4¢ per kilowatt-hour (half the national average) that translates into 2.5¢ per minute flowing down the drain. Consequently, the hot water for a 10-minute shower costs me 25¢ (50¢ in most places). That may not seem extravagant, but multiply the figure by the number of people in your family taking daily showers and you're looking at an ugly total by year's end.

Over time I've adopted tricks to keep the cost of showers low. Admittedly, some of them are the obsessions of a twisted mind, but at least half of them are practical—even for those of you who aren't quirky.

♦ Run the shower at low pressure. You'll get just as clean and make a huge divot in your water consumption. My shower can blast out five gallons of water per minute but I run it at a reduced pressure that delivers about one-and-a-half gallons per minute.

♦ If you enjoy strong water pressure, invest in a low-flow shower head. These shower heads maintain vigorous pressure by either mixing air with water or pulsing. The pressure feels good. Plus, if you install one in the guest bathroom, you won't stew over your visitor's long showers.

Low-flow shower heads cost as little as $6 at hardware and plumbing stores. Not much, considering they will save a family of four $2 to $3 a week. This product pays for itself in a few months which, by any standard of investing, is a coup.

Note: These shower heads are different from the flow restrictors utility companies distribute to reduce water use. Most people don't like the shower quality after inserting flow restrictors.

♦ Fancy low-flow shower heads can cost upwards of $40 and won't necessarily supply more satisfaction than the $6 models. Look at the July 1990 *Consumer Reports* to see how 34 different models stacked up. Some of the most expensive units received the poorest ratings.

Installation of all models is simple: Screw off the old head, screw on the new one, and shower off the sweat.

♦ If you want to soak in the luxurious ecstacy of hot water, take baths instead of long showers. The break even-point varies from house to house, depending on water pressure, shower head, etc. In my house, a shower longer than five minutes costs more than a bath (if the water is on full strength).

Calculate your own break-even point by plugging the drain to the bath and showering until the water rises to bath level.

♦ Take showers less often. Madison Avenue has the American public believing we need a daily fix of soap, shampoo, and deodorant. Sure, if you perspire an inordinate amount, exercise daily, have a physical job, work in a dirty environment—you'll want to avoid the odious stares of your fellows by bathing daily. But most Americans are idle and daily showers border on compulsive behavior—which proves the advertising gurus on Madison Avenue earn their high pay.

♦ The advertisement boys have their hooks in me, too—they have me cherishing clean hair. Long before the rest of me begs for soap, my limp hair demands shampoo. Rather than submitting to an unnecessary shower, I frequently wash my hair by kneeling alongside the bathtub and putting my head under the spigot. The procedure uses a fraction of the water (and time). I've also discovered I can turn on the shower, lean into the stall so that only my head gets wet, turn off the water, shampoo (still leaning into the stall), turn on the water, and rinse. The job takes less than two minutes and uses a gallon of water. What a bargain!

♦ Personally, I'm a promoter of military showers. Get in, get wet, shut off the shower, soap up, and then rinse. It's short, sweet, and cheap. Showers with a single control that mix hot and cold water (common in newer houses) make it easy to maintain the right temperature as you turn the water on and off. Military showers don't work well in older showers with separate knobs controlling the hot and cold water—it takes too much fiddling to get the temperature right. Solution: Get a new showerhead that has a lever to turn the water on and off at the nozzle (cost about $10 at hardware stores).

♦ Our house is cold in the morning and it takes true grit to go military. Jan's solution: preheat the bathroom with a small space heater (lots cheaper than keeping warm by staying in the shower). My solution (of which Jack LaLanne would be proud): morning calisthenics. Pushups, squat thrusts, and situps warm the blood enough that shutting off the water to soap up is no biggy.

♦ Plug the drain and let the warm shower water heat the bathroom rather than disappear down the drain.

He who nothing saves shall nothing have.
English proverb

Soaps and Cleaners

Most Americans spend hundreds of dollars each year on soaps and cleaners—body soaps, shampoos, face soaps, laundry detergents, dishwashing detergents, carpet shampoos, bathroom cleaners, oven cleaners, car-washing solutions...

In the *Formula* chapter, I listed recipes for excellent substitute cleaners that brew faster than a cup of coffee. Use those formulas and you'll find yourself with a small fortune to burn on pleasures greater than cans of toilet-bowl cleaner.

But not every cleaner has an easy-to-make substitute, and not everyone wants to take the time to make their own cleaners. Finally, some people just don't believe they can produce anything as potent and sterilizing as Proctor and Gambel. This chapter, therefore, offers you alternatives that won't clean out your wallet.

♦ Mystique. Elaborately packaged and expensive cleansing creams have a magical mystique, but tests show that few, if any, justify the expenditure. If you've been victimized by the hype surrounding an expensive, high-fashion cleansing cream, you'll save lots switching to a less expensive name-brand.

♦ More is less. The main difference among bar soaps on the market is not their ability to clean but their initial cost and their longevity. Soaps can vary from products like *Lux*, which cost well under a penny per use (cheap to buy and slow to shrink away), to *Eay di Gucci*, which costs over 30¢ per use (pricey to buy and very quick to melt away). Ironically, in one elaborate blind test, users ranked *Eay di*

Gucci in last place behind dozens of soaps costing as much as 50 times less on a per-use basis.

That trend was common: The cost of soaps had nothing to do with how they fared in the blind test. Expensive soaps costing a fortune could rarely compete with *Dove* which, with its moisturizing cream, delivered high user satisfaction at a reasonable cost. Meanwhile, the likes of *Lux*, *Palmolive*, and other low-cost bars rated good user satisfaction.

If you like an expensive soap because of its scent or association (maybe Elizabeth Taylor promotes it), fine. But don't deceive yourself: These "Gucci" products don't clean any better than *Lux* or moisturize any better than *Dove*, yet could easily be costing you an extra $40 a year to use.

♦ Laundry detergents. Non-partial tests show that some detergents do work better than others, but the differences among major brands are not large—all do a good job of cleaning. If you have young children who always seem to come home with grass stains on their pants and chocolate smeared over their shirts, then *Tide with Bleach* may be worth a higher cost. Most of us, however, are not rolling in dirt and can buy any major brand by price.

Look around and you'll find quality brands that are 30% to 50% less than the heavily hyped products seen on the television.

♦ Liquid or powder? Liquid laundry detergents are quicker to use and some are now as powerful as powders. But they are more expensive. For example, on a per-load basis the *Arm and Hammer* liquid costs twice as much as the *Arm and Hammer* powder, and a two-quart bottle of *Tide* is about 80% more than *Tide* powder.

♦ Life is a bleach. Store brands of chlorine bleaches are just as effective as name-brands like *Chlorox* and about 50% cheaper.

♦ For every room there is a cleaner. But you don't need a cleaner for every room. Case in point: An all-purpose cleaner will remove the dirt from the sink, toilet and tub as well as a bathroom cleaner, yet bathroom cleaners will cost about 50% more. If mold and mildew are problems in the bathroom, use liquid chlorine bleach (1 part bleach to three or four parts water)—it is extremely effective and costs much less than a bathroom cleaner.

♦ A stitch in time. Drain cleaners are extremely corrosive and, if your house has very old pipes, these chemicals could eat through the pipes and cause more problems than they solve. Better to practice an ounce of prevention by pouring boiling water down the sinks every week or two. See the *Formula* chapter for more drain ideas.

♦ Handle with care. You don't need a special soap for hand-washing delicate fabrics—liquid dishwashing detergent (most any brand) is gentle and will do an excellent job. It also does the job for much less money. To use: Add 1 teaspoon of detergent per quart of water.

♦ Much to-do about nothing. Commercials for laundry boosters promise you dazzling results. If, however, you compare the stain removal powers of most boosters to that of a good detergent alone, you won't notice a difference.

♦ Royal flush. Tinted, in-tank products may make your toilet bowl *look* cleaner, but if you think these products will keep your bowl clean without the occasional scrub, forget it. Mainly, these in-tank products just camouflage, rather than prevent, dirty bowls. That amounts to very few benefits for the bucks.

♦ Dirty hairy. What is shampoo? Mainly detergent with a few minor ingredients like scents. What is dishwashing detergent? Pretty much the same stuff. Considering that they are both basically detergent, you can legitimately question whether you should pay five times more for *Nexxus Therappe* than for *Ivory Dishwashing Liquid*. No you shouldn't, and a good washing (be it with shampoo or dishwashing liquid) will leave your hair clean and shiny.

Don't want to run the risk of getting a dishpan scalp? Then buy a cheap shampoo. When *Consumer Reports* evaluated about 60 of the best-selling shampoos—shampoos ranging in price from $1.50 per 15 ounces to $10 per 16 ounces—the professional beauticians who did the blind testing gave 54 of the shampoos nearly identical marks.

Price played no bearing on the performance; in fact, one of the $10 shampoos was one of the poorest performers. No shampoo gave hair more luster than another.

What about the notion that protein shampoos and secret conditioners "nourish" your hair? Rubbish. Hair is dead protein; you nourish it by eating properly.

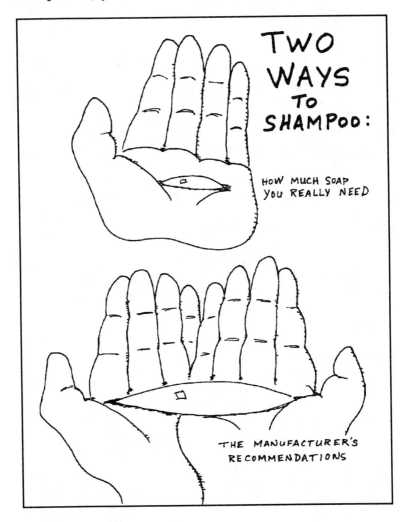

♦ Suds, suds, suds. That's how you test if the dishwashing water in the sink has cleaning power left; if it is still sudsy, it will still clean dishes. Typically, stronger dishwashing liquids (those producing the most suds from the least detergent) are cheaper to use because a teaspoon of detergent (measure it) does a load of dishes. Meanwhile, with some generic brands, it seems like you must add half the bottle to generate a solitary bubble of suds.

Name-brand products that give you the most bubbles for the buck include *Ajax Dishwashing Liquid* and *Sunlight*. Store-brands that are highly rated and cheap include *Kroger Mild White* and *A&P Dish Detergent*.

♦ Automatic cleaning power. Dishes that go into my dishwasher go in dirty (I just wipe off the particulate matter). The dishes may then sit for several days, so I need a good detergent—especially since I fill the machine's soap bin only about 3/5 full. Of the many name- and store-brands I've used, *Cascade* powder has given me the best results. It is mid-range in price and works well even with my water heater set at 120°F.

The cleaning power of liquid gels for dishwashers has improved greatly in recent years (*Palmolive Liquid Gel Lemon* is very good) but on a per-use basis the gels are 50% more expensive than the average powder.

♦ Couch potatoes. Yup, if you don't clean your upholstered furniture from time to time, it may become soiled enough to sprout tubers. Your best defense? Vacuum the upholstered furniture when you dust the rest of the furniture.

If it's too late for vacuuming and the couch looks more like a potato patch, you can rent an upholstery steamer. Though cheaper than hiring a pro, this is expensive unless you have lots of upholstery to clean or can split the cost with friends. Rental fees run $25 to $30 per day.

The cheaper (and easier) solution for small jobs is to buy a spray-on upholstery cleaner. Many brands don't work particularly well. The exception to the rule is *Blue Coral Dri-Clean Upholstery and Carpet Cleaner* (available at automotive stores), which produces results that compete with a steamer. Before you attack the couch, however, test the cleaner in an inconspicuous spot for adverse side effects, and don't use it on velvets and silks.

Note: Don't make the mistake of using *Blue Coral Velour and Upholstery Cleaner*. It doesn't work as well as the dry-cleaning formula.

Stains

"Out, out damn spot." Lady MacBeth was not the only person to utter those words. My wife mouths them, too. Seems like every time Jan dons a new blouse, spots swarm to her like mosquitos to bare skin.

Lady MacBeth had more at stake but Jan has legitimate concerns when a spot can ruin a $30 blouse. If she's lucky. On a bad day, spots can total a coat, carpet, or couch worth hundreds of dollars. Which explains why it's worth your time learning about spots—learning how to prevent them and how to remove them.

Taken to the extreme, spots are a complicated topic. Books have been written on the subject, and you may need such a book to remove caviar stains from an angora sweater. But the meat and potatoes of the subject are easily mastered. Pass this short course and you'll spend less money replacing spoiled goods and more at the theater yelling to Lady MacBeth, "Cold water—use cold water, you dingbat."

THE BASICS

◆ Procrastinate not. Take care of the stain immediately and you're most likely to succeed. Stains are like glues—they set up over time. If a garment needs washing, spending 50¢ to remove a stain now is a bargain compared to buying a new blouse later. If the item is a non-washable, get it to the dry cleaner fast.

◆ The wet head is dead. Most stains can be scraped, vacuumed, swept, and blotted up. Before you wet anything, remove as much of the staining agent as possible.

♦ Look before you leap. Don't douse a stain with water or other chemicals until you know what the stain is and what fabric it's on.

♦ Don't let the treatment kill the patient. Pretest your stain remover on a hidden part of the damaged goods. Make sure the "solution" doesn't worsen the problem.

♦ Keep it cool. Heat is rarely the right answer.

♦ Rub a dub, dub, dub—don't scrub a stain.

♦ Inside out. When possible, work from the underside of a garment and push the stain back out.

♦ Dry, dry, again. Air dry the items that you spot clean. If the remedy didn't work, you can try again.

PREVENTION THE BEST CURE

Using shaving cream to remove this stain and the dog's left ear to remove that one are the focus of most helpful hints articles and books about stains, but prevention is infinitely easier and more effective than salvaging a garment after the fact.

♦ Young children are the embodiment of walking stains, but you can limit their damage dramatically. Put a drop cloth under their high chairs to catch falling food and drink. Wipe their hands and mouths religiously after snacks and meals. Confine all eating to the kitchen (on the linoleum)—no walking around the house with food or drink. For young children, use bibs for all meals to protect clothing. Kids who have graduated out of high chairs should be seated on metal or wood (not fabric) chairs. If you're entertaining guests with young children, put towels under their chairs (and on the chairs if they have fabric cushions).

♦ Most stains walk in the door—on shoes. According to the American Carpet Association, shoes track 80% of the dirt into a home. Stop it at the doors with mats. You also may want to save yourself lots of vacuuming and stain removing with a no-shoes-inside-the-house policy. Shoes go off at the door and slippers go on. We use such a policy at our home—the carpet still manages to get stained, but at a dramatically slower rate.

♦ Kitchens and bathrooms are dens of stains. Don't carpet them.

♦ About 90% of the stains taken in for professional cleaning are food-related. You lower the odds of disaster by eating at a table. Meals with plate on lap, drink on floor and eyes on television are a dry cleaner's dream. So are buffets in which you invite dozens of friends to wander around the living room holding paper plates over your stuffed furniture and shag carpet. Nothing wrong with the buffet idea, just provide tables for guests to sit around. And give them real plates. Paper plates were probably invented by a dry cleaner's brother.

♦ The cooks and chefs who prepare food are also in great need of protection from food stains. Practice safe cooking and don an apron.

♦ Dress for the occasion. Have you ever changed a car tire, checked the oil, worked on a car without getting dirty? Not if you're human. Keep rags and overalls (or clothes that would otherwise be Goodwill-bound) in the car so you don't ruin an expensive suit should a tire blow en route to work.

Don't be lazy about donning protective clothing for dirty work around home. Wearing such clothing is both faster and cheaper than exorcising stains from clothes you care about.

GENERALITIES

♦ Greasy stains. These stains often require solvents, but because solvents will still work after laundering, try washing first. Pretreat the stain with detergent, then launder. Air dry. If this fails, treat the stain with an appropriate solvent.

♦ Non-greasy stains. These are tricky; washing removes some stains and sets others. Check the following section for specific recommendations. If none is given, try a cold water soak first and some gentle sponging. If this bombs, apply a little detergent to the spot. Still no luck? Apply some borax. As a last resort, try chlorine bleach— assuming the fabric can take it.

♦ Stains with a mixture of greasy and non-greasy parts should be treated for the non-greasy part first. Soak them in cold water and wash with detergent as described above. Let the garment air dry and then use a solvent to handle the remaining greasy component.

♦ Don't know what the stain is? Then follow these steps. If the first step fails, move on to the second step, and so on down the line.

1) Use a cold-water soak for 20 minutes, then pretreat the stain with liquid detergent and wait 30 minutes before laundering in the hottest water and with the strongest bleach the fabric can withstand. Air dry.

2) Use an enzyme presoak for an all-day soak followed by a five-minute wash in the hottest water the fabric can take. Air dry.

3) Dab dry-cleaning fluid onto the spot and wait 20 minutes before adding liquid detergent as well. Rinse well and air dry.

4) On whites, use a fabric color remover; on colors use a fabric rust remover. Air dry.

5) Make a solution of 1 part bleach (chlorine or all-fabric, depending on the material) and 2 parts water. Dab it on stain and then launder for five minutes in the hottest water the fabric can withstand. Air dry.

6) Use the garment for target practice. Aim for the #@&♦ spot.

THE NITTY-GRITTY DIRT BAND

There's more than one way to beat a stain. If you've got tricks that work for you, stick with them. But read through this section and shop for other weapons you can add to the arsenal.

♦ Alcohol. Rinse stain with cold water. If it stain persists, soak for 30 minutes in a solution of all-fabric bleach and water (1/8 cup all-fabric bleach per gallon of water). Then launder in warm water after rubbing the stain with detergent.

Old alcohol stains need an enzyme presoak before laundering.

♦ Blood. Soak garment in cold water, then rub. Launder in tepid water after rubbing extra detergent onto the spot. Get the last trace of blood from non-washables with hydrogen peroxide or borax.

For couches and carpets, rub the spot with an ice cube and then blot.

♦ Butter, margarine, cooking oil. Rub liquid shampoo on the stain and wash with the hottest water and strongest bleach that the fabric can withstand. Or spray with a prewash and launder after several minutes.

On carpet and upholstery, these and other greasy stains can be absorbed using cornmeal or treated with dry-cleaning fluid.

♦ Chocolate. Lick the stain clean—don't let any of that blessed sweet go to waste. Or rinse garments in tepid water before soaking for 30 minutes in a solution of warm water and all-fabric bleach, then wash. If stain persists, immediately rinse in cool water and apply a solution made from hydrogen peroxide and a few drops of ammonia.

♦ Coffee. Treat as a non-greasy stain with cold water or try the boiling-water treatment described under "Fruit.". If cream was in the coffee, use cold water, then detergent. A solvent may be necessary next. On carpet: Blot up what you can, then dilute with cold water and blot again. Repeat.

♦ Cosmetics. Dampen stain and rub in liquid detergent until stain vanishes. Wash in the hottest water the fabric can withstand.

♦ Crayon. Use an enzyme presoak, then launder garments in hottest water they can take. For crayon marks on the wall, rub the mark lightly with toothpaste, then wipe with a damp rag.

♦ Egg. Scrape off as much as possible before rinsing in cold water. Use an enzyme presoak followed by a cold-water wash (hot water sets the stain).

♦ Food stains. An emergency tactic for most food and beverage stains is to wet or dab the stain with club soda, then blot it up with a paper towel or napkin. Remember this when you're dining out and are away from your arsenal of specialized cleaners.

Similarly, women are wise to place a tiny canister of talcum powder in their purses. Spots from salad dressings, butter, or greasy foods can be sprinkled with talcum powder and brushed away in several minutes after the powder has absorbed the grease. If you don't have talcum powder, use salt or cornstarch in the same way.

♦ Fruit, berries, food coloring. Lay the fabric, stain-surface down, over a colander. From a height of several feet, pour boiling water through the stain.

♦ Grass stains. Grass and most plant stains can be removed by soaking garments in cold water first and then sponging the stain with denatured or isopropyl alcohol. Pretest to make sure the colors won't run.

♦ Gravy. Dissolve the starch with a cold water soak, then launder.

♦ Gum. Remove it from carpets by applying an ice cube to the gum. When the gum hardens, pull it off the rug. Chewing gum on garments can be hardened by putting the item in the freezer.

♦ Ink (ballpoint). Dab denatured or isopropyl alcohol around the stain and then on the stain. Next, place the stain on a paper towel and dab it from behind. Rinse well before rubbing in liquid laundry detergent and washing the item in the hottest water the fabric can take.

Alternately, spray the stain thoroughly with hair spray, allow it to dry and then launder the item. To get ink marks off vinyl or plastic, spray with hair spray. Let the spray sit several minutes, then wipe with a damp cloth.

♦ Mud. Let mud dry thoroughly, then chip off what you can; beat out the rest. If a stain remains, rub in a paste of liquid detergent and all-fabric bleach. Wash.

♦ Mustard. Soak all day in a solution of detergent and all-fabric bleach before washing.

♦ Paint (oil based). Scrape or blot off excess. Before the paint dries, dab on turpentine or thinner. Wait several minutes, then blot. Repeat dabbing and blotting until the entire stain lifts, then launder. Alternately, use mechanics' waterless hand cleaner as described under *Tar*.

♦ Paint (water-base). Rinse thoroughly with warm water. Apply enzyme presoak. Rinse again and launder.

♦ Pencil. Try rubbing the stain with a soft eraser.

♦ Perspiration. Wet new stains with ammonia, old ones with vinegar. Let the garment sit several minutes, then rinse and wash in the hottest water that's safe for the fabric.

♦ Product X. If an unknown (or old) spot mars clothing (that includes spots on garments at a garage sale), here's a recipe that neutralizes stains like white corpuscles kill pathogens. Add 1 cup chlorine bleach and 1 cup *Cascade* powdered dishwashing detergent to a bucket of very hot water. Let the stained item(s) soak all night, then launder normally. This recipe is amazingly effective, but because bleach is not always kind to fabrics, make it your last line of defense.

Another last-ditch approach for fabrics that cannot take bleach: Saturate the garment in hydrogen peroxide or lighter fluid for several hours, rinse, and launder.

♦ Ring around the collar. Rub shampoo into the collar several minutes before laundering. You don't need a special product for this job.

♦ Rust. Use water to dampen stain and then apply lemon juice mixed with salt; hold the stain over the steam of a boiling teakettle for several minutes before rinsing. If stain remains, try again.

♦ Shoe polish (wax). Scrape out excess polish with a dull knife and then clean the stain with a solution made from equal parts alcohol (denatured or isopropyl) and water. Launder. For white fabrics, use straight alcohol.

♦ Sink stains. Lay paper towels along the bottom of sink and dampen with chlorine bleach. Let the towels sit 30 minutes or longer. Alternately, rub a mixture of hydrogen peroxide (3% solution) and baking soda on the spots; let the mixture dry, then rinse it away.

♦ Tar. Use one of the waterless hand cleaners sold to mechanics (available at auto-part stores). Rub this into tar and grease stains. Blot up what you can. Repeat until the stain lifts, then launder.

For carpet, apply a small amount of dry-cleaning fluid, then blot. Repeat until all the tar vanishes.

♦ Tea. Rinse, then dab on a solution made from hydrogen peroxide and a few drops of ammonia. Rinse again and wash. Alternately, use the boiling water treatment described under *Fruit*.

♦ Tomato paste, sauce, and ketchup. Before the stain dries, spray on a laundry prewash, wait several minutes and launder.

♦ Urine & vomit. On carpets, blot up as much as possible (rather, have someone else blot up as much as possible). Gently sponge in a solution made from equal parts white vinegar and warm water and let the solution sit several minutes before blotting. Next, sponge on warm water and blot. Put a dry towel over the spot and weight it with heavy books.

♦ Wax. For upholstery or carpet, place a bag of ice cubes over the spill. Once the wax congeals, chip it off. To get the remainder, place a paper towel over the area and press it with a warm iron.

♦ Wine. Red wine: Immediately blot up what you can, then rub lots of salt into the stain. Let the salt absorb the wine for 10 to 15 minutes before brushing it off. Rinse the stain thoroughly with cold water, then wash the item if possible. For dried red wine, a mixture of hydrogen peroxide with a few drops of ammonia sometimes works. Soak the stain, then rinse it before laundering.

White wine and champagne: Rinse the stain thoroughly with cool water, then soak it with a solution made from hydrogen peroxide and several drops of ammonia. Rinse well before washing.

On carpet and upholstery. Instantly blot up what you can, then quickly dilute with cold water and blot again. Dilute and blot the area several times before rubbing generous quantities of salt into the stain. Sweep or vacuum the salt after 15 minutes.

♦ More, more, more. There are many staining agents not listed in this chapter. If you want a really handy (and inexpensive) chart with solutions to solve the problems posed by over 130 different stains, send $1 and a self-addressed stamped business envelope to the Carpet and Rug Institute (Box 2048, Dalton, GA 30722, 404-278-3176) and request their *Carpet Spot Removal Guide*.

WHEN ALL ELSE FAILS

Sometimes your best efforts fail and a stain decides to stick around. Then what do you do?

♦ Tear the spot out as though it were the heart of your worst enemy. Use what remains as a rag.

♦ Hack the garment into tiny pieces while muttering obscenities. Resurrect those little fragments in a quilt.

♦ With a huge knife, amputate part of the garment. Make a long-sleeve shirt into a short-sleeved one, long pants into shorts, a long skirt into a mini skirt...

♦ Sew an alligator or monogram over the stain.

♦ Pin a campaign button, brooch, or corsage over the spot, or embroider over it.

♦ Dye the entire garment a new, darker color, or try tie dying it.

♦ Dye the garment in the substance causing the stain.

♦ Reproduce the stain regularly throughout the item—like polka dots.

♦ Use the garment for yard work, car work, or other dirty jobs.

♦ If it's in the right spot, cut out the stain, restitch the edges, and let the low cut emphasize cleavage.

♦ Hang a rug or picture over a wall stain.

♦ Donate the garment to the community theater for their production of MacBeth.

A rich man may never get into heaven, but the pauper is already serving his term in hell.

Alexander Chase

Telephones

Many years ago my oldest brother helped me draft a speech for a seventh-grade contest: Eight Ways to Beat Big-Brother AT&T. The speech detailed how to slide slugs down the epiglottis of a pay phone, described the old dime-on-a-string trick, explained how chewing gum could dam up a small fortune inside the phone's coin return, and highlighted five other brilliant (if not completely legal) tricks. The presentation earned me pop fame among peers. It also earned me hours of detention when every phone and vending machine on school property became jammed with slugs, strings, and gum.

Granted, my speech was meant to humor more than inform, but some of my suggestions really worked. For years, for example, I used a pay phone to tell my mom when to pick me up from wrestling practice, and it never cost me a cent. I'd dial home, let the phone ring twice and hang up. That was our signal. I'd repeat the call (insurance that she had heard it), then amble down to the Coke machine for a free drink (the old, old machines with a collar throttling the neck of the bottles released their choke hold if the machine was unplugged).

I'm still aggressive about beating the phone company and the tricks I use all work—just don't tell the principal where you learned them.

♦ Most obviously, and perhaps most significantly, make your calls at the right time. Each long-distance carrier has slightly different times and rates but basically this is how the discounts work. From 8:00 a.m. to 5:00 p.m. on weekdays (caller's time), you'll pay full fare. From 5:00 p.m. to 11:00 p.m. (Sunday through Friday), rates fall 25%

to 33%. From 11:00 p.m. to 8:00 a.m., rates drop 40% to 50% below full fare. And on weekends (Saturday from 8:00 a.m. to 11:00 p.m. and Sunday 8:00 a.m. until 5:00 p.m.) rates drop 35% to 40% below full fare.

Note: Daytime calls on Christmas, New Year's, Independence Day, Labor Day, and Thanksgiving are charged at the early-evening rates, not the late-night rate. Daytime calls on other weekday holidays are not discounted.

♦ Hotels, airlines, and many mail-order businesses are open 24 hours a day. Call those that are long-distance for you in the evening or early morning when rates are low.

♦ Did you know the first three seconds of a telephone call are free? What can you accomplish in three seconds? From a pay phone you can tell a loved one, "Pick me up," or "I'm at the airport," and get your quarter back.

As a writer, I'm often calling long-distance to verify the accuracy of a number listed in an article. I dial the number and if the receptionist answers, "The XYZ Company," as I expect, I hang up. I've verified the number at no charge.

You can also save yourself a long-distance charge if you want to talk to a person and you hear the hollow sound of an answering machine on the opposite end. Hang up immediately and you won't pay.

♦ When I'm placing a long distance call, however, I usually don't mind the sound of an answering machine. That's a chance to leave a short message (costing very little) and to let the other party pick up the tab for the lengthier return call.

In fact, because I'm self-employed and pay for my own business calls, I often make long-distance business calls when people will be out to lunch or gone for the day. I leave messages and let them call me back on their dime.

♦ Use the ringing Morse Code described earlier to relay simple messages to friends and family. If you've driven home across the state after a family holiday, hanging up after two rings is a free way to tell those left behind, "I made it." Meanwhile, kids needing a ride home after school an make free calls from pay phones—two rings means, "Come get me."

♦ Most large manufacturers, hotels, airlines, and service industries maintain toll-free numbers. Use these toll-free numbers even if your contact has a normal number—very often the switchboard can transfer your call from the toll-free line to your contact's line.

If you're unsure whether the company maintains a toll-free number, check. Call the toll-free directory assistance (800-555-1212). Unlike normal directory assistance, this is a free call.

Often a company's toll-free number is not listed in directory assistance, so the first time you call a company, ask for its toll-free number. You'll be surprised how often you score an 800 number that can be used for future calls.

♦ Many phone companies now offer maintenance plans for the "free" repair of "inside" wires that break or malfunction. That "free" fix costs you between 30¢ and $2 a month (charges vary according to the carrier) and primarily pads the pockets of the phone company. Problems with "inside" wiring are relatively rare. Eight out of 10 times the company's wiring (i.e., the outside wiring) is at fault and this is always fixed at no charge to you—even if you don't own a maintenance plan. Say, "No thanks," when your carrier tries to sell you on such a plan.

♦ If you're still leasing a phone from the company, stop. When new phones can be purchased for as little as $10, and $25 buys a touch-tone phone with features like redial and mute, it's insane to pay $3 to $6 *per month* to lease an ordinary touch-tone phone.

Nonetheless, about 18% of phone customers do just that. Many of these customers claim they don't want to hassle with a phone that breaks. You don't need to hassle, just buy a new phone should an old one malfunction. With the money saved by terminating a lease, you can afford to buy three or four phones a year. Of course you won't need to—most phones operate for decades without a glitch.

♦ Confused about how you are billed for long distance calls charged to your calling card? With AT&T, it works like this: You are charged a surcharge for the first minute of the call (that charge ranges from 30¢ to around $1, depending on where you call). The rest of the call is billed at the direct-dial rate for that time of day.

To call collect, a surcharge of $1.88 is added to the direct-dial rates. And for person-to-person calls, a $3.50 surcharge is added to the direct-dialing rates.

While a calling card is one of the cheapest alternatives for placing long-distance calls away from home, the Universal Card from AT&T (a credit card) is an even better deal if you refrain from financing a monthly balance with it. The credit card has no annual fee and long-distance calls made with it are discounted by 10%.

♦ The cost difference is slight in using the calling cards of the big three long-distance carriers (AT&T, MCI, and Sprint)—unless you happen to be calling from a public phone managed by an "alternative operator service" (AOS). These AOSs, most often found at airports and hotels, exist primarily to net big profits for the company owning the facilities where the phones reside.

If an AOS is in use, MCI and Sprint automatically protect you from getting scalped because the AOS cannot intercept the the access codes you dial when using your calling card.

AT&T customers don't dial an access code and are, therefore, prone to becoming a host. These customers can protect themselves against parasitic pay phones by checking the information on the phone stating who carries the long-distance calls. Or they can dial 00 and ask. If the carrier is not AT&T, dialing 102880 gets customers in touch with an AT&T operator and delivers them from potential evil.

♦ Fax machines have changed the face of business in this country and, if you own one, they can change the face of your phone bill. Use them to send notes to friends or business contacts. Why fax when you can call? Well, to convey the gist of your message without all the expensive chit-chat accompanying a phone call. Or to send your messages late at night when phone rates are at their lowest (most fax machines can be programmed to send messages when you choose—e.g., after 11:00 p.m.).

♦ Calling directory assistance from a private phone is not free. Typically you'll get three or four free calls each month, then you are charged (between 25¢ and 60¢, depending on where you call) for each additional call to directory assistance.

The pay phones in most states, however, work by different rules, and you can call directory assistance within your area code for free. Sometimes when I need several listings, I'll run errands and stop at a pay phone while on my rounds—might as well take advantage of the system.

♦ These days the ubiquitous 900 numbers are a money-making scam. The money paid for these calls goes in part to the phone company and in part to the owner of the 900 number. Watch late-night TV and you get bombarded with 900 numbers: dial-a-joke, dial-a-prayer, 900-sextalk, 900-playmate.

These numbers cost about $2 a minute to call and stories abound of kids who have run up huge bills on 900 numbers. Solution? Tell your kids what these numbers cost and warn them that *they* will pay the full amount for any 900-number charges appearing on the phone statement.

♦ Phone companies offering speed dialing overcharge for the service. This service lets you touch two numbers on your phone and, presto, the phone automatically dials your friend in New York or your brother in Kenya (it also dials all the long distance codes or international codes you may be using). In Seattle, where rates for the service are mid-range, a $2.80 monthly service charge (plus a one-time installation charge of $10) buys you the ability to speed dial eight different phone numbers.

That's a lot to pay when you can buy phones for under $50 that will speed dial 28 different phone numbers. Buying such a phone will pay for itself in under two years which, compared to the monthly service charge, makes it an excellent investment.

♦ Call forwarding, a service that costs around $3 a month (plus about $10 for installation), reroutes your incoming calls to another number. If you need to answer calls elsewhere, the service is a valuable one. But if you're getting the service simply as a security measure to reduce the likelihood of burglary while you're away from home, the cheaper solution is to take the phone off the hook or to buy an inexpensive answering machine.

♦ The voice mail (personal secretaries) offered by phone companies has the unique ability to take messages when the phone line is busy—even when you're on the phone with someone else, a friend can leave you a message. Voice mail will also answer your phone and take messages when you are away from home. The cost of the service: about $6 a month plus the one-time installation charge of about $10.

The service is valuable for small businesses and individuals who spend an inordinate amount of time on the phone because a caller won't get a busy tone when you are talking to someone else. But for the average homeowner who isn't on the phone that much and whose friends really don't care if the line is busy from time to time, a $70 answering machine is a much wiser investment. It will take messages while you are away from the phone, it's easier to use, and over the long haul it's *much* cheaper than paying $6 each month.

♦ Hotels are notorious for nickel-and-diming their guests into poverty. You pay $200 a night for a room in a big city and what does that buy? Maybe a room phone for making free local calls? Not a chance. Local calls will run you a flat fee of 50¢ or $1 each. Toll-free numbers cost the same. Meanwhile, long-distance calls may have a flat fee of $1.50 to $2 added to the charges or a 25% to 30% surcharge added to the long distance bill.

To prevent this robbery, use the pay phone found in every hotel lobby—these phones eat quarters rather than dollars. Directory assistance and 800 numbers will be free. Use a calling card for long distance calls.

♦ When you dial a wrong long-distance number, immediately call the operator and report your error. The operator will usually strike that charge from your account.

Saving is a greater art than gaining.
German proverb

Vision

What is the difference between a $15 pair of sunglasses from Woolworth's and the $1000 gold-plated shades worn by Stevie Wonder? Not much when comparing the quality of eye protection. In a *Consumer Reports* review of sunglasses, the magazine reported that with few other products was there such a discrepancy between cost and quality. Roughly translated, Stevie got robbed blind.

Reading this was nothing new to me. As a merchandiser for an upscale mail-order company, I bought $8 frames for prescription sunglasses that we sold for $50—not an uncommon practice. Meanwhile, the glacier glasses we sold to skiers and climbers were bought for $4 and sold for $20.

The problem with the gamut of optical products— eyeglasses, sunglasses, contact lenses, reading glasses—is that advertisers can play so easily to your fears: What would be worse than losing or damaging your sight? How can you trust your sight to anything but the best? Using innuendo to instill doubt, companies muddy the waters about what you do and don't need. Let me help you see the picture more clearly.

♦ Sunglasses. Good ultraviolet (UV) absorption is critical for sunglasses. The same UV rays that burn bare skin can burn unprotected eyes, causing short- and long-term damage. Buy sunglasses that screen all UV radiation (100% filtration means the screening of rays between 290 and 380 nanometers). Most sunglasses (cheap and expensive) sold at outdoor specialty stores (skiing, backpacking, fishing shops) filter all the UV, but check.

After the UV rays, comes the violet/blue light (400 to 510 nanometers). Because recent evidence suggests these rays could be harmful to the eye as well, look for sunglasses that filter two-thirds or more of the blue light. Many manufacturers don't mention how much blue light their products filter, but nearly all lenses that meet the other criteria of good sunglasses filter out enough, meaning much of the blue-light hoopla is a marketing maelstrom. Beyond the filtration of UV and blue light, manufacturers boasting that their glasses screen more infra-red or mumbo-jumbo rays are creating hype—hype to hike prices.

Good sunglasses should also limit the visible light reaching the eye. Experts believe that on bright days only 10% to 30% of this light should pass through the lenses, making sunglasses with a 20% transmission rate a good general-purpose compromise. Test this by donning sunglasses and looking in a mirror; your eyes should be very difficult to see. Skiers and beach bums need even darker glasses and should not be able to see their eyes when performing the mirror test.

Sunglasses worth owning should not distort your vision so the lenses should be ground, polished, and capable of passing prescription eyewear specifications. Hold the sunglasses at arm's length and look at rectangular objects: The lines should be straight. If vertical or horizontal lines appear wavy or ragged, pass on the purchase.

Decent sunglasses should also be scratch resistant— i.e., made of glass, or covered with a scratch-resistant coating if made of plastic. Finally, they should be shatter resistant and—for the truest color transmission—tinted gray, green, or brown.

To get all this you don't need to spend a fortune. Use these tests and read the literature accompanying the glasses and you'll find products that pass muster for under $20. Pay two or three times more and you're paying much more than necessary.

◆ Eyeglasses. You are in no way obliged to buy prescription glasses from the doctor or clinic that examines your eyes. You are free to request your prescription and fill it elsewhere. Several years ago I followed this advice when I discovered I would pay $130 for lenses and frames at my doctor's clinic. I took my prescription (as well as the model numbers of a few frames) and ran to the *Yellow Pages*. Several phone calls later, I went to Eyes Rite Optical, a local vision-wear store that outfitted me with lenses and frames for $40.

Did I get a quality product? Yes. The lens blanks used by optical retail outlets come from a small pool of manufacturers. Scores of different companies will then grind the blank to fill a given prescription, but the quality of the finished goods is heavily regulated, meaning that the lenses are likely to be excellent whether you pay peanuts or pistachios.

Most optical retailers will carry, or have access to, the same frames. If you know the manufacturer and model number of a frame (usually marked inside one of the bands), a few phone calls will identify who's dealing and who's stealing. Remember, too, that if you want a Gucci name you pay a Gucci price. True, designer frames are quality products but you pay heavily for the snob appeal of the name. Look around and you're likely to find products of equal quality, whose styling pleases you, at half the price.

The warranty offered by any retailer should be examined before purchasing your glasses (or contact lenses). Finding a prescription that works involves a complex interplay between the eye and brain; it doesn't matter who makes the glasses, in a sizeable percentage of cases the finished product simply doesn't provide a satisfactory result. Before purchasing glasses (or contact lenses) you want to know whether you'll be charged if the lenses must be remade, if your prescription requires rechecking, or your frames need adjusting. Ask whether you will receive the same warranty even if your prescription comes from a different clinic. Find an outlet that guarantees your satisfaction, regardless of who checked your eyes.

♦ Lenses. I buy glass lenses for my spectacles because I value longevity. Plastic lenses have improved tremendously in modern times, thanks to scratch-resistant coatings, but they still don't hold up to glass in durability. Years after plastic lenses are pitted and scratched, glass still looks like new.

And on that sad day when the glasses fall and the frame splinters, the lenses will still be in top shape. Visit the optical center, pick a new frame for the lenses, and keep those chunks of glass alive.

♦ Frames. For the same reasons, metal is my choice in frames. Plastic frames quickly grow brittle and are prone to shatter when they take a sharp blow. Athletes engaged in contact sports like basketball or soccer are prone to break plastic frames with the regularity that weight watchers break diets. Metal frames, on the other hand, bend with the blows and can be bent back to their old selves with no appreciable damage.

♦ Contact lenses. Comparison shopping for contact lenses is easier than for eyeglasses—just ask different outlets for a price quote on a particular brand and model. Several years ago when my wife needed contacts, the doctor's clinic quoted her $150 for the Bausch and Lomb extended-wear contacts she wanted. Outrageous, she decided, for two slivers of plastic worth a dime. Jan brought her prescription home and called Eyes Rite. They sold the very same brand and model for $79.

Recently Costco, the membership warehouse we belong to, opened an eyecare center and Jan can order her Bausch and Lomb extended-wear contacts for $50.

Unfortunately, eye specialists are not required to relinquish your contact lens prescription after an eye exam—by law they need supply only your glasses prescription, which lacks some of the necessary information for fitting contacts. Call your eye specialist and make sure he or she agrees to give you your contact lens prescription before scheduling an appointment. Take your business elsewhere if a specialist won't cooperate because the contacts he or she is selling probably come with an unappetizing price.

The previous information about warranties for eyeglasses applies to contact lenses. Also, remember that not everyone who wants to wear contact lenses can. When ordering them for the first time, a store offering a good refund policy can protect you from a big loss if your eyes don't adjust.

♦ Contact lens solutions. Some manufacturers make much more off their saline and cleaning solutions than off their contact lenses. Minimize your contribution to their profits by buying their cleaning and saline solutions in bulk, and on sale, at discount pharmacies. Stock up with about a year's worth of solution when the price is right (shelf life for most saline and cleaning solutions is about 18 months).

Store-brand solutions like K-Mart's saline for sensitive eyes can offer savings of 25% to 50% over the name brands. Try them, they're safe. Don't stock up until you've tested a bottle, though. Agents in a new brand of solution may not bother most users, but may irritate your eyes. Switch back to your old solution (or one that has the same ingredients) if you suffer any irritation.

Mail-order purchase of name-brand solutions can make good sense. Check the *Mail-order Appendix* (under Medical and Optical Supplies).

♦ Reading glasses. By the time people with normal vision turn 45, most need glasses to read. This side effect of aging eyes is completely normal and is corrected by glasses that magnify print. You can pay more than $100 buying reading glasses from a specialist or you can pay $15 to $25 for good-quality, over-the-counter models (available at department stores and mass merchandisers around the country). These glasses are effective, perfectly safe, and meet regulations monitored by the American National Standards Institute and the FDA.

Over-the-counter reading glasses use numbers between 1.00 and 4.00 to denote their magnification. Find the strength that's right for you by reading a book with fine print. Start at low magnification (1.00) and try on different glasses until you hone in on the strength that works best.

Note: You can buy reading glasses without a prescription, but it's wise to have the health of your eyes checked by a specialist whenever your vision changes.

♦ Aging eyes. Members of the American Association of Retired Persons (AARP) have access to regional centers that provide eye exams, corrective lenses, and other eyecare products at a reasonable price. On average, the price AARP clinics charge for eye exams, glasses, and contacts is about 20% lower than purchasing the same goods and services at normal optical outlets.

The cities with AARP optical clinics include: Portland, OR; Kansas City, MO; Las Vegas, NV; Indianapolis, IN; Fort Worth, TX; and Richmond, VA. For more information call 800-456-2277.

♦ Glasses straps. Amazing how such little strands of cord, elastic, or neoprene carry such big prices.

The cheap solution: Make your own glasses straps. Actually, there's nothing to make. A 12- to 14-inch piece of clear, flexible tubing with an outside diameter of 1/4 or 5/16 inch (available at almost any hardware store) makes a strap for under 25¢. An equal length of 1/4-inch surgical tubing (available from medical-supply stores or with fishing supplies in many department stores) makes an even better strap for under 50¢. If you forget your strap while traveling, don't rush to the store: Dental floss between the ear pieces works fine—it's strong, inconspicuous, and cheap.

Glasses straps are especially valuable around the water. I know many sportsmen (yours truly included) who have lost glasses or sunglasses while windsurfing, sailing, rafting, boating, and kayaking.

♦ Miscellaneous. If you wear corrective lenses of any sort, ask your doctor for a copy of your prescription. Carry the prescription when you travel. Equally important, carry spare glasses or contact lenses when you travel. Buying replacement eyewear on a trip is inconvenient and, since you usually lack the time to comparison shop, costly.

Economy makes men independent.
                                    Chinese proverb

Water

Water is cheap. Around Seattle, where rates are about average, water costs about a penny per 10 gallons. Even at such insignificant rates, Americans use such vast quantities of water that the pennies add up fast.

The good news is that almost anyone can save tens of thousands of gallons a year with virtually no sacrifice: And because sewage rates throughout much of the country are based on water consumption, ten gallons of water saved actually translates into three pennies earned. The bad news is figuring out what to do with the coffee cans of pennies you're about to amass.

TIPS FOR DONALD-TRUMP TYPES

♦ Toilets are the biggest (and most sinful) use of fresh water *inside* the house. Each flush sends five to seven gallons of sparkling spring water swirling counterclockwise into odoriferous oblivion. And because each family member flushes about four times a day, toilets take their toll on your water and sewage bills. Saving a gallon or two per flush doesn't sound like a significant gain but it adds up to about 2000 gallons ($2 to $4) *per person* per year. Not bad considering these tricks accomplish that saving at no cost:

- Adjust or bend the bar to the float (inside the toilet tank) so the water shuts off at a lower level.

- Fill pop bottles, glass jars, dishwashing bottles, or juice bottles with sand and water and use them as displacement devices inside the toilet tank.

- Place clean bricks inside the toilet tank as displacement devices.

♦ If you're building a home or replacing a toilet, look at the ultra low-flush toilets that use a scant 1 to 1 1/2 gallons per flush. Some of these toilets are expensive but the Universal Rundle (Sears Catalog Number F42B-5560) has scored well in product evaluations and, at $110, costs less than most conventional toilets. Families using these toilets can save $30 to $45 per year on water and sewage bills.

♦ A leaking toilet (caused by a corroded flush valve) can silently spill over 150 gallons down the drain each day without you knowing it. In a bad scenario, eight gallons of water could leak out each hour which, at average utility rates, could cost $70 per year for the wasted water and another $80 for sewage charges.

How do you check your toilet for silent leaks? Put several drops of food coloring in the tank of each toilet. If colored water migrates into the bowl over the course of 15 minutes without flushing, you've got a leak.

Usually a bad flush-valve ball or corroded flush-valve seat (in the bottom of the toilet tank) causes the problem. Replacement kits cost under $4 (check hardware and plumbing stores) and take 20 to 30 minutes to install.

♦ If you can actually hear the toilet leaking, check whether water is spilling down the overflow tube inside the tank. If so, readjust or bend the float downward so the water shuts off at a lower level.

♦ Let the hose run while washing a car and you squander some 75 gallons of water. Use a hose-end nozzle to turn the water on and off.

♦ Sweep (rather than spray) your driveway and walkways clean.

♦ Most families double their water use in the summer by watering yards and plants. At the same time, many utility districts hike water rates, meaning you may be seeing red when your bill arrives. The *Lawn* chapter offers suggestions for reducing the summer spike.

♦ Xeriscaping. Water will become scarcer and more expensive in the future, which makes xeriscaping (plant selection and gardening practices that greatly reduce the need to irrigate) a logical practice. Xeriscaping relies on garden designs that retain rainwater, soil improvements to increase its water holding abilities, mulches that keep the soil moist, ground cover that is drought tolerant, and native plants that are suited to an area's rainfall.

For more information, order the booklet, *How to Xeriscape*, from the Texas Water Development Board (address to follow).

TIPS FOR JANE AND JOHN DOE

♦ A cold-water faucet dripping once every second loses 75 gallons of water a week—which in Seattle costs 7.5¢ in water and another 15¢ in sewage charges. That may not be incentive enough to hire a plumber at $45 an hour, but does cost $11.70 a year.

Fortunately, leaks are easy for anyone to fix. The booklet, *A Homeowner's Guide to Water Use and Water Conservation* (free from the Texas Water Development Board—address to follow) demonstrates how to operate on several standard faucets. Many library books also address the problem.

♦ Plug the sink (or use water held in a pot) to wash fruits and vegetables. Same goes for rinsing dishes for the dishwasher and for defrosting frozen foods.

♦ When you water, don't water the pavement.

♦ During summer droughts, use your gray water (e.g., bath and shower water) to water plants outside.

♦ If your water use is rationed in summer, give your trees and shrubs priority over the lawn. They are more expensive and harder to replace than grass and annual flowers.

TIPS FOR BEN-FRANKLIN TYPES

♦ Reuse the gray water from baths and showers (plug the shower drain). I use this water to hand wash clothes that need deodorizing but don't need to be sparkling clean (gym clothes, running shorts, gardening clothes). Friends use the water on their indoor plants—the soap won't hurt them.

♦ Use cooking water to water plants—saves water and puts nutrients into the soil. Egg water is especially good.

♦ A pitcher of water chilled in the refrigerator uses less water than running the tap until the temperature cools.

♦ Collect water during rainstorms. Your plants will appreciate the chlorine-free water.

♦ Place a bucket under the shower head (or tub faucet) while waiting for the water to warm. Use it for drinking, washing clothes, or watering plants.

MORE INFO

♦ Many excellent booklets for saving water are available through the Texas Water Development Board (P.O. Box 13231, Capital Station, Austin, TX, 78711, 512-445-1467). The information is practical, covers many measures discussed in this chapter in greater detail, and is free. Titles worth ordering include: *A Homeowner's Guide to Water Use and Water Conservation, Lawn Watering Guide, Water...Half-A-Hundred Ways to Save It, Sources of Leak Detection Equipment and Services, Sources of Water Saving Devices.*

Fortune knocks once at least at every man's gate.
English proverb

Water (Hot)

It doesn't take Einsteinian gray matter to understand the equation: Hot water down the drain equals money down the drain. It requires 540 BTUs to heat one gallon of ground water to the tank temperature of your water heater. Using average utility rates, those BTUs cost 1.25¢. So why do people waste hot water so wantonly? Are they brain-dead after work? Or have they never put two and two together to see what bad habits cost?

Following is a listing of the worst habits and some tips to keep your budget out of hot water.

♦ Brain-dead—running the hot water while shaving. This practice can waste 15 gallons of hot water (19¢). Instead, plug the sink and pour in a gallon of hot water.

Running the hot water while washing your face is less offensive but can still waste 5 to 7 gallons (6¢).

♦ Zombie—running the hot water continuously while rinsing dishes destined for the dishwasher can consume up to 16 gallons of hot water (20¢). In fact, many Americans waste more hot water preparing their dishes for the dishwasher than the machine itself will use. Any dishwasher worth its salt will clean filthy dishes—you just need to scrape off the scraps and crumbs. See the *Appliance* chapter for more about dishwashers.

♦ Numbskull—not fixing hot-water drips. You're going to fix it someday, so do it now. A drip every second wastes 75 gallons per week (94¢). That's a lot to tolerate when a 20¢ gasket solves the problem.

♦ Halfwit—overfilling bathtubs. A quick shower is the least expensive way to bathe. If you want the lingering luxury of a lengthy soak, however, remember that five inches of water (about 20 gallons) will immerse you nicely. You don't need to fill the tub to its 45-gallon capacity.

♦ Knucklehead—washing the majority of your clothing in warm or hot water. A large load of wash consumes 40 to 50 gallons of water. If that water is warm or hot, the energy costs can run upward of 50¢ per load (assuming average electric rates).

With modern detergents you'll get all but the filthiest clothes clean with the cold/cold or warm/cold cycles. In the process, you'll save money   because 90% of the cost of washing goes into heating water.

♦ Simple Simon—not insulating your water heater. When you want to conserve heat what do you do? Put on a coat. Do the same for your hot water heater (especially if it's located in a cold garage or basement). Fiberglass-insulated blankets made for water heaters will reduce your hot-water bills by as much as $30 a year. Before purchasing a blanket from a local department store, call your utility company—many supply free (or very inexpensive) blankets.

Note: More and more new water heaters have built-in insulation. Check your unit's manual, or lay your hand on the heater. If it feels warm, it needs insulation.

♦ Pinhead—long, long showers. See the *Shower* chapter for rantings and ravings on this subject.

OTHER HOT WATER SAVERS

♦ People commonly heat their water to 140° F—which is considerably hotter than necessary. For every 10° F you turn down the thermostat, you'll save 6% on your hot-water-heating bills. Try 120° first—this is the new recommendation from the U.S. Department of Energy. Not all dishwasher detergents dissolve at this temperature, but try it. If you have trouble with the dishwasher, try a new detergent or reset the thermostat to 130° and try again.

Many water heaters have two thermostats. In this case, turn the top control to the desired temperature and set the bottom control 10° F cooler. Note: Turn off the power at the fuse box before resetting the thermostat.

♦ If you buy a new dishwasher, paying an extra $30 for a booster heater that raises incoming water to 140° F is well spent. The booster heater lets you turn the main water heater down to 120°, which saves you $20 to $30 a year and pays for the booster heater in fewer than two years.

♦ Install low-flow faucet aerators on the bathroom and kitchen faucets. These inconspicuous devices screw onto the end of faucets and reduce water flow by 40% to 50%. Because air is mixed in with the water, however, the spray feels just as strong and is just as useful for washing hands or rinsing dishes.

Low-flow aerators cost $3 to $4 (available at hardware and plumbing stores) and pay for themselves quickly.

Note: Don't mistake these aerators with conventional screen aerators that don't restrict water flow.

♦ Double up. Let kids share the same bath water. Or take your bath first before having your children bathe in the same water.

♦ A short shower uses about 10 gallons of water, versus the 25 gallons of water used for a bath. Consequently, a hand shower for a showerless tub will pay for itself quickly.

♦ Turn off the water heater when you leave home for longer than a weekend.

♦ Use cold water when running the garbage disposal.

♦ After wintertime baths, don't empty the tub until the water cools. The energy stored in the warm water will help heat the house.

♦ In summer, place dark-colored water containers on the window sill (or outside) to heat water. Might as well let nature heat your water.

♦ Hot-water pipes passing through basements or crawl spaces should be wrapped with insulation. Covering them with foam-wrap insulation has a 1- to 2-year payback.

An even cheaper alternative is to slice fiberglass batting (lengthwise) into strips that are 7 1/2 inches wide. Wrap these strips around the pipes and secure them with staples.

Note: Don't use foam tubing on the pipes of a steam boiler—the foam can melt.

Mail-Order Appendix

The following pages list many outlets selling goods and services by mail. Many of these outlets charge considerably less for their wares than the average retail store. Most have operated for many years; when known, the firm's first year of operation has been placed in parentheses at the end of the listing.

This list is far from comprehensive. You'll often find many reputable, specialty outlets in the back of special-interest magazines. The *Wholesale by Mail Catalog* (Harper-Collins Publisher, 10 E. 53rd St., New York, NY 10022) is also an excellent source for some 500 mail-order businesses selling animal supplies, art materials, electric appliances, automobiles and accessories, boats and accessories, camera gear, smoking needs, clothing, furs, footwear, baby supplies, maternity clothing, craft supplies, farm and garden needs, food and drink, health and beauty supplies, furniture, linens, jewelry, gems, watches, leather goods, medicines, office supplies, stereo equipment, computers, sports equipment, surplus goods, tools, hardware, toys, games...

ART SUPPLIES

♦ American Frame Corporation, 1340 Tomahawk Dr., Maumee, OH 43537, 800-537-0944. Free catalog of frames (metal and wood), picture glass, matboard. (1973)
♦ Art Supply Warehouse, 360 Main Ave., Norwalk, CT 06851, 800-243-5038 or 203-846-2279. Free catalog of paints, pigments, pens, brushes, and scores of other art supplies.
♦ Crown Art Products Co., 90 Dayton Ave., Passaic, NJ 07055, 201-777-6010. Free catalog of craft supplies, art supplies, and frames. (1974)

AUTOMOBILES, BOATS, MOTORCYCLES

♦ American Automobile Brokers, Inc., 24001 Southfield Rd., Suite 110, Southfield, MI 48075, 313-569-2022. Sell American and some import cars with minimum markup. Shop locally, then get a price quote from this firm. (1972)

♦ Car/Puter International, 499 Sheridan St., Suite 400, Dania, FL 33004, 800-722-4440 or 305-921-2400. Free brochure tells you how they can help you find out the dealer's cost and locate the local dealer with the lowest markup. (1964)

♦ Cherry Auto Parts, 5650 N. Detroit Ave., Toledo, OH 43612, 800-537-8677 or 800-472-8639 (in state). Free brochure of used and reconditioned foreign auto parts.

♦ Clinton Cycle and Salvage, 6709 Old Branch Ave., Camp Springs, MD 20748, 800-332-8264 or 301-449-3550. Free price list of salvaged motorcycle parts. (1971)

♦ E & B Marine Supply, 201 Meadow Rd., Edison, NJ 08818, 800-533-5007. Free catalog of marine supplies. (1946)

♦ Euro-Tire, 567 Route 46 West, Fairfield, NJ 07004, 800-631-0080 or 201-575-0080. Free catalog of European and domestic tires and shocks. (1974)

♦ Goldbergs' Marine Distributors, 201 Meadow Rd., Edison, NJ 08818, 800-BOATING. Free catalog of boating supplies and equipment. (1946)

♦ Nationwide Auto Brokers, 17517 West 10 Mile Rd., Southfield, MI 48075, 313-559-6661. Free brochure describing their price quote process. Use these quotes to negotiate a better local price. Can also have them ship you a car at quoted price. (1966)

♦ TeleTire, 17642 Armstrong Ave., Irvine, CA 92714, 800-835-8473 or 714-250-9141. Free brochure listing domestic and imported tires.

BOOKS, MAGAZINES

♦ American Family Publishers, P.O. Box 62000, Tampa, FL 33662-2000, 800-237-2400. Clearinghouse for magazines: rates often lower than from the publishers.

♦ Barnes and Noble Bookstores, 126 Fifth Ave., New York, NY 10011, 201-767-7079. Free catalog of discounted books, records, cassette tapes, video tapes. (1873).

♦ Consumer Information Center, P.O. Box 100, Pueblo, CO 81002. Free catalog listing many free and cheap booklets with consumer-oriented info: energy conservation, home improvement, travel, nutrition, electronics...

♦ Daedalus Books, P.O. Box 9132, Hyattsville, MD 20781, 301-779-4224. Free catalog listing of deeply discounted literary works. (1980)

♦ Discount Books and Video, P.O. Box 928, Vineland, NJ 08360, 800-448-2019 or 609-691-1620. Free catalog lists discounted books, tapes, videos, CDs. (1984)

♦ Edward R. Hamilton—Bookseller, Falls Village, CT 06031-5000. Free catalog of discounted books (all subjects).

♦ Publishers Clearing House, 101 Winners Circle, Port Washington, NY 11050, 516-883-5432. Ask about subscription prices for specific magazines. Prices often below what publishers charge.

♦ Tartan Book Sales, 500 Arch St., Williamsport, PA 17705, 800-233-8467, Ext. 507 or 717-326-2461, Ext. 507. Free catalog listing used, undamaged, hardbound books. (1960)

CLOTHING

♦ Chadwick's of Boston, One Chadwick Place, Box 1600, Brockton, MA 02403, 508-583-6600. Free catalog of women's clothing.

♦ D & A Merchandise Co., 22 Orchard St., New York, NY 10002, 212-925-4766. Brand name underwear, lingerie, socks, and hosiery for men, women and children. Catalog costs $1.50. (1947)

♦ Fall River Knitting Mills, Inc., P.O. Box 4360, Flint Station, Fall River, MA 02723, 800-446-1089 or 508-679-5227. Factory outlet for sweater and knitwears for men, women, and children. Free catalog. (1911)

♦ Huntington Clothiers, 1285 Alum Creek Dr., Columbus, OH 43209, 800-848-6203. Free catalog lists conservative styles of men's clothing.

♦ L'eggs Showcase of Savings, L'eggs Brands Inc., P.O. Box 748, Rural Hall, NC 27098, 919-744-1170. By buying direct, women can get big discounts on irregular underwear and hosiery.

♦ National Wholesale Co., 400 National Blvd., Lexington, NC 27292, 704-249-0211. Free catalog listing many brands of women's underwear and hosiery. (1952)

♦ Paul Frederick Shirt Co., 140 W. Main St., Fleetwood, PA 19522, 215-944-0909. Make men's dress shirts for many different labels. Buying direct here allows for sizeable discounts. Catalog costs $1.

COMPUTERS, PRINTERS

♦ Computer Discount Warehouse, 2840 Maria, Northbrook, IL 60062, 800-326-4CDW or 708-498-1426. Computers, accessories, monitors, software.
♦ Fast Micro, 3655 E. LaSalle St., Phoenix, AZ 85040, 800-441-FAST or 602-437-0300. Computers, accessories, software, printers.
♦ Micro Warehouse, 1690 Oak Street, P.O. Box 1590, Lakewood, NJ 08701, 800-367-7080 or 908-370-0518. Computers, accessories, software. Free catalog.
♦ Midwest Computer Works, 350 Lexington Dr., Buffalo Grove, IL 60089, 800-669-5208 or 708-459-6883. Computers, accessories, printers.
♦ PC Connection, 6 Mill Street, Marlow, NH 03456, 800-243-8088 or 603-446-7721. Computer accessories, software.
♦ Browse magazines like *PC Magazine* for additional mail-order sources.

COSMETICS AND TOILETRIES

♦ Beautiful Visions, 810 S. Broadway, Hicksville, NY 11801, 516-576-9000. Free catalog listing big discounts on name-brand toiletries and cosmetics. (1977)
♦ Beauty Boutique, P.O. Box 94520, Cleveland, OH 44101-4520, 216-826-3008. Free catalog listing big discounts on name-brand toiletries and cosmetics. (1970s)

ELECTRONICS AND APPLIANCES

♦ Bernie's Discount Center, 821 Sixth Ave, New York, NY 10001, 212-564-8758. Call for price quotes on appliances, audio components, and TVs. (1948)
♦ Crutchfield Corporation, 1 Crutchfield Park, Charlottes-ville, VA 22906-6020, 800-336-5566. Free catalog of home and car stereos, telephones, and video equipment. (1974)

◆DAK Industries, 8200 Remmet Ave., Canoga Park, CA 91304, 800-DAK-0800. Free catalog of audio, video, computer, and electronic goods.

◆ Foto Electric Supply Co., 31 Essex St., New York, NY 10002, 212-673-5222. Price quotes on TVs, large appliances, video gear, and cameras. (1962)

◆ Illinois Audio, 12 E. Delaware Pl., Chicago, IL 60611, 800-621-8042 or 312-664-0020. Free price list of audio and video equipment, and components. (1971)

◆ International Electronic World, Moravia Center Industrial Park, Baltimore, MD 21206, 301-488-9600. Free catalog of audio and video components. (1950)

◆ Percy's Inc, 19 Glennie St., Worcester, MA 01605, 508-755-5334. Price quotes on large appliances, office machines, TVs, copiers, audio components. (1950s)

◆ Sewin' In Vermont, 84 Concord Ave., St. Johnsbury, VT 05819, 800-451-5124 or 802-748-3803. Free brochure and price list of sewing machines and accessories.

MISCELLANEOUS MERCHANDISE

◆ Comb Direct Marketing Corp, 720 Anderson Ave., St. Cloud, MN 56372-0030, 800-328-0609. Free catalog listing discounts on brand-name items being closed out or liquidated. Computers, stereos, sewing machines, videos, telephones, tools, watches, furniture, sports equipment...

◆ Damark International, 7101 Winnetka Ave. N, Brooklyn Park, MN 55428, 800-729-9000. Free catalog listing discounts on brand-name items being closed out or liquidated. Computers, stereos, sewing machines, videos, telephones, tools, watches, furniture, sports equipment...(1986)

◆ Sears, Roebuck and Co. Not the lowest prices but still offer good value. Catalogs available from local stores or by calling 800-366-3000. Catalog cost: $5 (refunded with first purchase).

MEDICAL AND OPTICAL SUPPLIES

◆ American Association of Retired Persons, 1909 K St. N.W., Washington DC 20049, 800-456-2277 or 703-684-0244. Members of AARP have access to the mail-order pharmacy for prescription and over-the-counter medications. Call for price quotes.

♦ Contact Lens Replacement Center, P.O. Box 1489, Melville, NY 11747, 516-491-7763. Send self-addressed stamped envelope for price list for name-brand but deeply discounted hard, soft, extended wear, disposable, and gas-permeable contact lenses. Supply current prescription. (1986)

♦ The Eye Solution, Inc., P.O. Box 262-H, Galion, OH 44833, 419-683-1608. Free catalog of name-brand products for cleaning, disinfecting, and lubricating contact lenses. Also sell sunglasses.

♦ Hidalgo, 45 La Buena Vista, Wimberley, TX 78676, 800-950-8086. Free catalog for discounted prescription eyeglasses and sunglasses. Try-on program lets you order three frames for trial before purchasing.

♦ Medi-Mail Inc., P.O. Box 98520, Las Vegas, NV 89193, 800-331-1458. Free brochure describing services. Call for price quote on both prescription and over-the-counter medications.

♦ Pharmail Corporation, P.O. Box 1466, Champlain, NY 12919, 800-237-8927 or 518-298-4922. Free price list of the most common medications or call for a price quote on a prescription or over-the-counter drug.

OFFICE SUPPLIES

♦ Penny-Wise Office Products, 4350 Kenilworth Avenue, Edmonston, MD 20781, 800-942-3311 or 301-699-1000. Free catalog of office supplies, equipment and furniture.

PET AND VET SUPPLIES

♦ The Dog's Outfitter, P.O. Box 2010, Hazelton, PA 18201, 717-384-5555. Free catalog of products for dogs and cats. (1969)

♦ The Kennel Vet Corporation, P.O. Box 835, Bellmore, NY 11710, 516-783-7516. Free catalog of dog, cat, and horse products. (1971)

♦ United Pharmacal Company, P.O. Box 969, St. Joseph, MO 64502, 816-233-8800. Free catalog of products for all kinds of pets. (1952)

PHOTOGRAPHY SERVICES

All of the following outlets offer high-quality film processing and print making, and they charge about half of what you'll pay at local photography or department stores. Send away for brochures listing services and prices.

♦ A Positive Kolor, 11037 Penrose Street, Sun Valley, CA 91352, 818-768-5700.

♦ Clark Color Labs, P.O. Box 96300, Washington, DC 20090, 301-595-5300.

♦ Custom Quality Studio, P.O. Box 4838, Chicago, IL 60680. Send away for a mailer.

♦ Mystic Color Lab, P.O. Box 144, Mystic, CT 06355, 800-367-6061.

♦ Skrudland Photo, 5311 Fleming Court, Austin, TX 78744, 512-444-0958.

PHOTOGRAPHY AND VIDEO EQUIPMENT

♦ Adorama, 42 W. 18th St., New York, NY 10011, 800-223-2500 or 212-741-0052. Cameras, lenses, film, camcorders, binoculars, darkroom supplies, accessories. Call for price quote or catalog.

♦ Bi-Rite, 15 E. 30th St., New York, NY 10016-7080, 800-223-1970 or 212-685-2130. Call for price quote or catalog. Cameras, lenses, film, camcorders, TVs, electronic office equipment.

♦ B&H Photo, 119 W. 17th St., New York, NY 10011, 800-221-5662 or 212-807-7474. Cameras, film, lenses, darkroom supplies, camcorders, and video supplies. Call for price quote or catalog.

♦ Cambridge Camera Exchange, 7th Ave. and 13th St., New York, NY 10011, 800-221-2253 or 212-675-8600. Cameras, lenses, film, binoculars.

♦ Camera World, 500 S.W. 5th Ave., Portland, OR 97204, 800-222-1557 or 503-227-6008. Cameras, lenses, camcorders, accessories.

♦ Focus Camera, 4419-21 13th Ave., Brooklyn, NY 11219, 800-221-0828 or 718-436-6262. Cameras, lenses, accessories, film, camcorders, darkroom supplies.

♦ You'll find many other mail-order sources in the back of magazines like *Popular Photography*.

RECORDS, DISCS, TAPES, VIDEOTAPES

◆ BMG Compact Disc Club, P.O. Box 91412, Indianapolis, IN 46209-9758. Club with very good introductory offer. Unlike many clubs, membership can be cancelled after the purchase of just one disc. Write for their introductory offer.
◆ Bose Express Music, 50 W. 17th St., New York, NY 10011, 800-233-6357. Huge selection of discounted CDs and cassettes. Catalog $6 (refundable with first purchase).
◆ Publishers Central Bureau, One Champion Ave., Aveneal, NJ 07001-2301, 201-382-7960. Free catalog of deeply discounted records, books, videotapes, cassette tapes.
◆ See the 'Books and Magazines' section of this appendix for additional sources.

SPORTS EQUIPMENT

◆ Bike Nashbar, 4111 Simon Road, Youngstown, OH 44512-1343, 800-627-4427 or 216-782-2244. Free catalog listing bicycles and accessories for the serious rider. Reasonable savings compared to purchasing retail.
◆ Cabela's Inc., 812 13th Ave., Sidney, NE 69160, 308-254-5505. Free catalog of hunting, fishing, and camping equipment.
◆ Campmor, 810 Route 17 North, P.O. Box 997-C, Paramus, NJ 07653-0997, 800-526-4784 or 201-445-9868. Camping, backpacking, and climbing supplies at good prices. Free catalog.
◆ Recreational Equipment Inc., P.O. Box 88125, Seattle, WA 98138-2125, 800-426-4840 or 206-575-3287. Free catalog of camping, backpacking, walking, canoeing, bicycling, skiing, and climbing supplies. Reasonable prices on the gamut of outdoor sports equipment.

YOUR CHOICE

◆ Send me a note listing your favorite mail-order sources. Which ones have really great prices or a combination of good prices and service?

Index